The Azerbaijan crisis of 1946 represented a landmark in the early stages of the Cold War and played a major role in shaping the future course of Iran's political development. In this book, Louise Fawcett presents the first comprehensive study of the five-year struggle for control of Iran which culminated in the crisis of 1946.

Dr Fawcett examines both the Iranian domestic scene and the role played by the three great powers. In the first part, she explores the causes, course and consequences of the Azerbaijan crisis from an Iranian perspective. She considers the extent to which events in Azerbaijan were the product of local conditions, the position of the central government and the role of the Azerbaijan Democratic party. The author then looks at the policies of the Soviet Union, the United States and Britain, and their impact not only on Iran, but also on the relationship between these three war-time allies. Dr Fawcett argues that the Iranian crisis was a far more complex affair than has hitherto been realised. It brought into play the competitive and often conflicting relationship between not only the United States and the Soviet Union, but also between Britain and the two superpowers.

This study is based upon newly released documents in Britain and America, Persian language newspapers and memoirs, and on Russian sources. It is firmly located within the international relations literature of the Cold War and breaks extensive new ground. *Iran and the Cold War* will be widely read by students and specialists of both international relations and Middle East studies.

IRAN AND THE COLD WAR

Cambridge Middle East Library: 26

Editorial Board

The *Cambridge Middle East Library* aims to bring together outstanding scholarly work on the history, politics, sociology and economics of the Middle East and North Africa in the nineteenth and twentieth centuries. While primarily focusing on monographs based on original research, the series will also incorporate broader surveys and in-depth treatments.

Cambridge Middle East Library

Iran and the Cold War

The Azerbaijan Crisis of 1946

LOUISE L'ESTRANGE FAWCETT

MacArthur Scholar and Junior Research Fellow in the International Relations of the Developing World, Exeter College, Oxford

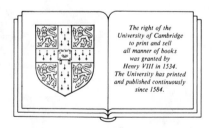

The right of the
University of Cambridge
to print and sell
all manner of books
was granted by
Henry VIII in 1534.
The University has printed
and published continuously
since 1584.

CAMBRIDGE UNIVERSITY PRESS
CAMBRIDGE   NEW YORK   PORT CHESTER
MELBOURNE   SYDNEY

Published by the Press Syndicate of the University of Cambridge
The Pitt Building, Trumpington Street, Cambridge CB2 IRP
40 West 20th Street, New York, NY 10011-4211, USA
10 Stamford Road, Oakleigh, Victoria 3166, Australia

First published 1992

Printed in Great Britain at the University Press, Cambridge

A catalogue record for this book is available from the British Library

Library of Congress cataloguing in publication data

Fawcett, Louise L'Estrange.
  Iran and the Cold War: the Azerbaijan crisis of 1946 / Louise l'Estrange Fawcett.
  p.   cm. – (Cambridge Middle East Library: 26)
  Includes bibliographical references and index.
  ISBN 0 521 37373 5
  1. Iran – History – Mohammed Reza Pahlavi, 1941–1979. 2. Azerbaijan (Iran) –
History. I. Title. II. Series.
  DS318.F38 1992
  955.05'3 – dc20 91–3774 CIP

ISBN 0 521 37373 5 hardback

To Eduardo and Beatriz Andrea Ramona

Contents

Acknowledgements

This book began as a doctoral thesis completed at St Antony's College Oxford in 1988. My first thanks go to John Gurney for all his valuable guidance. I am also grateful to Adam Roberts, Avi Shlaim, Fred Halliday and Roger Owen for their support and helpful suggestions, and to Faraneh Alavi Moghaddam, whose classes helped me to improve my Farsi.

I would like to thank the ESRC for financing part of my research, including a fieldwork trip to Washington. I have received the assistance of the staff at the Public Record Office in Kew and the National Archives and Library of Congress in Washington, as well as of the librarians of St Antony's College, Oxford, to all of whom I am grateful. Finally I would like to thank all my family, friends and colleagues who have, in different ways, helped and encouraged me during the writing of this book. To my parents I owe a special debt of gratitude for all their support over the years. My husband, Eduardo Posada, and my daughter, Beatriz Andrea, have been my constant inspiration.

Introduction

When the Germans attacked the USSR in the summer of 1941 and the Soviet government hastily forged an alliance with the Western allies, Iran, despite its declared neutrality, was quickly drawn into the Second World War. Apart from the country's strategic position which made it the obvious route for allied supplies to reach the USSR, Iran had, during the previous decade, developed a close and thriving economic relationship with Germany. This relationship, so valuable to Iran, provided the allies with an excellent reason to overrun the country and turn it over to the war effort. In the autumn of 1941, after the Shah of Iran, Reza Pahlavi, had repeatedly procrastinated over the question of expelling the large numbers of Germans then present in the country, Soviet and British troops invaded. The two old rivals, in scenes reminiscent of earlier times when a spheres of influence agreement had been signed to mark out British and Russian interests in Persia, now proceeded to establish zones of occupation in the north and south of the country. Reza Shah was forced to abdicate, to be succeeded by his son, the young, inexperienced and initially pliant, Muhammad Reza. Iran's economy and communications network were soon harnessed to the allied war effort, the country becoming an artery through which millions of tons of goods and supplies were transported to the USSR.

The management of the supply line, and the provision of special assistance to Iran during the war, brought large numbers of American troops and advisers to Iran to add to the already considerable Soviet and British presence. The United States hoped that Iran would provide a model for allied cooperation in the war, and later a testing ground for the principles of the United Nations. Instead it became a battlefield of conflicting interests in which national pride, security considerations, the struggle for control of oil resources and the hearts and minds of the Iranian people all played a part. The war effort provided the pretext for the pursuit of the different national interests of the three great powers, and turned Iran into one of the earliest non-European theatres of the Cold War.

While the allied occupation thrust Iran onto the international stage and foreshadowed a major transformation in the country's external relations, it also opened the way for profound internal changes. The removal of an authoritarian ruler paved the way for a 'quasi-parliamentary regime',[1] but the limits of Iran's experiment in democracy were increasingly defined by external interests and pressures. While a new spectrum of political opportunities presented themselves during this period, giving rise to considerable popular expectations, the success or failure of the emerging political groupings was closely connected to the relations which they sustained with foreign powers. Both Britain and the Soviet Union tried to wield their influence to promote parties or individuals likely to favour their respective interests. The result was a polarisation of Iranian politics: on the right were the pro-British or pro-American groups, on the left those who associated with the USSR. There was, however, an important middle ground occupied by a group of independent politicians, their most famous representative being Muhammad Mussadiq, who advocated a non-aligned foreign policy.

This internal power struggle was thus conditioned by the parallel struggle for Persia that developed between Britain, the United States and the USSR. This conflict ranged not only East against West, but also West against West, as the three powers each sought to mark out their stake in postwar Iran. A succession of crises, in large part the product of foreign intervention, with which the Iranian government was ill equipped to deal, led to a final denouement in 1946. The USSR firstly promoted the creation of two autonomous regimes in Iran's northwest province of Azerbaijan, and then refused to withdraw its troops from Iran as stipulated under an agreement signed with Britain and Iran in 1942 until it had won some important concessions from the Iranian government. At this juncture the US government decided to intervene in Iran and teach the USSR an early lesson in containment. The Iranian crisis, which had been quietly simmering for nearly five years, had begun in earnest. The story of the crisis, and its significance both for Iran and for international relations, is the subject of this book.

Until quite recently the 'Iranian' or Azerbaijan crisis of 1946 has been assigned a rather modest place in Iran's political history, and an even more modest place in the annals of Cold War history. Most historians and political scientists, with a few notable exceptions, have dealt with the crisis in no more than a few pages, or at most a chapter, in a broader work on Iran[2] or the Cold War.[3] Some more complete accounts are to be found in different histories of Iran's foreign relations, but many of these are now outdated.[4] It is surprising that the Iranian crisis should have received relatively little scholarly treatment. On the one hand, the unfolding of events in Azerbaijan, the culmination of five years of allied wrangling over Persia, helped to shape the future course of the country's political development. On the other hand, they provided an excellent example of problems faced by the victorious wartime allies in redefining their own relationships, and in shaping the postwar world.

The Iranian crisis displayed all the characteristics of a classical Cold War conflict.

The 'rediscovery' of the international significance of events in Iran in the 1941–7 period can be ascribed to two main factors. The first is the heightened interest in Iran generally as a result of the events surrounding the Iranian Revolution of 1979. The second is the move away from orthodox and revisionist theories of the origins of the Cold War. The so-called 'post-revisionist' school, by extending the scope of its enquiry from the two major actors in the Cold War to a range of lesser, yet nonetheless significant actors in the conflict, have opened the way for a reassessment of a whole range of Cold War issues.[5] These two developments, together with the publication of a number of works based on recently released archival materials,[6] have resulted in a spate of new publications on all subjects relating to Iran, not least on the turbulent decade of the 1940s.[7]

It is not therefore the task of this book to rescue the Iranian crisis from obscurity, for that job has already been done. However, recent literature on Iran or the Cold War has not, as yet, made the crisis its only, or principal focus. Indeed, with very few exceptions, most of the existing works on the subject are over twenty-five years old.[8] In short, we now know that what happened in Iran during and after the Second World War was somehow important, but the picture that most of us have is at best a hazy and incomplete one. This book sets out to fill in the gaps, and in describing the events surrounding the Iranian crisis of 1946 to demonstrate its importance in both an Iranian and international context.

The book is divided into two parts dealing respectively with the internal and external dimensions of the crisis. The division, it could be argued, is a somewhat artificial one, given the close interplay of domestic and external factors, a constant of Iran's modern history, and especially of the period under discussion. Yet it is nonetheless helpful, both in finding out what really happened in Azerbaijan, and in establishing the role played by the Iranians themselves in the unfolding of events. The first three chapters thus examine the causes, course and consequences of the Azerbaijan crisis, viewed, as far as possible, from an Iranian perspective. They assess the extent to which events in Azerbaijan were the product of local conditions as opposed to external intervention, as well as examining the strategies adopted by the central government to deal with the situation. There is a short chapter on the Azerbaijan Democratic party which effectively ruled Azerbaijan for one year (December 1945 to December 1946). This focuses in particular on the personalities involved in the party while also examining its relationship with the communist Tudeh party, the subject of some controversy.

The second part of the book, comprising the last three chapters, looks at Soviet, American and British policy in Iran during and immediately after the

Second World War. It analyses the policies of the three powers in Iran and assesses the impact of these policies, not only on Iran, but also on the relationship between the three wartime allies. While not neglecting the traditional East–West perspective on the early origins of the Cold War, this book argues that the Iranian crisis was in reality a far more complex affair, bringing into play the competitive and often conflicting relationship between not only the United States and the USSR, but between Britain and both the USSR and the United States.

This attempt to go beyond existing stereotypes places this work within the so-called post-revisionist literature on the origins of the Cold War. Certainly the Iranian crisis does not fit comfortably into either orthodox or revisionist interpretations previously on offer, which attribute the 'blame' for the Cold War to the Soviet Union and the United States.[9] Both approaches suffer from two failings: they underplay or even ignore not only the Iranian contribution to events, but, less explicably, that of Britain. The Iranians, as discussed in the early chapters of this book played a far more important role in directing their own affairs than is generally allowed. Britain, for its part, as the most important international actor in Iran, both before and during the war, had a hand in virtually every major wartime development in Iran, including that of turning the country into an early Cold War theatre. Any account that places responsibility for the latter development solely on American or Soviet shoulders (or both) falls far short of the mark.[10]

While sharing some of the general conclusions of the post-revisionist school on the origins of the Cold War, this book does not attempt to slot itself into any special pigeon-hole. The reader will find no models or formulas designed to assist our understanding of what happened in Iran in the period under study. Iran's past, like its present, stubbornly refuses to fit into a neat package. The approach is unashamedly historical. It attempts to describe the events of the period in a lucid and scholarly way and secure for the Azerbaijan crisis of 1946 its proper place in Iranian and international history.

1 The roots of the Azerbaijan crisis

A number of explanations have so far been offered as to the origins of the Azerbaijan crisis. These may be divided crudely into four categories. The first, favoured by conservative Iranians, particularly the Shah and his supporters, but also some Western writers, holds that the whole Azerbaijan affair was the product of Soviet intervention and was without historical or indigenous roots.[1] A larger group of Western and Iranian writers, while not neglecting the Soviet factor, do recognise the existence of a popular element in the Azerbaijan rebellion, which is explained in terms of the distinctiveness of the province and the feeling of injustice on the part of the local population at its unfair treatment by the central government.[2] Yet another group of Iranians, mostly of left-wing political persuasion, have underplayed the Soviet element, and emphasised the Azerbaijan revolt as part of a broader, nationwide movement demanding fundamental changes.[3] Finally, the Soviet version of events, as yet unexposed to the winds of *glasnost*, holds that Azerbaijan's history was part of a national liberation struggle, of which Azerbaijani nationalism was just part of a general reaction against the tyranny of the government in Tehran.[4]

Neither the first nor last explanations stand up to rigorous analysis. Soviet intervention is not a sufficient single explanation of the Azerbaijan crisis, but nor can it be excluded altogether. For the same reason, authors in the third category have often failed to provide a comprehensive picture of the Azerbaijan rebellion. The search for internal rather than external causes of the crisis is a useful corrective to the 'Soviet intervention explains all' school but it tends to go too far the other way. While a version of the truth seems to lie between the second and third categories, both also suffer from the weakness that in explaining the roots of the Azerbaijan crisis, they pay undue attention to the peculiarities of the province's history. Azerbaijan is identified as having special problems and grievances, radical tendencies, which at times led the province on the road towards provincial autonomy and even secessionism. In Azerbaijan radicalism and separatism have been seen as synonymous.

This chapter questions the above assumptions, and will try to demonstrate that while Azerbaijanis are quite rightly seen to have been part of the mainstream of Iran's twentieth-century radical movement, their manifestations of separatism and autonomy were neither typical nor representative of the majority of the population. Rather they were the product of particular circumstances and conditions, of which outside intervention was one important factor and the chronic weakness of the central government another. Despite the province's distinctiveness in terms of racial descent and language – differences that are shared with a number of other provinces – Azerbaijan's contemporary history has demonstrated an attachment to a strictly Iranian nationalism.[5] This attachment was reinforced, not weakened by the centralising and modernising trends that took place during the first half of the twentieth century.

Before reviewing the early twentieth-century history of Azerbaijan, a few general observations about the province should be made.

Firstly, any understanding of Azerbaijan's history must take into account the geographical location of the province. Straddled by Turkey to the west and the Caspian Sea to the east, Azerbaijan's northern border is shared exclusively with the Soviet Union. Azerbaijan was a frontline victim of successive Turkish and Russian invasions of Iran: after the second Mongul invasion in the thirteenth century, Tabriz had briefly been the capital of the Mongul Empire; five centuries later, during the period of Ottoman decline, the Russians stripped Persia of her Caucasian territories.[6]

Despite the impact of Turkey and Russia on Azerbaijan and the close cultural links that exist between the Iranians of Azerbaijan and the Turks and Russians who live around their borders, the idea of a greater Azerbaijan, under either Turkish or Russian auspices has held little appeal. Azerbaijanis shared the general feeling of hostility and mistrust felt by all Persians towards their neighbours' pretensions. The existence of trading and commercial links did not change this picture. When the first stirrings of Persian nationalism were felt at the end of the nineteenth century, Azerbaijanis were among the movement's most prominent adherents. The ties that bound Azerbaijan to Iran were always stronger than the forces working against national unity.

Religion was an important factor in this picture. Islam was a major unifying force in Iran, the spiritual centre of the Shi'ite faith. The Turks are Sunnis, and while the USSR contains significant Shi'ite and Sunni minorities, Islam had never been the official state religion and following the 1917 Revolution was seriously proscribed. While Iran's holy places achieved widespread fame among Russian Muslims, Russia held no similar appeal for Iran's faithful.[7]

Apart from the uniting force of religion, Azerbaijanis were conscious of their province's integral and often glorious role in Persian history. They were prominent actors in the major political developments leading to the Constitutional Revolution, and present in all important walks of Iranian life.

Their own sense of belonging to Iran was wholly shared by the rest of the country which never doubted that Azerbaijanis owed their allegiance to Iran. Aside from the government's perennial concern about maintaining Iran's territorial integrity against both internal and external threats, Azerbaijan was an important trade centre and source of agricultural products. In 1938–9, when Azerbaijan's population was estimated to represent about 20 per cent of the national total, the province supplied about one-quarter of the country's needs in items such as wheat, barley, lentils and wool; held the same proportion of the country's total number of sheep and goats, and produced about one-third of its tobacco, almonds and cooking fat.[8]

Azerbaijan was also significant in industrial terms. In 1941 the town had eighteen factories, including five textile mills.[9] Its relatively high urban population stimulated a migratory movement to other major towns. Azerbaijanis were thus to be found throughout the country. Demographic changes and industrial growth assisted the province's integration with the rest of Iran and diminished the sense of provincial distinctiveness. This did not mean that Azerbaijanis lost their affection for their own language and culture, but simply that they also owed allegiance to a broader national consciousness, which they themselves had helped to create.

The language question is often seen as proof of Azerbaijan's distinctiveness and as a cause of the province's resentment against Tehran. The inhabitants of Azerbaijan speak Azeri, a Turkish dialect which distinguishes them from the Farsi-speaking majority, and some had resented Reza Shah's efforts to 'Persianise' the country and suppress the use of local languages. In addition, Persian speakers tended to disparage Azeri, regarding it as a language imposed by Mongul barbarians.[10] As one British historian writing at the end of the nineteenth century noted, there was 'no love lost' between the northern and southern races.[11] Nevertheless, the old antipathy had been overcome to some extent by the forces of modernisation and national integration, and it would be wrong to assume that Reza Shah's demise gave way to a resurgence of provincial feeling such as to inspire revolt against Tehran. Azeri was, after all, but one of many minority languages in a country where Farsi was the first language for less than half the population. Iran had long been obliged to accommodate to its linguistic differences, and while Reza Shah's policies were provocative to some, educated Azerbaijanis were prominent among those who believed that a common language was essential to the country's future progress and development.

Another factor making for the unity of Azerbaijan with the rest of Iran is that the majority of its inhabitants are not tribally organised. This is in contrast with other linguistic minorities such as the Kurds, Baluchis and Qashqa'is, whose cultural and kinship bonds made them particularly resistant to centralist tendencies.[12] While both tribal and provincial unrest in twentieth-century Iran were linked to periods of internal instability and external intervention, the two had little else in common. This was one of the reasons why the Kurdish rebellion of 1946 was quite different from that of Azerbaijan. Although both were subject to a high degree of foreign interference, there was more Kurdish sentiment behind the Mahabad republic than there was Azerbaijani sentiment in the Tabriz national assembly. Significantly the former also proved to be less amenable to Soviet influence. The Kurds are Sunni Muslims and their members are distributed throughout Iran, Iraq and Turkey. Unlike the Azerbaijanis, their links to the Iranian state are relatively weak, as demonstrated by continuing Kurdish support for the creation of a greater Kurdistan.[13]

The purpose of these introductory comments has been to stress the ties that bind Azerbaijan to Iran. That the province possessed certain distinctive characteristics is clear, but these do not, in themselves, provide the key to the 1946 rebellion. Part of the answer lies in Azerbaijan's radical tradition, but this radicalism was by no means exclusive to Azerbaijan. What gave Azerbaijani radicalism its particular colouring was the province's susceptibility to Russian influence. The story of the Azerbaijan rebellion of 1946 is that of the forward march of Iran's radical and nationalist movement which was, more than once, diverted from its tracks by the exigencies of Soviet policy, and by the belief that the USSR would assist its cause.

Azerbaijan: from the last Qajars to the Second World War

Towards the end of the nineteenth century, when the first signs of organised dissent to the century-old Qajar dynasty were observed, Azerbaijanis were prominent among the protestors. Qajar decadence and corruption, which had brought the state to near bankruptcy, were important factors in the mobilisation of opposition, but so too was the influence of Western movements and thinkers.

Ultimately the Qajars lacked the internal dynamic, financial means or the efficient army which were needed to sustain their dynasty and to achieve reform and resurgence in a period of internal upheaval. Gradually they lost control of the slim consensus on which their power was based. The last Qajar monarch, Ahmad Shah, left for Europe in 1923, although it was not until 1926 that Reza Shah was crowned as head of the new Pahlavi dynasty.[14]

One of the Qajars' efforts to gain finance, the awarding of concessions to foreigners, caused major public protests in 1872, and again in 1891–2 when two Europeans were awarded major economic concessions, the latter being a total monopoly over the exploitation and distribution of tobacco. The 'Tobacco Regie' provoked a national outcry in which Tabriz citizens played a dominant role in the popular movement against the 'bartering of rights to foreigners and unbelievers', which led to the concession's repeal in 1892.[15]

This demonstration of early 'nationalist' sentiment, culminated in a period of popular protest and political unrest from 1906 to 1911, known as the Constitutional Revolution because the protestors obliged the Shah, Muzaffar al-Din, to grant the country's first constitution and convoke its first national assembly or majlis. During the revolution, and the civil war which followed, the country was divided into groups which fought for the retention of the constitution or for its removal.[16]

Once again Tabriz was at the centre of the confrontation. Azerbaijan deputies were predominant in the first assembly, and when the new Shah, Muhammad Ali, attempted to undo the constitutionalists' work, and crushed the assembly by force, Tabriz formed the core of provincial opposition. The town was besieged by the Shah's forces from June 1908 to April 1909. Its resistance was a testimony to the strength of feeling that the constitutional movement had aroused in Azerbaijan, and demonstrated the province's attachment to the ideals of the Iranian nationalists. The siege threw up local heroes, whose names are still revered: Sattar Khan, the illiterate horse dealer, and Baqir Khan, a bricklayer who performed heroic acts and mobilised popular support for the defence of the town.[17]

The siege finally ended with the arrival of Russian troops. Nevertheless, developments in Tabriz had kept the nationalist movement alive. By July 1909 Tehran was in nationalist hands once more. Muhammad Ali was deposed, and in August the second national assembly was convened.

The nationalist struggle in Iran was closely linked to the revolutionary developments taking place in neighbouring Russia. In Tabriz, certain political societies affiliated themselves with the Baku Social Democrats, a party consisting mainly of exiled Persians and Russian Azerbaijanis. It was this offshoot of the nationalist movement, a precursor to the Persian communist party, which would later try to wrest the initiative from the leaders of the Gilan and Azerbaijan rebellions; its members were also to predominate in the later creation of the Azerbaijan Democratic party.[18] It was perhaps inevitable that the constitutional movement in Iran should be coloured by events in Russia. In Tabriz in particular the association between the Social Democrats and the nationalists gave the province the appearance of greater radicalism. The more extreme demands of the Russian Social Democrats were, to some degree, superimposed on Iran's broad-based popular movement.

In the second assembly Azerbaijanis predominated among the radical deputies and came into increasing conflict with the conservatives and moderates. The fragile alliance that had sustained the unity of the nationalist movement was soon eroded as divisions in the assembly increased. Meanwhile, foreign intervention further helped to hinder the efforts of the constitutionalists. The signing of the Anglo-Russian convention in 1907 dismissed hopes that either power would lend its support to the nationalist cause. If Persian nationalism stood for anything it was the rejection of external interference in the country's affairs. Yet the convention provided the precedent for further intervention, both in the prewar years when Iran's internal condition deteriorated, and during the war itself when military conditions dictated it. In 1915 Ottoman troops had also invaded Iran, turning the country into a battlefield of conflicting internal and external pressures.[19]

Although the Iranian provinces, and in particular Azerbaijan, had played an important role in the constitutional movement, there was no real distinction between the local struggle and the national one. It was assumed that a 'genuine' constitutional government would pay due consideration to the special needs of the provinces and recognise the regional diversity which characterised Iran. Provincial autonomy was not, therefore, a demand to be associated with the Constitutional Revolution.

This picture changed somewhat with the experience of foreign occupation, war and finally the Russian Revolution. During the Russian occupation, most Tabriz citizens, but especially the intelligentsia, increased their dislike of the Russian forces, who had been in evidence since 1909. A series of incidents between Russian troops and the local population increased the tension.[20] By the time of the October Revolution, hostility towards Russia, and frustration with central government policy produced a potentially volatile mixture of ingredients. Provincial groups prepared to take independent action to satisfy their grievances. Many were as much against the central government and the occupation as they were for anything else, but all were influenced by events in neighbouring Russia. Such was the case with a small guerrilla force, known as the Jangalis, formed in Gilan under the leadership of Mirza Kuchik Khan.

Because of the countrywide state of discontent, the potential for such manifestation had existed before the October Revolution. The Gilani move-ment, for example, preceded it.[21] Nevertheless the revolution was important in supplying encouragement, and sometimes practical assistance, to local rebels. In general it was welcomed by Iranians who saw it as the means to end the occupation and establish a more egalitarian relationship with their northern neighbour. Britain was now perceived as the main obstacle to the nationalist dream of an Iran independent of foreign influence.[22]

In the northern provinces, the revolution had a special impact. Russian troops in Azerbaijan rebelled and were subsequently recalled. Meanwhile the Bolsheviks gave encouragement to nationalist forces by renouncing both the Anglo-Russian Agreement and 'all tsarist claims on Persia'.[23] A number of provinces declared open rebellion against Tehran. In Gilan, Kuchik Khan's movement gather momentum.

The Gilan rebellion was directed against Tehran and its capitulation to foreign pressures. The Jangalis demanded the cancellation of unequal treaties, the evacuation of British forces, administrative autonomy for Gilan and the defence of Islamic principles. Initially the movement was neither separatist nor communist but its focus shifted during the civil war in Russia, which brought the Red Army into northern Iran, and by the creation of the Adalat party which challenged Kuchik's leadership of the local rebel movement. The Adalat party, which consisted of former Social Democrats and Bolshevik sympathisers, soon became an important force in northern Iran. One of the party's first acts was to join forces with the Jangalis, and following a congress in Enzeli, during which it changed its name to the more familiar Persian communist party, it declared that it had formed with the Jangalis a 'Soviet Socialist Republic of Iran'.[24] The link between the Jangalis and the Russian revolutionaries having been sealed, Kuchik's struggle took on a different aspect; it now carried with it the hopes of the young Bolshevik regime and its Persian allies.

The initial advantage that accrued to Kuchik's movement from his alliance with the communists was short lived; he soon lost both local and national support. Paradoxically, it appears that Kuchik had been reluctant to seek Bolshevik support but had been urged on by his more radical colleagues.[25] Moreover, he was no communist, and contrary to Russian expectations could not be persuaded to become one. This was the comment of one Soviet observer:

We do not conceal the fact that the composition of the new government is far from communistic. At the present moment it unites those who have risen under the slogan of 'away with England' and 'away with the Tehran government which has sold itself out to England'. The cabinet consists of the democratic petty bourgeois elements of northern Persia.[26]

Kuchik soon quarrelled with his communist colleagues, yet he continued to lose popular support. Few Persians wished their country to pass from Russian to Soviet tutelage. Meanwhile there were rumours that the Gilan regime was carrying out anti-Islamic policies. The 'Gilan Republic' finally collapsed following the successful *coup d'état* by Sayyid Ziya Tabataba'i and Reza Khan which brought the Qajar dynasty to an end.[27] By pledging to restore national unity and signing a new treaty with the Soviet government, Reza Khan undermined the last props of the Gilan regime. His own Cossack troops supplied the military force required to retake the province. In the ensuing conflict, both Kuchik Khan and the communist party leader, Haydar Khan, were killed, and many of their supporters fled to the Soviet Union.[28]

While the Gilan revolt provided an example of the Soviet government's early efforts to garner the support of overseas nationalist movements, it was ultimately more important as a bargaining counter in negotiations with Tehran. In this respect it had much in common with the later Azerbaijan rebellion, in that the fate of each movement rested on the exigencies of Soviet policy. Arguably, the Gilan rebellion had a stronger root than did the Azerbaijan uprising. Kuchik Khan was an Iranian nationalist who joined forces with the communists in the belief that he could strengthen his cause;

there was, as we shall see, no comparable leader among the Azerbaijan Democrats. Nevertheless the strong degree of continuity between the two movements was demonstrated by the Social Democrat–communist party origins of many of their leading members.[29]

The Azerbaijani Democrats of the 1940s probably had more in common with their Gilani forebears than they did with the followers of a parallel movement in Azerbaijan which emerged in 1917 under the leadership of a local religious man and prominent Democrat, Muhammad Khiabani. Khiabani and Kuchik Khan shared certain goals *vis-à-vis* their policies towards the central government, but Khiabani, unlike Kuchik Khan, unequivocally rejected Soviet support. Nevertheless, Khiabani's movement had prospered in the wake of the Russian Revolution, and won further support for its anti-British stance. At a Democrat conference in Tabriz, Khiabani changed the local party's name to the Firqih-i Dimukrat Azerbaijan. A petition was sent to Tehran demanding the fulfilment of constitutional rights, the establishment of provincial councils, and the appointment of a governor general who could be trusted by the people of Azerbaijan; it also voiced the now familiar complaints about unequal provincial representation and budgetary allocations.[30]

Khiabani's movement met with little resistance, and he soon took control of Tabriz, establishing his own provincial government. He renamed the province 'Azadistan' or land of freedom. Khiabani's goals were essentially reformist and nationalist, but also reflected provincial frustration at the central government's abandonment of the constitution and its succumbing to foreign pressures. Khiabani was thus able to exploit popular discontent and seize the local initiative. He solicited neither the support of the Russians, nor that of the communist party and distanced himself from the Gilan movement. Therein, perhaps, lay his weakness, for, in the absence of outside assistance, there was insufficient local or national interest in his movement to sustain it. With Khiabani facing growing opposition from within the province, a concerted initiative from Tehran soon brought his reign to an end.

Despite the considerable attention that both the Khiabani and Kuchik rebellions have received, it is doubtful that either demonstrated a genuine desire for provincial autonomy. They were rather products of local dissatisfaction at the government in Tehran, as well as being part of a general reformist trend, which had commenced with the constitutional movement, but whose effects continued to be felt for some time. Left to their own devices both provincial leaders would have been satisfied with a government in Tehran which respected constitutional rights and reconvened a representative and effective national assembly to implement nationwide reforms. It is not surprising that they gained inspiration from the Bolshevik experience, which not only seemed to accord with some of their democratic and reformist ideals, but also broke completely with the old pattern of Russo-Persian relations. Yet

Kuchik's decision to join forces with the Persian communists and to accept Bolshevik support proved detrimental to his cause. Persians were alarmed by Bolshevik activities, particularly by reports that Moscow had dispatched hundreds of 'communists' to Iran to support Soviet ambitions there. Ultimately the Bolshevik connection detracted from the movement's popular support, while the Persian communists became increasingly identified with the Soviet Union. The party's Baku origins and its early history sealed the link with the new Soviet state.

The Persian communists had shared the Bolshevik experience and felt the revolutionary euphoria. They were perhaps just as eager to support the Soviet cause as they were to bring about changes in Iran. Although there were differences among the party's leaders, as demonstrated by the contrasting approaches propounded during the party's first congress in Enzeli in July 1920, their loyalty to the USSR was not in question. As one congress resolution stated, it was the duty of the Persian communist party to 'fight jointly with Soviet Russia against world capitalism and to support in Persia all forces opposed to the Shah's government'.[31] The appointment of Haydar Khan as party leader after the Baku Conference of Eastern Peoples in October of the same year, also demonstrated deference to Russia. Its first elected leader, Sultanzadeh, had been critical of the general line adopted at Baku.[32] Subsequently the party was obliged to accept the Soviet abandonment of the Gilan Republic in favour of a *rapprochement* with the Tehran government which resulted in the signing of the Soviet–Persian treaty of February 1921.[33] The subsequent withdrawal of Red Army forces obliged the party to take refuge in Baku once more. This defeat of the 'Persian revolution' owed as much to the changing estimates of the local situation by Bolshevik leaders as it did to their desire to conclude agreements with neighbouring countries to make the young Soviet state less vulnerable to hostile attack.[34]

The loyalty of the Persian communists to the USSR is of particular significance, since it was from their ranks that many members of the future Azerbaijan Democratic party were drawn. Their introduction to Russian revolutionary ideals, and their enforced period of exile under Reza Shah helped sustain their close links with the USSR, and correspondingly distanced them from Iranian reality. This was less the case with the Tudeh party, whose members were, in general, drawn from a younger group of European-educated Marxists with weaker Soviet links.

In consolidating his position, Reza Khan faced continuing outbreaks of unrest around the country including two further rebellions in Azerbaijan and Khurasan. These were short lived however, and were soon overcome by Reza Khan's superior military forces. In these different uprisings against the central government which followed the First World War, it is true that Azerbaijanis played a central role, and that both Soviet influence and the province's own radical tradition were important factors in inspiring unrest. Nevertheless there was no indication of genuine autonomist sentiment in the province. Most of the rebellions, inside and outside Azerbaijan, were spontaneous responses to local conditions caused by the war and central government policies. If anything, Kuchik Khan and Khiabani's efforts showed a desire to rescue the constitution rather than to establish autonomy for Azerbaijan. Secession was a threat used to put pressure on Tehran, but was not an end in itself.

The manifestations of tribal and provincial unrest that had characterised the first two decades of the twentieth century were largely to disappear as Reza Khan established himself in power. Although also a product of the revolutionary mood that prevailed during this period, the different rebel movements had, to a large extent, depended for their success on foreign intervention and the debilitation of the central government. When these conditions no longer prevailed, such manifestations gradually died down. The constitutional movement had taken root in Persian hearts and minds; the defence of the constitution remained the goal of Persian reformers and radicals. Even if its achievement remained out of reach for the next twenty years, the centripetal forces which went hand in hand with the progress of Iranian development continued to triumph over the still existent, but slowly diminishing centrifugal ones.

The rise to power of Reza Shah, as he became in 1926, was to mark the end of the old Iran, a 'giant bazaar', characterised by the loose network of power and shifting alliances.[35] Reza Khan broke from the Qajar mould and set himself the joint tasks of building a strong army, which the Qajars had always lacked, and deploying it to assert Tehran's authority over the country. Reza Khan was a nationalist, but not a constitutionalist: he wanted a strong centralised state, but was not interested in a political consensus. Although during his reign he continued to pay lip service to the majlis, he preferred to concentrate power around the army and a few chosen individuals. He shared the views of prominent contemporary thinkers, of whom Ahmad Kasravi was one notable example, that modernity, national unity and development were desirable goals, but these, he believed should emanate from his concept of authoritarian and centralised power, not from constitutional government.[36]

The advent of Reza Khan thus spelt the end of the already divided and proscribed democratic movement. Although the democrats could take some comfort from the abrogation of the bilateral treaty with Britain, and the final withdrawal of foreign troops, negotiated by Reza Khan in 1921, many of their earlier achievements were nullified by the increasingly repressive policies of his regime. An integral part of Reza Khan's campaign was to crush permanently the residual manifestations of unrest in the provinces. Reza Khan had been commander of the Cossack brigade which had overcome the Khiabani rebellion; by 1921 his troops had meted out the same fate to the Gilan and

Khurasan rebels.[37] Between 1921 and 1926 when Reza Khan crowned himself Shah-in-Shah, thus inaugurating the new Pahlavi dynasty, he had further consolidated the army and launched a series of successful campaigns against the country's once powerful tribes.[38]

Reza Shah's policies were to earn him considerable opposition and the lasting hatred of certain sections of the population, yet he secured public support by shifting his alliances with the country's powerful interest groups and by winning the confidence of conservatives and moderates who were fearful of the consequences of the radical tendencies thrown up during the last years of the Qajar dynasty. He thus obtained a 'genuine' majority in the Constituent Assembly vote which gave its support for the establishment of the Pahlavi dynasty.[39]

Reza Shah's policy towards the provinces and tribes – one historian described the latter as 'the most sordid chapter' of his reign[40] – undoubtedly caused bitterness and resentment. However, it would be wrong to assume that the provinces were held in a state of abject repression, and were waiting for the first opportunity to reassert themselves. This view ignores the multifaceted nature of the provincial movements during the Constitutional Revolution, their strong nationalist component, and perhaps most important, the fact that the provinces played an important role in Reza Shah's efforts at national modernisation and integration.

As has already been suggested, it was doubtful that the majority of the local population had been united behind the rebellions of Kuchik Khan and Khiabani, particularly with respect to their autonomist demands. However the existence of these movements, and the subsequent appearance of the Azerbaijan Democratic party, which shared at least some of their goals, has led to the assumption of continuity with the implication that the autonomous spirit had been kept alive throughout the Reza Shah years. This continuity was in many ways more apparent than real, and was the result of a coincidence of factors, of which Soviet interference was the most important. Of the local elements who supported these movements, only one group can be clearly identified: the Persian communist party. The Persian communists may have helped to fuel local discontent, particularly since many originated from the Azeri-speaking and Armenian communities. However, the party's efforts were seriously compromised during the Reza Shah period: firstly because of the exigencies of Soviet policy, and secondly because of Reza Shah's own anti-communist measures. After the party's second congress at Urmiah in 1927, at which it took a 'sharp turn to the far left', and thenceforth condemned Reza Shah as an 'imperialist stooge', many of its members were arrested or forced into exile.[41]

Among those arrested were Pishihvari and Uvanissian,[42] both important figures in the later debates between the Tudeh and Azerbaijan Democrats. Of those who escaped to the Soviet Union, some disappeared in Stalin's purges. The survivors formed the core of the Azerbaijan Democrats, although a few chose to join the group of younger Marxists who later formed the Tudeh party. Among the latter group were those Persian communists who questioned the party's rigid subordination to the USSR.

A sympathetic view of the Reza Shah period would point to his achievements in the economic field; his improvements in communications, the most notable landmark of which was the Trans-Iranian railway; his reestablishment of order throughout the country; a certain success in foreign policy, particularly in his relations with neighbouring countries, of which the Sa'adabad Pact of 1937 (between Iran, Iraq and Turkey) was one example; and his work in the fields of public health, education and justice. However, even sympathetic observers recognised his serious limitations: 'Like many nationalists, he was more intent on the independence of his country than on the freedom of his people.' Others note that despite some 'striking results' in Reza Shah's reform programme, the upper and middle classes were the first to benefit, while progress in the economic field was unbalanced, with emphasis on high prestige projects.[43]

There is no doubt that many of Reza Shah's policies were unpopular, particularly in the provinces. The absence of any form of local self-government, the Shah's contemptuous attitude towards linguistic minorities, and his anti-religious policies have all been singled out as special motives for provincial discontent. Azerbaijan, because of the Shah's special dislike for Turkic-speaking groups, its 'deep commitment' to Shi'ism, its 'indigenous intelligentsia' and high level of urbanisation is held to have experienced particular hardship and frustration.[44] Yet there is little evidence of a real link between the different manifestations of Azerbaijani unrest that existed in the Reza Shah and post-Reza Shah periods. To assume that there was such a link is to ignore the evidence of Azerbaijani patriotism, and the province's participation in Iran's development process. While provincial resentment undoubtedly existed, it seems unlikely that this was responsible for the extreme demands which surfaced after 1941. As during the 1917–25 period, the prevalence of unrest in the early 1940s was not necessarily indicative of a nascent revolutionary or autonomist movement, but of a mixture of general discontent at the country's condition and a genuine desire for change and reform. Once again, discontent in Azerbaijan was the more readily exploitable because of the presence of Soviet troops. Outside interference gave special prominence to the rebellious elements of the province. The existence in Azerbaijan of certain groupings with particular grievances against Tehran also contributed to the impression of unrest in the province.

One difficulty in establishing the origins of provincial discontent, in the post-1940 period, lies in the confusion which prevailed throughout the country after the joint allied invasion and occupation and the forced abdication of Reza Shah. There was widespread confusion and unrest, but much of this was the product of allied propaganda and public dislike of the occupation. A return to the Reza Shah style of government was clearly considered unacceptable, but few of the new political groupings that emerged during this period offered concrete alternatives, while several of them were closely linked to one or other of the occupying powers.[45] It is thus difficult to ascertain the extent to which the demands for the redress of provincial grievances, or the later calls for autonomy, were the true reflection of popular will, or merely of foreign influence. One thing is clear: both Britain and the USSR were willing to kindle the separatist issue when they felt that this might serve their interests.

The demand for the redress of grievances suffered under Reza Shah was real enough, and the realisation of constitutional rights which had been so seriously circumscribed during his reign was the goal of many reformers. In the provinces, there was new interest in the establishment of provincial councils. Although it has been suggested that Reza Shah's modernisation policies had aggravated the traditional conflicts in Iranian society and widened the gap between the capital and the provinces,[46] there is no evidence that the Azerbaijanis of 1941 were more militant than those of the constitutional period, or were any less attached to constitutional goals. Despite the fact that some Azerbaijanis had resisted Reza Shah's language restrictions, and religious minorities had demanded the right to practise their faith, there was no evidence of mass protest on Reza Shah's departure. This was in contrast to the tribally organized Kurdish areas of West Azerbaijan where there was widespread unrest and rumours that the Kurds were planning to create an independent state.[47]

The underlying mosaic of tribal and ethnic diversity that had characterised Qajar Iran had not disappeared, although the tribes would never regain their former importance, but on it had been superimposed the concept of a broader allegiance to Persian nationalism. While this concept was still weak in certain areas, it had grown stronger in Azerbaijan which had itself provided much of the impetus to the nationalist movement and supplied some of the country's greatest contemporary thinkers, of which Ahmad Kasravi, Khalil Maliki and Hasan Taqizadeh are but three well-known examples. Dislike of Reza Shah should not be confused with dislike of belonging to Iran. Nationalism in itself was desirable, but not the despotic nationalism of Reza Shah. What was called for was a fusion of the values enshrined in the constitutional movement with the awakened nationalist mood. The failure to achieve this, through the inability or unwillingness of ruling elites and the intervention of foreign powers, encouraged the search for more radical solutions.

From the allied invasion to the declaration of autonomy

Two foreign observers, commenting on the conditions in Azerbaijan prior to the rise of the democrat movement in the 1940s, concurred in the feeling that

Azerbaijan was not ripe for rebellion. An economic report by the British consul in Tabriz in 1937 found that local initiative had been sapped by government intervention and that Azerbaijan could in no way be described as an independent economic entity. Moreover, the report found that labour was without 'mass consciousness' and class feeling was 'non-existent'. Indeed, the most powerful social force in Azerbaijan was the 'all embracing Islam'.[48]

A later report by the American consul in Tabriz echoed these words. Azerbaijan was in a state of 'supine dependence', politically it was 'immature'. Moreover, it found that there was 'absolutely nothing of a nationalist nature which can be considered unredeemed in this province . . . any suggestion that the province was out of place in its sovereignty was a fantasy plucked out of thin air'.[49] Significantly, the American report also stressed the 'dominant and dominating force' of religion in the lives of the Azerbaijani people, and continued in a vein more appropriate to describing the years preceding the Khomeini revolution, noting that the mosque in Azerbaijani towns was 'virtually the only cultural center available to fully 95% of the people of this province . . . it is interesting to note that the mosques in Azerbaijan frequently become extemporaneous political forums . . .' Such forums may have constituted the basis for an attack against the government, as during the Tobacco Regie or the Constitutional Revolution, or indeed in 1941 and 1979, but the mosque would not have encouraged any move towards provincial autonomy especially with Soviet support.

If the religious convictions of the Azerbaijani people made unlikely a spontaneous provincial uprising, and tended to reinforce, rather than to weaken their national ties, the province certainly shared the mood of uncertainty and discontent which prevailed throughout the country at the beginning of the occupation. Iran had been humiliated by the allied invasion. The Shah may not have been popular, but his ignominious demise, and the pathetic performance of his army, which fled in confusion at the allied advance, contributed to a sense of national defeat. In addition, the enforced rupture of links between Iran and Germany – then the country's most important trading partner – was greatly resented. The war was felt to be distant from Iran's immediate concerns, and Iranians were understandably reluctant to share the privations which the allied war effort involved. Although not required to fight, Iranian soldiers and citizens had lost their lives in the allied invasion, while the economic losses to the country were immeasurable. Food was in constant short supply, and the cost of living increased by 800 per cent between 1939 and 1944, dropping only slightly in 1945.[50] Rich and poor alike suffered from allied requisitioning which increased the sense of national grievance.

Despite the gloom surrounding the circumstances of the occupation, there was room for optimism on the political front. Press and political freedoms which were impossible under Reza Shah now permitted a flourishing of new parties or loose political groupings and a variety of newspapers. Few of these groupings achieved the status of party in the Western sense of the term, with the important exception of the Tudeh, created in 1941 by a group of Marxist intellectuals who had been arrested in 1937 for their communist activities and were released following the allied invasion. The only other party which achieved a comparable level of organisation was Sayyid Ziya's National Will party (Hizbih-i Iradih-yi Milli) created in 1944 as the successor to his Fatherland party.[51]

The majlis itself was essentially unchanged in its appearance and composition. Preparations for elections to the 13th majlis had already commenced under Reza Shah, and the new assembly, which first met soon after his departure, looked remarkably like its predecessor. This proved to be to the advantage of the young Shah since it allowed him continued control over military matters: a privilege that proved to be invaluable in his later consolidation of power.[52]

Despite the apparent continuity, the absence of strong central authority, characteristic of the Reza Shah period, in which parliament had been little more than a rubber stamp, permitted the new assembly to act as a forum for discussion and debate in a manner previously impossible. Another new departure was the formation of parliamentary factions (*fraksiuns*). Important in the context of Azerbaijani developments was the Azerbaijan faction: a group of provincial deputies, mainly of Qajar aristocrat origin, but with certain pro-Soviet sympathies.

While the greater activity of the majlis was a welcome development, the assembly remained in many respects an unwieldy body. It was the scene of shifting alliances and unstable majorities, as witnessed by the rapid change of ministries during the occupation period. This lack of continuity was a serious source of weakness in a country already debilitated by the effects of the war.[53] Yet despite the limitations of the majlis, and the efforts of the allies, notably Britain, to dispense with its services altogether, the assembly not only survived, but succeeded in passing some important pieces of legislation. Perhaps its most notable achievements in terms of future developments, were the passing of two bills, one banning the negotiation of oil concessions with foreign powers, and another preventing the holding of elections while foreign troops were on Iranian territory. These and other important measures passed during the occupation period, to be discussed in this and in further chapters, demonstrate that the majlis could not be written off merely as a cumbersome and inefficient body.

The composition of early wartime cabinets was conditioned by the predominance of British influence in Iran. While Britain was severely critical of Iran's politicians and its political system, the post of prime minister was consistently filled by candidates likely to support British interests in Iran. Soviet interests were poorly represented in the capital, a fact of no small significance since it led the USSR to concentrate its efforts on exploiting its position in the northern zone of occupation.

In Azerbaijan, aside from the presence of its own forces the Soviet position was strengthened by the existence of certain groups which had particular grievances against the central government and which, for different reasons, maintained close links with the USSR. Apart from containing some of Iran's religious minorities, including members of the Christian Armenian and Assyrian communities, whose bonds with the Iranian state were weak, Azerbaijan was also the point of entry for Iranian exiles who had been living in the USSR. Among the latter were members of the old communist party. There were also a considerable number of former migrant labourers, known as *muhajirin*, also believed to be particularly susceptible to Soviet influence.[54] It was such groups, bolstered reportedly by Soviet Caucasians who had followed Soviet forces into Iran, which gave Azerbaijan's unrest its unique flavour.

Despite the obvious potential for exploitation in the Soviet zone, there was little evidence, at least during the early occupation, of any widespread popular sympathy for the USSR. On the contrary, the arrival of Soviet forces produced a hostile reaction from the local population, which, if British reports are to be relied on, was more pro-German than pro-Russian.[55] The overwhelming impression of Azerbaijan in this period was one of disorganization and confusion, making difficult any identification of the different currents of opinion. The picture was further complicated by the tight control that Soviet forces came to exercise over their zone, which stretched from Mahabad in the west to Mashad in the east (see Map 1). Strict censorship laws restricted the circulation of news, while Soviet propaganda was most effective in obscuring the reporting of local events.

The early agitation in Tabriz was directed therefore against both the Persian administration and the Soviet occupation. The merchant community, the pulse of Iranian public opinion, was 'obstructive', shutting the bazaar and restricting business activities.[56] Many merchants had enjoyed lucrative trade links with Germany and were dismayed by the sudden rupture in relations. The upper classes of Tabriz were also hostile, and a large-scale exodus to the capital was reported, although there was evidence of some cooperation among big landlords who were anxious to protect their local interests.[57] Most government officials had deserted their posts, either before or soon after the arrival of Soviet forces. This wholesale departure of the Azerbaijani elite created a power vacuum in the province. The absence of local officials, and the dismemberment of the army and police force, while weakening Tehran's control over the province, gave extra powers and

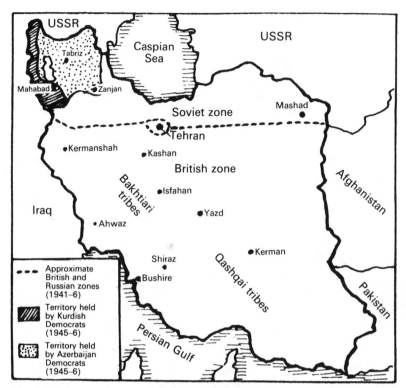

Map 1 Allied zones of occupation and boundaries of the Azerbaijan and Kurdish regimes

responsibilities to the Soviet occupying forces. It also gave greater prominence to local discontented elements.

If the absence of local authorities, and the administrative confusion that prevailed, played into Soviet hands, so too did the continuing pro-Germanism of the population. Popular sympathy for the German cause, even if exaggerated by the allies to explain their drastic invasion measures, helped the USSR to justify the need to impose its authority forcefully throughout its zone of occupation.

Amid the confusion which prevailed in Azerbaijan, it was possible to identify certain groups who initiated the first concentrated offensive against Tehran, and from whose adherents the Azerbaijan Democratic party would later take shape. All were in some way linked to the Soviet Union, and in turn received Soviet encouragement. These groups, and in particular their autonomist tendencies have received considerable attention. Their existence has been linked to Azerbaijan's turbulent past, as well as explaining the sudden rise of an autonomist movement. It does seem however, that the claims made for the popular basis of an Azerbaijan rebel movement have been exaggerated, as have the province's historical grievances, and its desire for 'home rule'.[58] Although selective citing of British and American archival sources may give a contrary impression, the unrest that existed in Azerbaijan was neither widespread, nor representative of the population as a whole, but was limited to certain clearly defined groups.

Perhaps the most significant of these was the local Armenian community, who together with a smaller group of Assyrians formed an important minority in Azerbaijan.[59] Armenians had played an important role in Iran's civil war which followed in the wake of the Constitutional Revolution, but they had also been closely identified with the pro-Bolshevik Social Democrats and later with the Persian communist party. During the civil war, Armenian radicals had organised a short-lived takeover in Rasht with the help not only of the Russian Social Democrat and Social Revolutionary parties, but also the Armenian Dashnaks from the Caucasus, an extremist group which supported Armenian independence.[60] It was not clear to what extent the Dashnaks, or other Soviet Armenians, played a role in the manifestations of autonomy in the early 1940s. They may have been among the immigrants from Transcaucasia who crossed over into Iran in the absence of border controls at the beginning of the war. Their presence in Persian Azerbaijan has been confirmed by different sources, and they undoubtedly contributed to the early unrest.[61] Not only were the Armenians a potentially divisive force in the province, but they were also particularly vulnerable to Soviet exploitation.

The links between Iran's northern Christian communities and the central government had never been strong, but they were particularly strained during the Reza Shah period. Religious minorities suffered from his national unification policy, which jeopardised their religious and educational activities. Once central government control was removed, the local Armenian and Assyrian communities at once demonstrated their assertiveness. They identified closely with the Soviet occupying forces, and staged demonstrations in different towns throughout the Soviet zone. In Tehran, the Armenian community also maintained close contacts with the Soviet forces and published three opposition newspapers.[62]

It was in Armenian organised meetings in Tabriz that the first calls for the 'separation' of Azerbaijan were heard. Local Armenian leaders praised the Soviet troops, vilified the Iranian administration, and called for the province's independence and annexation to the USSR.[63] Armenians were also among the early adherents of the Tudeh party, although their separatist tendencies soon made them uncomfortable bed-fellows; they also constituted an important element in the creation of the Azerbaijan Democratic party.

While the status of Iran's Armenians, their links to the USSR and radical political tendencies made them a focus of discontent in Azerbaijan, they could hardly be described as representative of the local population. The traditional distrust between the Muslim and Christian communities meant that the latter were generally unpopular. Their unpopularity increased with the arrival of Soviet forces, when arms were distributed and a local security force improvised among Armenian irregulars to help keep order in the province. Although soon disbanded, this 'police force' provoked local hostility and strengthened the links between the Armenians and the USSR, since the community now sought Soviet protection against possible acts of revenge by the local Muslim population.[64]

Another important group associated with the early unrest in Azerbaijan was the *muhajirin*. The movement of labour from Iran's northern provinces to the Caucasian region predated the Russian Revolution, and these migrant Iranian workers were linked to radical activities both in Russia and in Iran. They numbered among the Persian communist party's early followers and many later transferred their sympathies to the Tudeh and the Azerbaijan Democrats.

Consular sources also refer to other 'discontented' elements, describing them 'communists', 'democrats', or simply 'the rabble'.[65] Without further identification it is impossible to say exactly who such individuals were. The picture is a confused one, and is not made any clearer by the tendency to lump together all the different manifestations of unrest in the province. Was the 'angry crowd' which protested against a sugar shortage in Tabriz composed of the same individuals who were busy organising local committees to demand regional autonomy, the removal of local officials and the use of Azeri?[66] With the existence of a number of different and sometimes conflicting reports, it is difficult to draw definite conclusions about the early unrest in Azerbaijan. The evidence, however, is not suggestive of a widespread popular movement, although Soviet propaganda tended to promote such an impression. It can be no coincidence that the most radical expressions of unrest in Azerbaijan came precisely from those groups who, for different reasons, enjoyed close links to the Soviet Union.

Added to the confusion created by the Soviet presence, was that produced by British propaganda against Reza Shah, German propaganda against the allies and both Persian and Turkish alarmism about Soviet intentions. It was difficult to trace coherently the thread of events or to discover who was directing them, particularly in view of the prevailing lawlessness and parallel unwillingness of either the USSR or the Persian administration to take the initiative for restoring order in the province. In a report at the end of 1941, Britain's consul in Tabriz, Cook, pointed to the difficulties in identifying any political movement, but warned of the discontent which lay below the surface, as manifested by the secret meetings calling for a break with Tehran, the 'Turcophile parties, Bolshevik machinations and Armenian intrigues', while German agents spread rumours against the Russians, and the province still hoped for the arrival of the German army from the Caucasus.[67]

The signature of a Tripartite Agreement between Britain, Iran and the USSR in January 1942 put an end to some of the speculation about allied and German intentions, temporarily alleviating the disturbed conditions of Iran's major towns. The agreement legitimised the Soviet presence and gave it an air of permanence: whatever the wishes of the local population, the Soviet occupying force would henceforth call the tune in northern Iran, as did their British allies in the south.

Given the prevailing conditions, Tabriz proved to be an excellent location for the promotion of a pro-Soviet party, especially one which could incorporate in its programme some of the province's long-held grievances against the capital. The opening of a branch of the Tudeh party in Tabriz, early in 1942, supplied some of the political direction that had previously been lacking. However the party's attempt to unite the province's different protest groups was ultimately unsuccessful as the Tudeh Central Committee frowned on the extreme regionalist demands of its provincial members. This problem was reflected in the party's local organ *Azerbaijan*, which while dwelling on the national concerns of the Tudeh, also dedicated considerable space to provincial issues. The paper's editor, Shabistari, who would later renounce his links with the Tudeh, was a passionate advocate of the Azeri language.[68]

Since the Tudeh aspired to rapid expansion of its membership on a broad democratic front, it felt bound to welcome Azerbaijan's various radical groups under the party's umbrella. It was hoped that, in time, these potentially divisive elements would be induced into the mainstream of the party with only a minimum of concessions to local demands. Even when this hope was not realised the party was still unwilling to sever the link with its northern colleagues, an action which would detract from its image as the only party which united Iran's reformist elements. The possibility of creating a new party which might better serve the interests of the northern radicals and those of the USSR remained, however, open.

Despite the evident contradiction between the Tudeh's activities in the capital and the provinces, the party continued to prosper in Tabriz. At the end of 1943, the Tudeh's provincial branch in Azerbaijan was referred to as the 'largest in the country'.[69] The party also began to attract support among the region's factory workers. There was some competition from an existing workers' organisation led by a popular local leader, Khalil Ingilab. Ingilab's activities were privately frowned on by the Tudeh, particularly since he took recourse to the strike weapon, the use of which the party carefully avoided because several Tabriz factories were supplying Soviet war orders. In time, Ingilab was displaced and his organisation affiliated to the Tudeh-controlled Central Council of Trade Unions.[70]

The Tudeh's labour related activities in Azerbaijan did not diffuse the autonomy issue as the party might have hoped. One obstacle in this respect was the attitude of the USSR, whose interest in the provincial question helped to provide much of its momentum. In effect there were two radical forces at work in Azerbaijan: the Tudeh party, which was trying to spearhead a nationwide democratic movement, and local separatist elements enjoying Soviet protection. At first the divisions between these two groups were obscured, because of Soviet propaganda and the Tudeh's desire to present a united front. Their differences would later emerge more clearly.

While all these developments were taking place, a mood of discontent prevailed in Tabriz, as in much of the country, as a result of the privations caused by the war. Although allied policies were much to blame for the situation, it was often the Persian government which became the target of popular hostility. Certainly, attitudes towards the Soviet Union mellowed with the experience of the occupation. Local merchants, obliged to abandon their German contacts, now looked to the Soviet market where profits could be made from the new demands arising from the war. Landowners too accommodated themselves to the presence of Soviet forces, avoiding a conflict which might threaten their interests. There was to some extent a marriage of convenience between the occupying forces and the local population. Among the lower classes, Soviet propaganda appears to have had some success, particularly among factory workers, although among the more conservative peasantry, still bound by semi-feudal ties to their landlords, it had less impact.[71]

The susceptibility of Azerbaijan to Soviet influence, the weakness of the central government and the absence of other political parties gave the Tudeh an unique opportunity to thrive. When preparations for the 14th majlis elections began in mid-1943, the central government regarded the Tudeh in Azerbaijan as a serious danger. Local industrialists feared that their workers, encouraged by the intense propaganda campaign, would now vote for the Tudeh, and representations were made to the British consulate for assistance. Although landlords remained confident that the peasants would follow their lead, the propertied classes in general felt that the Soviet Union would try to 'cook the election' and pack the majlis with their supporters.[72]

Capitalising on the hopes and fears of the local population, the Tudeh in Tabriz organised a broad electoral platform known as the Free Front which incorporated democratic and leftist groups. The Free Front, distinct from, though associated with the Freedom Front – an association of liberal press editors, sympathetic to Tudeh goals – pledged its opposition to the reelection of the Tabriz governor general and other Azerbaijani officials.[73] Meanwhile the Tudeh posted election stickers throughout Tabriz, calling on the electorate to join the fight against corruption, bribery and food shortages.[74]

The political rallies which continued through the autumn and winter of 1943 gave the impression of an imminent 'liberal' victory. Alarmed at the course of events, Prime Minister Suhaili, during his second term in office (February 1943–March 1944), briefly suspended electoral preparations in Tabriz on the grounds that the Soviet consul general was promoting his own candidates.[75] This action, together with the calming effects of the Declaration on Iran, signed by the allies at the end of 1943, brought a brief respite from the tension.[76]

As the election results became known early in 1944, it was clear that the much feared Tudeh landslide had failed to materialise. Indeed it was the constitutional issue which contributed to a major redefining of political alliances, not the influence of foreign powers. With only five Tudeh candidates elected nationwide by the end of 1943, the British minister, Reader Bullard remarked that 'the bogey of Russian intervention in the elections in the north proved to be a small one'.[77] The majlis convened early in 1944 before the Tabriz elections had been completed, and there was a last minute burst of Tudeh activity in an attempt to improve the party's position. Further lists of candidates were produced and demonstrations organised. Transport to the polls was provided for Tudeh voters, although local authorities obstructed the party's efforts by closing the voting booths at 6 pm making it difficult for workers to vote.[78]

It was during these final electoral preparations in Tabriz that two figures emerged who would soon come to dominate the political scene in Azerbaijan, Ja'far Pishihvari and Muhammad Biriya. Pishihvari was promoted as a Tudeh candidate for the 14th Majlis, while Biriya gave a series of preelection addresses in favour of Tudeh and pro-Soviet candidates. In one rally in early March, Biriya described Azerbaijan's '22 years of oppression' under Reza Shah and called on the population to elect 'liberal candidates' to ensure 'better food and future security'.[79]

In the final shuffle of candidates in Tabriz it was difficult to discover who were the Tudeh and Soviet candidates, and whether these were one and the same. The Soviet consulate in Tabriz supported Tudeh nominees but also sponsored some non-Tudeh candidates, one example being a local merchant with commercial links in the USSR. Pishihvari, as further discussed in chapter 2, was not a typical Tudeh candidate, and his inclusion on the Tudeh list was probably the result of Soviet pressures. Certainly, as a War Office report noted 'the Russians did not confine themselves to supporting left-wing parties'.[80]

In the event, of the nine representatives elected in Tabriz, only Pishihvari and one other Tudeh candidate were successful. Neither took up their seats because the committee supervising the elections later refused to ratify their credentials. Even had they been accepted, two extra Tudeh deputies from the north would have made little difference to the overall showing of the party, for it secured only 7 out of a possible 50 seats. As a party the Tudeh had done well, but it is misleading to speak of a party victory for the Tudeh was the only party which carried its organisation into the majlis. The allegiance of other deputies proved to be ephemeral and they reorganised themselves into factions as before.[81]

Contrary to expectations, Soviet intervention had failed to change the face of Iranian politics. In Azerbaijan, Gilan, Khurasan and Mazandaran, Tudeh and Soviet influence made but a slight impression; outside the northern provinces their impact was negligible. There were sixty new faces in the majlis, but its pro-Western or independent elements predominated as before. The voting pattern in Tabriz in particular – less than one-third of the population voted – revealed the limitations of Soviet and Tudeh influence.[82] So far, fears of an imminent communist takeover had proved to be greatly exaggerated.

The results of the 14th majlis elections were, in many respects, a watershed for the Tudeh and the USSR. Their policies had thus far failed to produce a lasting impression, and it was clear that new strategies were called for. While the Tudeh was pushed closer to the USSR and greater radicalism, the latter also started to look for new ways to extend its influence (see chapter 5). The separatist issue, which had been kept alive through Soviet support to local sympathisers, now assumed greater importance. The Tudeh, which thus far had sought to avoid reference to provincial differences, was obliged to shift its position. By the party's first congress in August 1944, provincial grievances had become an important issue: northern delegates were allowed to speak in their native Azeri, and the party's new programme granted some 'modest concessions' to the provinces.[83]

Pressures from the north had affected the party in other ways. The rejection of Pishihvari's credentials as a majlis deputy provoked a hostile reaction from the Soviet authorities in Tabriz. While the Tudeh central committee had ultimately supported Pishihvari, probably under Soviet pressure, it had little to say about the rejection of his credentials. Nevertheless the Soviet propaganda attacks and outbreaks of worker unrest in Tabriz which greeted this decision were bound to implicate and draw in the Tudeh. As the political temperature rose in Tabriz, and relations with Tehran took a downward turn, the Tudeh could hardly afford to pass up the opportunity of exploiting the situation. The party now focused its efforts on a new campaign to prevent the appointment by Tehran of a new 'reactionary and conservative' governor general of Azerbaijan.[84]

Representative of the changing direction and tempo of events in Azerbaijan were the activities of Biriya. In August, the British consul reported that Biriya had presided over the amalgamation of the Tudeh union, the local workers' union, and the anti-fascist party into what was called the 'workers' council of Azerbaijan'.[85] This was seen as the fruition of Tudeh efforts to secure control of the local trade union movement. Yet the workers' council, while affiliated to the Tudeh-controlled Central Council of Trade Unions, could also be turned into a weapon against the Tudeh when the autonomy movement gathered momentum.

The pace of change in Azerbaijan was further accelerated after the spurning of the Soviet oil mission at the end of 1944. It was during and after the majlis debates over oil concessions took place that the demand for the autonomy of Azerbaijan resurfaced with new vigour. The oil crisis also prompted a further reconsideration of popular attitudes towards both the Tudeh and the USSR, while contributing to a realignment of political forces which was ultimately to the disadvantage of the left. The pro-Soviet groupings in the majlis were now reduced to one – the Tudeh – while the conservative elements gained new supporters.[86]

Another event which strengthened the right was serious worker unrest in Isfahan. A confrontation between millowners and their workers drew in the southern tribes who assisted in suppressing the Tudeh-supported labour uprising. The loss of support for the left as a result of the Isfahan riots was reflected in the withdrawal of a number of newspaper editors from the Freedom Front, and in the success of a counter-offensive against the Tudeh headed by Sayyid Ziya and his own Independence Front. Alarm at the situation in Isfahan also enabled prime minister Sa'id to pass an emergency bill giving extra funds to the war ministry.[87]

The Tudeh had not yet reached the peak of its power, but it was already losing important supporters which in the long run helped to close off its political options. The process which would transform the Tudeh, literally 'the masses', party into a small and disciplined pro-Soviet communist party had already begun, although its results would not be apparent for several more years. In the short term, the downturn in the fortunes of the reformist deputies and the corresponding improvement in the position of conservatives increased Soviet and Tudeh frustration. While the Soviet Union sought to improve its position, many Tudeh members also concluded that foreign support was essential in their struggle for power. The need for the party to redefine its position was made more pressing as a result of the Soviet demand for an Iranian oil concession.

The background to the 1944 oil crisis lay in the Iranian government's desire to award an oil concession to the United States. Talks with the Americans encouraged first Britain, then the USSR to press for similar claims.[88] The appearance of a Soviet official in Tehran demanding an extensive concession, to cover some 216,000 square kilometres in the northern provinces, revealed at once the conservative and anti-Soviet composition of the majlis, while also forcing the Tudeh into open identification with the USSR. Most majlis members applauded Sa'id's decision to postpone discussion of oil concessions until after the war. Sa'id claimed that privately even Tudeh members had sympathised with his decision, but publicly the party moved to a position of unqualified support of the Soviet demand.[89] Freedom Front newspapers, after some defections, condemned the government's decision and organised demonstrations in major cities.[90] The Independence Front, bolstered by new supporters, endorsed the government's position.[91]

While the capital remained divided on the oil question, Azerbaijan was solidly behind the USSR. Even the usually pro-government newspaper *Akhtar-i Shomal*, supported the Soviet case. Many Azerbaijanis appear to have been convinced by the economic benefits the concession promised to bring. As the end of the war approached, local factories which had managed to keep going with Soviet war orders now faced the threat of closure. The Soviet oil concession was seen as a way of avoiding the economic collapse of the province. The British consul remarked how 'Tabriz workers are generally aware that factories are near collapse and their interest lies in stability and new industry.'[92]

Pro-Soviet propaganda, and the threat of reprisals failed to secure the passage of the oil concession, but did result in the resignation of Sa'id. This proved to be a poor reward for Soviet and Tudeh efforts, particularly since his departure was followed by the introduction of a new bill by deputy Muhammad Mussadiq, who had played an important role in the rejection of the Soviet oil demand, to prevent the negotiation of any further foreign oil concessions.[93] Nevertheless, the new prime minister, Bayat, was regarded more favourably by the Soviet Union, and by early 1945 much of the agitation resulting from the oil issue had died down.

Attention shifted to Azerbaijan once more where the oil question gave new impetus to the anti-government campaign. It was difficult to determine the true state of public opinion in Azerbaijan because of the effects of the Tudeh and Soviet propaganda campaign. One new departure was the linking of the oil question to provincial grievances against Tehran:

It seems that speakers are treating the grant of an oil concession as only part, or as a consequence of a wide programme of administrative and social reforms, calling amongst other things, for the establishment of freely elected town and provincial councils and the transfer of great proprietors' land to the peasants.[94]

The purpose of the councils, according to a Tudeh representative in Tabriz was to protect the 'freedom and rights of the people' by expediting central government measures 'only if they were in the popular interest'.[95]

The growing agitation and political activity in Tabriz were invariably linked to the Tudeh, although there was no evidence that the party had come any closer to supporting the separatist tendencies which were resurfacing in the province. The Tudeh leadership would make no further commitment to autonomy beyond that of endorsing the idea of provincial councils. Yet it increasingly appeared that the party's central committee was no longer in total command of the Tabriz branch. In Azerbaijan, the British consul noted, the Tudeh appeared to be: 'rather more than a party in the ordinary sense of the term. Its activities and authority seem constantly to overlap with not only those of the local workers' unions, but even those of the local government. Party members take on a police role in the streets.'[96]

Soviet influence was partly responsible for these changes. Vice-Consul Wall thought that the Azerbaijan workers' council was falling under Soviet control, while Biriya went about Tabriz accompanied by two Soviet soldiers. At the height of the oil concession crisis, when Tabriz was the scene of daily anti-government demonstrations, Soviet troops prevented the local police and military from using force against the protesters. Although agitation temporarily subsided in January after the departure of the Soviet oil mission, the period between the oil crisis and the official formation of the Azerbaijan Democratic party in September 1945 saw a gradual deterioration in central government authority in the province.[97]

In early 1945, the new prime minister, Bayat, was still grappling with the repercussions of the oil crisis. His success in defusing Soviet anger was at least partly due to a secret promise he made to the Soviet ambassador that he would support the establishment of an Irano-Soviet joint company to exploit Iran's northern oil.[98] He also showed leniency towards the Tudeh. In his attempt not to alienate the left, however, Bayat upset some of his own supporters. Their displeasure increased when the prime minister secured the removal of the controversial American financial advisor, Arthur Millspaugh.[99] Many majlis members felt this was the wrong moment to risk American disapproval and wanted Bayat removed. The potential of majlis forces to shift their allegiances was nowhere more clearly demonstrated than in the brief premiership of Bayat. He took up the position in November 1944 with the support of the right, when he left in April 1945 he enjoyed the support of the left.

In Azerbaijan, Bayat could do little. He removed the Tabriz mayor, a future Democrat, because of his 'liberal' sympathies, but otherwise failed to stop the prevailing trend, which was the gradual unseating of all *persona non grata* to the Russians.[100] In April the provincial governor general and the governor of Tabriz were forced to leave. The Tudeh's position continued to weaken. There was a growing gap between the party's national programme and the exclusively provincial focus of Pishihvari, Biriya and their associates.

While the latter gained prestige and new supporters, the local Tudeh branch seemed discredited. It took the blame for the threatened closure of Tabriz factories like the Pashminih wool and Khusravi leather plants. The Tudeh programme had promised to create new industries, yet the province now faced imminent economic collapse.[101]

The government's anxiety over the situation in the north led to attempts to get the Iranian question raised at the various allied conferences, in particular that of Yalta, early in 1945. By placing the international spotlight on Iran it was hoped that the occupying powers would refrain from further interference and perhaps even accelerate their plans for withdrawing their troops. From the Iranian viewpoint, the conference was unsatisfactory in that no concrete assurances were given, however it did at least oblige the great powers to turn their attention to Iran's problems. The obstructive attitude of the USSR at Yalta and later at Potsdam was, in the long term, decisive in securing American support for Iran.

As the northern crisis deepened, Bayat's own position became increasingly untenable. After failing to win a vote of confidence in April, he resigned, to be replaced by Ibrahim Hakimi. The latter's premiership proved to be even shorter. His promise to appoint ministers 'without political bias or conviction' failed to rally the necessary majority, and his administration fell within a few weeks.[102]

The end of the war in Europe in May 1945 brought little relief to the Iranian domestic scene. If anything the internal crisis worsened with the controversial appointment of Muhsin Sadr as prime minister on the one hand, and the more desperate policies of the USSR on the other. Sadr's choice of ministers and his proposed anti-Tudeh measures alienated the majlis and public opinion, provoking a new government crisis. Even the Shah warned of the possible consequences of Sadr's reactionary and repressive policies.[103] The government crisis which followed provided the ideal environment for a new attack on Tehran's authority in Azerbaijan. Although Sadr was able to curb Tudeh activities in the capital and southern towns, the virtual absence of central government control in Azerbaijan meant that his policies had little impact. Perhaps the most important consequence of Sadr's election from the point of view of northern developments was the paralysis of government business which followed the boycott of parliament by Tudeh, Liberal and Independent parties in protest against his policies. Numerically sufficient to prevent a quorum, this group obstructed the functioning of the majlis during a critical three-month period. By September, when the deputies had managed to resolve some of their differences, the Azerbaijan and Kurdish Democratic parties had already declared their existence.

The months May to September of 1945 witnessed intense activity throughout Azerbaijan. In the western regions, Qazi Muhammad assumed leadership of the Kumalah – a local group of Kurdish nationalists – and was said to be organising his own army in Mahabad.[104] In the east, future Democrats, using the Tudeh front, organised demonstrations against Sadr. The editor of *Azerbaijan*, Shabistari, promised 'vigorous action' if the government continued to ignore the province's demands. Meanwhile, Biriya, with the help of the workers' union, organised road blocks to prevent local merchandise, destined for Tehran, from leaving the province.[105] Azerbaijan's independence was soon to be achieved.

In July there were celebrations in Tabriz to mark the third anniversary of the Freedom Front. Local Tudeh leaders were conspicuously absent from the rallies, and it was the pro-Soviet *Kharvar-i Now* which took the lead in the press attacks against the capital while taking pains to stress Azerbaijan's special friendship with the USSR.[106] Events continued to move swiftly. In early August there was a riot at the municipal prison in Tabriz resulting in eighteen casualties. Soon after there were seven deaths in a clash between the Tudeh and a conservative landlord in the village of Liqvan outside Tabriz. Considerable alarm was caused by these two incidents and a government commission was sent to Tabriz to investigate. The commission's work was inconclusive, but infuriated the left who attacked the commission as a collection of 'reactionary elements'. A list of demands was sent to Tehran, which included a 'fair hearing' for the Tudeh, the appointment of a sympathetic governor general and better representation of provincial interests.[107]

The crisis in Azerbaijan was infectious. In mid-August a mutiny took place at the Mashad garrison in neighbouring Khurasan. Some of the forty-odd deserters were subsequently captured and killed. Others survived and were rumoured to be among the volunteers for the Azerbaijan Democrats' local militia or 'peoples army'.[108] By the end of August Tehran was placed under martial law, the army was purged and a ban placed on all political meetings. In Azerbaijan however, the opposition to the government went from strength to strength. 'Dress rehearsals' for the Democrat takeovers took place in Tabriz and Maragheh, when armed rebels briefly seized control, forcing local officials to leave their posts.[109] These events, as the US consul remarked, proved to be merely the prelude to greater acts of daring. Order was temporarily restored, but the time was now right for Pishihvari and his supporters to capitalise on the local unrest and the deadlock in Tehran and show their hand.[110]

Pishihvari officially announced the creation of the Azerbaijan Democratic party (ADP) on 3 September 1945 with the publication of a party manifesto. This was followed by the announcement of the local Tudeh branch that it had decided to affiliate with the Democrats. Biriya's workers' council of

Azerbaijan followed suit. The newspaper *Azerbaijan* became the new party's official organ.[111] The formation of the ADP was followed, a few weeks later, by that of the Kurdish Democratic party, after Kumalah leaders returned from a visit to Baku.[112]

Pishihvari had made a clean break with the Tudeh. His party espoused different goals, and in his manifesto he had carefully avoided reference to either the Tudeh or the Freedom Front. He also refrained from occupying the recently vacated Tudeh premises.[113] The Democrat leader brought together the discontented elements of Azerbaijan under the banner of his new party: Armenians, Assyrians, *muhajirin*, old communist party members, and some Tudeh members all had a place. Soviet Caucasians and members of the Soviet army were also active in the new party's foundation.

Between September and December of 1945 the Azerbaijan Democrats directed their efforts towards consolidating their control over Tabriz and other major towns in east Azerbaijan. The Kurds followed a similar pattern, although the boundaries of their future 'republic' were smaller. The Democrat takeovers met with little resistance due to the presence of Soviet forces, who had both kept to a minimum the numbers of Iranian troops stationed in Azerbaijan and now prevented the arrival of any reinforcements. Qazvin was the northernmost point to which government troops were allowed to proceed.[114] The gendarmerie and army commanders in Tabriz did not formally surrender until December, but they played little part in resisting the Democrat advance. There were reports of isolated clashes between the gendarmerie, supported by the local Shahsavan tribe, and Democrat supporters, but the general picture was one of resignation. The Iranian army commander in Tabriz favoured surrender, believing that resistance was futile.[115]

The early statements issued by the ADP dwelt on the neglect of provincial affairs by the capital. The stated task of the Democrats was to establish the 'rights' of the Azerbaijani people which had been denied to them by successive governments. The intransigence showed by Tehran had obliged the people to take matters into their own hands.[116] The ADP programme and subsequent 'declaration of autonomy' were a synthesis of the different demands for provincial reform. The most important of these were: the establishment of an autonomous government in the province, the official use of the Azeri language, better representation in Tehran and a more equal distribution of revenue. The Democrats also pledged to fight corruption, end unemployment, improve the position of the peasantry, and bring prosperity to Azerbaijan.[117]

The Democrats were anxious to avoid alienating foreign powers, and their programme advocated friendly relations with all 'democratic countries, especially with the allies'. At the end of September they sent a petition to the Council of Foreign Ministers meeting in London, drawing attention to the conditions prevailing in the province.[118]

Iranian officials, forced to leave Azerbaijan, described Pishihvari's demands as 'seditious', and saw the creation of the ADP as part of a Soviet plan to annex Iranian Azerbaijan. Most majlis deputies, with the exception of the Tudeh were united in condemning events in the north: 'Recently a Democratic Party has been formed in Tabriz. A party which was democratic only in the sense that it had been content to borrow the name of democracy ... no truly patriotic Azerbaijani had any share in its formation.'[119] The government however did promise to adopt a more 'vigilant' attitude towards Azerbaijan and 'spare no effort in improving the lot of peasants and workers'.[120] Sadr's attempt, however, to appoint a new governor general provoked further Azerbaijani outrage. His choice, Sayyid Farrukh, who had been minister for the interior during the Suhaili administration, surprised Reader Bullard who thought Farrukh to be 'unsuitable for any high post, being small-minded, headstrong and violent'.[121]

Most majlis deputies were united in their desire to prevent the establishment of an autonomous Azerbaijan, but there was otherwise little accord between them. After a period of mutual recriminations over the northern situation, there was a growing realisation that the present state of affairs should not be allowed to continue. Sadr was as unwelcome to the USSR as he was in Azerbaijan, and his continued presence in power was seen as an unnecessary provocation. A replacement had to be found, and Hakimi was brought forward once again as a compromise candidate. Before Sadr's resignation, however, his supporters were successful in securing the passage of two important bills: one to secure an increase in the military budget, the other to postpone elections until allied troops had withdrawn from Iranian soil.[122]

The return of Hakimi in October 1945 did little to defuse tension in Azerbaijan, although Farrukh's appointment as governor general now seemed unlikely. As local party branches were set up throughout the province, the Democrats held their first party congress in early October, when they announced their intention to establish 'full autonomy' for the province. At the same congress came news of the Kurdish campaign, and of a new harmony between the Firqih Dimucrat – as the ADP was locally known – and the Kumalah.[123] This understanding proved to be fraught with obstacles, but from the viewpoint of Tehran, the spectre of Azerbaijan united in rebellion was an imposing one.

If Hakimi was a less controversial candidate than Sadr, he had no more intention of negotiating with the Democrats, but, like his predecessor, he was unable to prevent their advance. The Democrats were armed and could rely on Soviet support to prevent the arrival of the Iranian army. Gendarmerie posts were systematically overcome and Democrat forces took control of communications. By mid-November the hastily assembled Democrat militia had moved north to control the area around Maraghih, and south in the direction of Zanjan. After the announcement that the 'first phase' of its organisation was complete, with party committees set up in all major towns in east Azerbaijan, the party called its first 'national' congress in Tabriz on 20 November 1945.[124]

About 650 delegates attended the congress which formed itself into a constituent assembly, drawing up a fourteen-point declaration. This document reiterated the main points of the Firqih's earlier manifesto and appealed to the 'five great democratic powers' to support Azerbaijan's demand for autonomy and self government 'like any other nation'. The declaration also charged the assembly with the task of appointing a national committee to implement its resolutions and to oversee preparations for the election to the Azerbaijan majlis, to be convened in December.[125]

As voting commenced, the Democrats continued to consolidate their hold over the province. By the end of November Zanjan had fallen to Democrat forces. Hakimi could no longer dismiss the ADP as 'a group of ignorant people who, in the last few days, have caused some regrettable incidents at certain places in the Third and Fourth Departments'. In what was intended to be a conciliatory gesture, he appointed the former Prime Minister Bayat as governor general of Azerbaijan with instructions to implement 'wide ranging' provincial reforms.[126]

Bayat tried to win the confidence of the Democrats. He claimed that as prime minister he had intended to introduce provincial councils, and now promised that a large sum (40 million rials) would be set aside for social reforms and a public works programme in Azerbaijan, and offered to replace 'reactionary government employees'. It was a case of too little, too late. As Vice-Consul Wall commented, Bayat's efforts were simply ignored. After fifteen fruitless days in Tabriz, he returned to Tehran.[127]

Elections for the Azerbaijan majlis took place in the week ending 3 December. Candidates were required to be literate in Azeri, between the ages of 27 and 80, and 'friendly' to the aims of the Democrats; all Azerbaijanis over the age of 20 could vote. One hundred representatives were duly elected to take their seats in the majlis which held its first session on 12 December 1945 in a Tabriz theatre. Only the Soviet consul general responded to the Democrats' invitation to all foreign representatives to attend the opening ceremony, at which Pishihvari was approved as prime minister and charged with the task of selecting a cabinet.[128]

Tabriz had not, as yet, officially fallen under Democrat control, although its militia already occupied strategic points outside the town. On 12

December the Iranian gendarmerie surrendered, followed, two days later, by the army garrison. The Iranian government troops stationed in Ghazvin retreated to Hamadan.[129] With Azerbaijan's autonomy now a *fait accompli*, the Kurds soon followed suit. Qazi Muhammad and his supporters had for some time exercised *de facto* control over the Kurdish regions, but this situation was made official on 15 December with the inauguration of the 'Kurdish People's Government of Mahabad'. In January 1946 Qazi Muhammad was elected president of the 'Kurdish Republic'.[130]

2 The Azerbaijan Democratic Party

Studies of the Azerbaijan Democratic party tend to fall into similar categories to those described in chapter 1 in explaining the origins of the Azerbaijan crisis. One view of the ADP holds that there was little to distinguish it from the Tudeh and that both parties received their orders from Moscow.[1] Another finds clear distinctions between the two parties and rejects the theory of Soviet predominance.[2] Yet another draws on each of the above schools of thought, but adds little that is new to our understanding of the nature of the ADP.[3] Again it is in a mixture of the above views that the truth probably lies. This chapter will consider the structure and goals of the Azerbaijan Democratic party, and look critically at the above approaches. Was the ADP synonymous with the Tudeh, and was the ADP really controlled by Moscow? The analysis offered so far in this book suggests the answer is no to the first question and a qualified yes to the second.

It is not difficult to see why many commentators have regarded the ADP as an offshoot of the Tudeh. Some of their professed aims were similar, both were closely aligned with the USSR and significantly, the Tudeh appeared to offer the ADP its unconditional support. If the dissolution of the local Tudeh branch was not an act of self-destruction, how could its affiliation to the ADP be explained except in the above terms? The action of the Tudeh party, as one sympathiser explained, represented an attempt to unify all the democratic forces of the province and to realise the 'legitimate demands of the Azerbaijani population'.[4]

Those unhappy with the above explanation could argue that the replacement of the local Tudeh branch was a mere propaganda move. The party's limited success in other areas could have prompted a new initiative in Azerbaijan where its potential field of action was greater because of the presence of Soviet troops. The term 'dimucrat' moreover, had a more attractive ring than 'tudeh'; at least so thought one British official: 'while not all can belong to the Tudeh, *everyone* can be a Democrat'.[5] The creation of a new party with a new name might thus be regarded as a Tudeh ploy to widen the party's appeal. By recalling the Democrats of the constitutional movement, the ADP might also enhance its popularity by emphasising its moderation, and the historical continuity in its programme and goals.

Despite certain similarities between the two parties, to regard them as one and the same is misleading. To do so neglects the early history of the Tudeh and instead draws a straight line from the Persian communist and the early 'nationalist' movements in Azerbaijan and Gilan to the Azerbaijan Democrats. Ervand Abrahamian has decisively demonstrated the different roots of the Persian communist party's founder members and those of the Tudeh as it was reformed in 1941.[6] Much had changed in the intervening years. National unity was seen as a prerequisite for development and was demanded by intellectuals of all political persuasions. Part of the weakness of the Qajar state was explained in terms of Iran's cultural and ethnic diversity and the decentralised nature of government control. Regional autonomy movements were encouraged by the Persian communist party; the Tudeh regarded them as dangerous.

The Tudeh's position on the nationality question was defined by one of the party's intellectual forebears, Taqi Arani. An Azerbaijani by birth, Arani advocated a centralised state and the abolition of minority languages including his native Azeri. He once defined Azerbaijan as a 'vital and deadly problem for Iran', and insisted that Azerbaijanis wished to relearn Farsi, which they had forgotten as a result of successive Mongol invasions.[7] When Arani died, his views were incorporated into the Tudeh's programme which stood unequivocally for a united Iran. In 1941, contemporary Iran did not, however, fit so neatly into the Tudeh's plans. The modernising and centralising trends of the Reza Shah period were at once incomplete and at the same time disrupted by the allied invasion which tended to exaggerate old tribal and regional divisions. The removal of the old Shah and the greater freedom of expression which followed unleashed a flood of complaints from the provinces. The provinces felt neglected by a centralised system which had inevitably favoured the interests of the capital. They now demanded better treatment and representation. The question of accommodating regional interests was to pose a problem for which Tudeh ideologues were poorly prepared.

The rapid growth of the Tudeh and its expansion to the provinces, already referred to in chapter 1, was of course a welcome development for the Tudeh. But the need to embrace the provincial question, eventually required a policy change. Azerbaijani members brought their regional grievances to the Tudeh forum, while a rethinking on the language issue was made urgent by the fact that a majority of Azerbaijani delegates could not even speak Farsi.[8] Clearly the ethnic question could not be ignored, but, rather than introducing fundamental policy changes, the Tudeh hoped that by making a minimum of concessions to the provinces, party unity could be sustained. Thus at the party's first general congress in August 1944 only vague assurances were given to pay 'greater attention' to provincial needs, although the party programme was amended to include a clause on freedom of language.[9] Nevertheless the Tudeh remained firm in its resolve not to further succumb to regional pressures, and at the same congress reaffirmed its hostility towards 'separatist tendencies'. At the second congress a further blow was delivered to the provinces when the Tudeh launched a nationwide literacy campaign in the teaching of Farsi.[10]

Without the physical presence of Soviet troops in Iran, it is likely that the Tudeh would have been able to contain the provincial problem. The encouragement of provincial grievances by the USSR made the party's task more difficult. The Tudeh was placed in a paradoxical situation: it owed part of its strength to Soviet inspiration and support, yet the USSR's position on the provincial question was potentially damaging to the party. In the long term, Soviet policy in Azerbaijan seriously compromised the Tudeh. Many of its members could not accept the subordination of their interests to those of the USSR which such a policy implied.[11]

The timing of events in Azerbaijan provides another clue to the degree of Soviet influence. Although minority groups in Azerbaijan had been calling for provincial autonomy since 1941, it was only after the majlis decision regarding oil concessions that the movement started to gather real momentum. By the end of 1944, the simultaneous call for a Soviet oil concession and for provincial autonomy was heard in Azerbaijan. The fortunes of the provincial movement were closely linked to the general trend of Soviet policy in Iran. It flourished when the latter became more urgent in its search for long-term influence, and floundered when the USSR believed its demands had been satisfied.

While the history of the growth of the provincial uprising seemed also to be closely bound to the Tudeh, this was deceptive. Most Tudeh members in Azerbaijan were ready to press for modest concessions to the provinces, but stopped far short of what the Democrats ultimately demanded. The alliance was an uneasy one in the early months of 1945, but by the summer most Tudeh members distanced themselves as the Democrats prepared to take control in Tabriz. There had been a difference in emphasis between the goals of the Tudeh central committee and those of its Azerbaijani branch, but the gulf dividing the Tudeh and the Democrats was far wider. The ADP was not therefore an extension of the Tudeh's provincial branch. It was essentially a Soviet backed creation and drew its support from local pro-Soviet elements and from former communist party members, who also enjoyed strong links with the USSR.

A source of confusion over the Tudeh's position lay in the party's failure to condemn openly the situation in Azerbaijan, or indeed to criticise Soviet policy. The party was not, at least between 1944 and 1946, the pro-Soviet monolith that it would later become. Its position on the Azerbaijan question merely reflected the belief that if any international support for its cause were forthcoming it must come from the USSR. There were certain party ideologues, those who emerged the stronger when the Tudeh finally split in 1947, who later would argue for the subordination of national interests to those of the Soviet Union. For the moment however, they were silent[12]

During 1945, Tudeh influence in Azerbaijan was, with Soviet collusion, progressively undermined. In the 14th majlis elections the USSR had supported non-Tudeh candidates, and this policy continued with regard to appointments in Azerbaijan. In an attempt to reverse the trend, the Tudeh announced a purge of the Azerbaijan branch in the summer before the ADP takeover. Khalil Maliki, strongly committed to national and linguistic unity, was sent to Tabriz to check autonomous tendencies within the party and to strengthen the Tudeh as a counterweight to Pishihvari's activities.[13] Maliki's efforts were useless. For a short while the two parties existed uneasily alongside each other. Soviet influence however, proved too strong for the Tudeh. The infrastructure of the new party had already been laid down by the work of Pishihvari and his colleagues, with the backing of the USSR and local pro-Soviet elements. The Tudeh in Azerbaijan was thus unceremoniously dissolved, and 'incorporated' into the ADP.[14] The party's central committee had apparently not been consulted, and was taken by surprise at the rapid course of events.

Pishihvari made no secret of the distinction between the Tudeh party and his own. In a description of the steps leading to the ADP's formation, he recalled:

In those days in Azerbaijan, there was no political organisation apart from the Tudeh. The latter had acquired a bad reputation and become ineffective. The Freedom Front, created through the efforts of Shabistari and myself, which consisted of old liberals and constitutionalists, had retained its purity, but lacked the power to fight. Thus following long discussions over a period of three days, between Shabistari, Padigan and myself, we decided to form the Democratic Party of Azerbaijan . . .[15]

Former Tudeh members who supported the creation of the ADP included Padigan, mentioned above, Qiyami and Biriya. Biriya's participation was important. As president of the Azerbaijan workers' council, he effected the affiliation of his movement to the ADP. The other leading members of the ADP had no links to the Tudeh, but like Pishihvari, owed allegiance to the old core of the original communist party, and had in general participated in the nationalist rebellions of the early 1920s.

The Tudeh's lack of involvement in the ADP was confirmed by its apparent ignorance of events in Azerbaijan. If Padigan was party to the discussions with Pishihvari about the ADP's creation, he did not pass this information on to Tehran. Tudeh leaders knew nothing of the decision to dissolve the local party branch. When they did find out, they were both surprised and annoyed. Khalil Maliki summoned an extraordinary meeting of the central committee, and called on members to denounce Pishihvari's action and refuse recognition of the new party. Only the intervention of the Soviet ambassador in Tehran prevented the publication of a message to this effect.[16] One former Tudeh member denounced the creation of the ADP in an article in the liberal daily *Sida-yi Iran*, in which he claimed that the Soviet embassy had organised the conversion of the local Tudeh branch into the Democratic party and had instigated the demand for provincial autonomy.[17]

The Tudeh was careful not to publicly show its displeasure. Following Maliki's failed attempt at intervention, the party kept quiet, and was soon to be heard cautiously sanctioning some of the Democrats' demands, insisting that the situation in Azerbaijan had been brought about by the neglect of successive governments.[18] Nothing however, could disguise the extreme anxiety of Tudeh members when the ADP proceeded to set up its independent government apparatus and to replace Farsi with Azeri as the official language of the province. Nevertheless, to the world at large, a façade of solidarity was maintained, helped coincidentally by the government's suppression of the party's main newspaper *Rahbar* from September to November 1946.

In contrast to the Tudeh's reticence in discussing Azerbaijan events, the Soviet press was full of praise. Similarly, Pishihvari's initial contacts with the Tudeh were minimal while his links with the Soviet consulate in Tabriz were close.

An illustration of the different goals of the two parties could be found in their respective programmes. The Tudeh programme, as far as possible, treated the country as a single unit and promised to 'defend to the utmost, the independence of Iran and the integrity of its soil'. Despite minor concessions to Azerbaijan, it tried to eliminate the need for special treatment of the provinces. The ADP, in contrast, considered that Azerbaijan's problems took priority over all other national issues, and its programme, while promising to 'respect' Iran's independence, also called for an autonomous Azerbaijan.[19]

Another major difference between the programmes of the two parties was over participation in the government. The Tudeh programme envisaged the party's participation in Iran's parliamentary system, and thus provided a platform from which the party could campaign in the majlis elections. The ADP programme rejected Tehran's authority. Because of the nature of its demands, it was a statement of non-participation. The Tudeh sought changes within the system, the ADP outside. Significantly, the Tudeh programme at no point endorsed the use of force, as a means of achieving its political goals. In this respect the ADP's decision to form its own army was unprecedented.

To summarise, the Tudeh's early programme was national in scope and essentially moderate in its demands.[20] It emphasised the necessity for a broad-based democratic government to implement a wide range of social and economic reforms with an emphasis on labour legislation and land redistribution. The ADP programme was local in scope and more extreme, at least in its provincial demands: the establishment of provincial councils with wide powers of autonomy, the substitution of Azeri for Persian as the official language, the increase to twenty in the number of Azerbaijani representatives in the majlis and a fundamental readjustment of tax arrangements whereby taxes collected in Azerbaijan would no longer be sent directly to Tehran. As noted earlier, the amendments to the Tudeh programme made as a result of provincial representations fell far short of such demands. Had the ADP merely been an offshoot of the Tudeh, why had the latter not adopted a more sympathetic attitude towards provincial grievances? It is easy to misconstrue the actions of the Tudeh party, such as its cautious endorsement of provincial councils, and conclude that it had already paved the way for the assumption of power by the ADP. However the Tudeh's idea of provincial councils was that they should play a strictly limited role in local affairs, not that they should be the means of achieving autonomy for any particular province.[21]

It was Soviet pressure that forced the Tudeh to reassess its attitude towards the provincial question, just as Soviet pressure had earlier reversed the Tudeh position on foreign oil concessions. The Democrat press in Azerbaijan insisted that the Tudeh and ADP were united in their goals,[22] yet the reserve displayed by the former continued well into 1946. Tudeh newspapers restricted their comments on the northern situation, and what they did say accorded, as far as possible, with the party's own broader reformist views. Azerbaijan developments were explained in terms of general nationwide disaffection rather than in terms of provincial grievances. No public reference was made to the ADP's link with the USSR.

It was impossible for the Tudeh to keep silent for long. When the Democrats came under attack in the national press, the party rose to its defence. To a series of hostile articles in *Ittila'at*, one of which claimed that as soon as foreign forces had left Azerbaijan, the population would 'punish the democrats, traitors of the nation, as they deserved', the Tudeh paper *Iran-i Ma* responded: 'The newspaper *Ittila'at* is deceived, the world will not allow Azerbaijan to be silenced again.'[23] Nevertheless, the Tudeh press was also careful not to take responsibility for statements made by the Democrats. Even if it did not openly criticise the ADP the Tudeh continued to disassociate itself from the latter's radical policies, particularly with regard to the language and autonomy questions. *Iran-i Ma* insisted that the ADP was not separatist, and expounded on the great affection which Azerbaijanis felt for the Iranian nation. In a further series of articles in December, the paper stressed the importance of Farsi as the national language and as the 'source of civilisation' for the entire country, including 'our dear Azerbaijani fatherland'.[24]

The Tudeh's official organ *Rahbar*, when it reappeared, was even more reticent about discussing the Azerbaijan situation, the absence of comment being a sure indicator of the paper's displeasure. In March, Khalil Maliki wrote an article contrasting the forces of dissolution and development inside Iran, referring to the central government and the 'forces of democracy' but made no mention of the ADP. Later he spoke of the possibility of the Azerbaijan example serving as a model for other provinces, but warned that the ADP should not profit from its experience by taking 'unilateral' actions. Another writer described the situation in Azerbaijan as merely one element of a broader countrywide struggle against the ruling class.[25] In conclusion, the reserve of the Tudeh press served only to confirm the distance between the party and the activities of the Azerbaijan Democrats.

It was true that the Tudeh approved of sections of the ADP programme, particularly those related to labour questions and the redistribution of land. As Pishihvari tried to implement a series of social and economic reforms in the province, the Tudeh made more of the common interest of the two parties.[26] The divisions between them were to some extent obscured with the passage of time, but the Tudeh came no closer to accepting the ADP position on language or provincial autonomy. It was, in fact, the ADP which moderated its tone on the language issue because of the need to reach an agreement with Tehran. This also helped to bring the two parties closer together.

In November 1946 the ADP and the Tudeh, together with other sympathetic groupings, joined forces for the purposes of presenting a united front in the forthcoming majlis elections. The old divisions remained however, in what proved to be a short-lived alliance as the ADP was officially dissolved in December. Subsequently the proscribed group of Azerbaijani Democrats who comprised the Firqih-in-exile, continued their separatist propaganda from the USSR, once more independent of the Tudeh.[27] It was not until 1960, when the Tudeh retrospectively admitted its neglect of the nationality problem, following a lead taken several years earlier by the USSR, that the two parties formally merged. Following the merger, delegates of the two parties agreed on a common programme, in which the Tudeh accepted that, despite the shared history of the Iranian peoples, Iran was a 'multi-national state'.[28]

Following its official demise at the end of 1946, there is little evidence to suggest that the ADP enjoyed any real support. This fact might of course be explained in terms of repressive government policies, but perhaps more important was the absence of Soviet propaganda which destroyed any illusions about the existence of a broad-based popular movement in Azerbaijan. Azerbaijanis no doubt still believed that provincial affairs were neglected by Tehran, yet the majority did not question the resumption of central government control despite some of its unpleasant consequences. The province remained a vital and integral part of the national economy, while Azerbaijanis, as before, constituted an important element in the professional, intellectual and political life of the country.

Those who hold that the ADP had its origins deep in Azerbaijani history, and reject the theory of Soviet predominance, point to the party's continued existence as evidence that the party had indigenous roots. Similarly, they argue that the privation suffered in Azerbaijan during the Reza Shah period, the change in status experienced by the province since Qajar days, together with the influences of the Khiabani movement and early communist ideas, could all be taken to indicate the existence of a specifically Azerbaijani democratic movement, pulling away from the constraints of central government. Thus the ADP, albeit aided by the special circumstances of the allied occupation in 1941, was simply a new manifestation, but essentially a continuation of this trend. A superficial look at the background of ADP leaders tends to support this argument, for they were, in general, as discussed below, the same early Persian communists who had supported the earlier uprisings in Gilan and Azerbaijan.

The 'continuity' thesis is appealing, but has one serious weakness: it depends on the conviction that there existed in Azerbaijan a genuine popular movement which desired provincial autonomy. As argued in chapter 1, there is considerable evidence which points away from this conclusion. Azerbaijanis saw themselves as Iranians first and foremost, regardless of their racial extraction, unlike the Kurds, who, as one observer noted, saw themselves as Kurdish 'first, last and always'.[29] The province's role in the constitutional movement, and its contribution to the modernising processes of the twentieth century, demonstrated a greater desire to promote national integration than regional autonomy. The idea that Azerbaijanis were self-reliant or sought independence was a myth nurtured either by those who felt persecuted by central government policy, or by those who sought to further Soviet aims in Iran.

There is no doubt that many Azerbaijanis wanted change; so did a large number of Iranians from all over the country. Whether they desired provincial autonomy was less certain. The mood of the province was hard to ascertain in view of the intense Soviet and Democrat propaganda. Nevertheless, there was no evidence of massive support for the ADP. There were few large demonstrations, and the electoral turn-out in the crucial 1944 elections was low. The pro-autonomy groups in the province were ill defined, far from homogeneous, and probably few in number – according to one observer, the original movement was composed of 'only some 200 persons'.[30] Moreover, as noted in chapter 1, they were unpopular with the population at large and could not be said to have been representative of it. It may be true that the USSR and the Tudeh party had won some support among the local population, support which the ADP inherited, but the latter could not be described as a popular movement. For most of the Azerbaijan population, their interest in the Democratic party went only as far as obtaining redress for their grievances; it stopped far short of what the ADP leaders were demanding.

If it is difficult to find genuine local support for the ADP, must it then be assumed that its leaders were no more than Soviet creatures? Since many of them were also active in the Persian communist party and the Gilan and Azerbaijan uprisings, were these too only manifestations of Soviet power and influence? Some general answers to these questions have already been suggested in chapter 1, but a few general observations may help to clarify this issue further.

There were clearly elements of continuity between the democratic movements of the 1920s and the 1940s, but this continuity does not, in itself, prove that the movements were purely indigenous in origin. Many of the personalities involved spent much of the intervening period in exile in the USSR. Their absence from Azerbaijan, even if it was the result of circumstances beyond their control, prevented the very continuity which was necessary for the democratic movement to put down deep roots. In contrast to the Tudeh, moreover, whose leaders were busily reorganising their party in the 1930s, the organisation of the ADP appeared to be a very last-minute affair. The Tudeh grew rapidly, but the ADP had little or no gestation period. Pishihvari himself only returned to the province late in 1944. As one Tehran deputy commented at the end of 1945: 'Although the formation of a political party required long preparation, the Democratic Party had, in only two months, developed sufficient strength to challenge the government.'[31] The speed with which the party was organised and the lengthy period of exile of its leaders, does point strongly to the conclusion that Soviet influence had been a crucial factor in its formation.

It would be wrong however to assume that the ADP leadership had no genuine desire to implement reforms in Azerbaijan. Nor should their historical role as the vanguard of a pro-Soviet communist movement be belittled. Yet if the Azerbaijani leaders were united behind a single cause, it was that of the Soviet Union. This was both comprehensible and acceptable in the post-1917 period, when Iran's young communist movement, like those elsewhere, identified closely with the USSR and shared its revolutionary euphoria; it was less so in 1945. Herein perhaps lay a critical difference between the ADP and Tudeh leaders. The former, who had witnessed the

45

Bolshevik revolution at first hand, and were well schooled in the doctrines of international communism, were unconditional in their support for the USSR. The latter, at least in the period under discussion, were not.

Pishihvari's own close links with the Soviet Union, and the timing of his decision to found the ADP, tend to point away from the conclusion that the democratic movement was the product of local circumstances and conditions. Rather, they reinforce the impression that Soviet influence was the predominant factor in the development of the democratic movement in Azerbaijan. It can be no coincidence that the ADP's creation coincided almost exactly with the end of the war with Japan, which marked the beginning of the six-month period, after which, according to the Tripartite Treaty, the allies should withdraw from Iran.

The desire to link Azerbaijan's radical history to the events of the 1940s has led to the assumption that separatism was an integral part of that history. Yet Azerbaijan's very radicalism, free from Soviet interference, would surely have represented no more than one of the many voices throughout the country calling for changes and reforms.

It is difficult to see how provincial autonomy could have been in the interests of the majority of the population of Azerbaijan. Once in power, the ADP encountered serious economic problems, demonstrating just how poorly equipped the province was for any sort of autonomous existence. Most Azerbaijanis soon felt deceived. As one disillusioned Democrat member, showing his party badge, told an American official in Tabriz: 'You see this . . . It is all I have to show for what we gained by the new government. Pishihvari and the others ride around in fine cars, but all I get is a button to pin on my coat.'[32] The best way for Azerbaijanis to resolve their provincial grievances was to seek the accommodation for their interests in Tehran. This did not necessarily exclude the possibility of provincial councils in the future, although the political climate in the 1940s was not appropriate for the devolution of power from the capital. This more moderate path is surely the one that Azerbaijanis would have chosen, had they been free from outside influence.

A closer look at the background of the individual members of the ADP tends to confirm the view that there were substantial differences between the ADP and the Tudeh and that the Azerbaijan movement owed its existence to Soviet support. As already noted, only a small number of Tudeh members joined the ADP. This was despite their obvious attachment to the province and the fact that they had already been prominent spokesmen for its grievances. Only one former member of the local Tudeh branch, Biriya, went on to play an important role in the new party.

There were certain characteristics common to all the ADP leaders, that is, those who were elected to the ADP 'national committee' in November 1945,[33] as well as those who were subsequently appointed members of the provincial cabinet.[34] Of those about whom data has been obtained, all but one were born in Iranian Azerbaijan and all but one were Azeri speaking; all had participated in the formation of the Persian communist party and in either the Jangal uprising in Gilan, the Khiabani rebellion in Azerbaijan or both, and all had spent part of the 1920s and 1930s in the USSR; only one, Biriya, was a founder member of the Tudeh, four others had at some time been associated with the Tudeh, but of these two left in 1943 and two in 1945. Only Biriya had been a member of the Tudeh at the time of its dissolution.[35]

It was thus a certain mix of characteristics which made up the background of the ADP leaders. It was not a sufficient condition to be Azerbaijani, or a member of the Persian communist party, or even to have spent years of exile in the USSR. Several Tudeh members shared one or more of these characteristics with the ADP yet remained loyal to their party. Why then did some former communists join the Tudeh, while others remained aloof until presented with the possibility of joining the ADP? A combination of the above factors was clearly important, but Abrahamian has also drawn attention to the importance of educational background. Intellectuals with a 'Persianised' education joined the Tudeh, while the Azerbaijani movement was in the hands of Russian trained men, not of Persian émigrés who had returned from pre-Nazi Germany, as was the case with many Tudeh members.[36]

The Tudeh were influenced by, and indeed were part of the centralising and modernising trend that prevailed in Iran in the early part of the century. In contrast, the ADP founders were Azerbaijani intellectuals, educated outside the state system and exposed therefore to quite different influences. Many of these differences can be explained by the age of the individuals involved. ADP members were, in general, older, and had therefore not been exposed to the 'Persianising' trend, although the intellectual processes behind it had already been set in motion. The younger intellectuals who later joined the Tudeh, regardless of their origins, were educated in the new philosophy, and represented a new generation. Significantly, no young Tudeh members joined the ADP although a few older Azerbaijanis did join the Tudeh. Of the latter, Ali Amir Khizi and Ardishir Uvanissian are two interesting examples, worthy of special mention. Both were from the older generation of Azerbaijanis, yet remained loyal to the Tudeh party.

Ali Amir Khizi was born in Tabriz in about 1900. Like many future ADP members, he participated in both the formation of the Persian communist party and the Jangali movement. In contrast to the later Democrats, however, Amir Khizi was a founder member of the Tudeh, and had been imprisoned and later released in 1941 with other members of the 'fifty three'.[37] The Tudeh sent him to Azerbaijan in 1942 to help organise the local party branch.

His principal task there was to persuade the Azerbaijani workforce to join the local Tudeh union and withdraw their support from the local union leader, Ingilab, who had upset Soviet and Tudeh plans by instigating strikes. Amir Khizi subsequently became head of the local Tudeh branch. He favoured the establishment of provincial councils and the introduction of moderate reforms in Azerbaijan, but did not sympathise with the ADP's more radical demands, and left Tabriz soon after the party declared its intentions.[38]

Back in Tehran, Amir Khizi argued that the 'force of circumstances' and especially the 'danger of imperialism' had given the Azerbaijani people no choice but to take over the provincial administration.[39] In other respects however, he shared the Tudeh's general skepticism over Azerbaijan developments. Despite his own Azeri background, Amir Khizi's loyalties to the Tudeh were stronger than any attraction he may have felt for the ADP.

Ardishir Uvanissian, like Amir Khizi, was a veteran of the Persian communist party. A Christian of Armenian extraction, Uvanissian was born in Rasht but was educated in Tabriz. He had spent some of his youth in France and the USSR. He returned to Iran in 1933, but was arrested for his communist activities the following year.[40] Like Amir Khizi, Uvanissian was a founder member of the Tudeh; he was also regarded as one of the party's leading theorists. He was a dominating figure at the party's first general conference, which produced modifications to the party programme following complaints from the provinces. He was elected to the 14th majlis as Armenian and Assyrian representative, and although his name was indisputably linked to the USSR owing to the close Soviet link with elements of these minorities, his candidature was accepted unlike that of Pishihvari. He was not involved in the discussions over the dissolution of the local Tudeh branch in Azerbaijan. His support for provincial reform did not extend as far as Pishihvari's claims for autonomy, and he too left Azerbaijan soon after the new party appeared. Despite his ethnic roots, Uvanissian considered himself as an Iranian rather than as champion of the distrusted Armenian minority, a factor which may help to explain his continued affiliation to the Tudeh.

Amir Khizi and Uvanissian both had been closely involved in the Tudeh's early activities, and it was this fact, perhaps more than any other which distinguished them from the ADP leaders. In general, the most active ADP members were those who had the fewest links with the Tudeh. There were, of course, exceptions, notably Biriya, who was the only Tudeh member to enter the provincial cabinet. A Tabrizi who had spent many years in the USSR, Biriya returned to Iran in 1941 where he immediately joined the Tudeh. He was soon sent to Azerbaijan, and was active in the organisation of the labour movement in Tabriz. He later became head of the local pro-Tudeh union and his name was linked to a period of political and labour disturbances in Tabriz prior to the formation of the ADP. Biriya was a power orator and in his speeches often referred to the need for provincial autonomy in Azerbaijan. Biriya's switch in party affiliation proved particularly important for the ADP. It helped give the party the appearance of unity while also securing the support of the local union. Biriya was selected as a national committee member in November and was subsequently appointed minister of education. He was regarded as one of the most able men in the provincial administration, and was certainly one of the most active.[41] Following the fall of the Democrat regime, he fled to the USSR, returning to Iran after the 1979 revolution where he died in 1985.[42]

No other ADP member had similar links with the Tudeh. The case of Shabistari, for example, was more typical. Born in Soviet Azerbaijan and a veteran of the Persian communist party and the Khiabani uprisings, Shabistari appeared to possess all the necessary qualifications for membership of the ADP. He was a Tudeh party member between 1941 and 1943, during which time he was appointed local party chairman in Azerbaijan. In 1943 he resigned from the Tudeh to found the 'Azerbaijan Society' but continued to edit the newspaper *Azerbaijan*, which later became the official organ of the ADP. A prominent activist in the summer of 1945, Shabistari was also present at the discussions over the creation of the ADP. He later became president of the Azerbaijan majlis.[43]

Two other former Tudeh members, Padigan and Oiyami, were also elected to the ADP's national committee. Both were veterans of the Khiabani uprising, and subsequently joined the Tudeh, but later switched their affiliation to the ADP. Padigan became the party secretary and Qiyami a Supreme Court judge.[44] Other members of the Democrats' national committee had no links with the Tudeh, and tended to have similar backgrounds. Javid, who became minister of the interior, was born in Azerbaijan but educated in Baku. A member of the Adalat party, Javid participated in the Gilan uprising, after which he fled to Baku. He later returned to Iran where he spent some years in prison, and in exile in Kashan. He reappeared in the capital in 1941.[45] Kaviyan, who became the ADP's defence minister, was also born in Azerbaijan and educated in Baku. He had participated in both the Khiabani and Gilan rebellions and subsequently returned to Soviet Azerbaijan. On his later return to Iran, Kaviyan was imprisoned until 1941.

Little is known of the remaining three national committee members: Ilhami (who became finance minister) Rafi'i and Ali Shams, but they were not linked to the Tudeh. Nor were the remaining cabinet members: Azima, minister of justice, Mahtash, minister of agriculture, Urangi, minister of health, Kabiri, minister of post and telecommunications and Rasuli, minister of commerce and economy.[46]

Taken as a group, of the fifteen ADP members who were either elected to the national committee or who became ministers – some were both – only five, including Pishihvari, had previously been linked with the Tudeh. Of these, two had only been members for a short period. The theory of continuity between the two parties rests therefore on three men alone: Qiyami, Padigan and Biriya.[47] Of these, only Biriya had a record of intense political activity within both parties, and must therefore be regarded as the exception in an otherwise fairly constant pattern of ADP party membership.

The background of Ja'far Pishihvari, the ADP leader, conforms in all important details to that of other party members. Born in Tabriz in the late 1880s or early 1890s, Pishihvari had spent much of his youth in the USSR, including some years as a school teacher in Baku. He was linked to early radical activities in both Russia and Iran, participating in the Russian Revolution of 1905 and offering his support to Sattar Khan during the constitutionalist uprising in Tabriz. He was among Iranian exiles who formed the Adalat party in Baku and continued to play a leading role in the Persian communist party, as it was subsequently known. Like other colleagues who joined the ADP, Pishihvari had played a prominent role in the Gilan movement, and was elected to the executive committee which headed the short-lived Soviet Republic of Gilan.[48]

Little is known about Pishihvari's life between the fall of the Gilan Republic in 1921 and his imprisonment by Reza Shah in 1930. Some time after the Gilan uprising, he returned to Baku, but during this period he also appeared in Tehran, where he was involved in labour activities and edited the newspaper *Haqiqat*.[49] He was active in Iran again in the early 1930s and was imprisoned with other communist activists. In prison, he was later joined by future Tudeh members of the group known as the 'fifty-three'. These were important formative years for the Tudeh, but fellow inmates recalled how Pishihvari distanced himself from the Arani group, regarding them as inexperienced and their plans as idealistic.[50] On his release from prison in 1941, Pishihvari immediately became involved in the surge of political activities in Tehran. He appears to have briefly joined the Tudeh, but by 1943 was publishing his own newspaper, *Azhir*. The latter, although proclaiming itself to be a member of the Freedom Front, was frequently critical of Tudeh policies. When Pishihvari stood as Tabriz candidate for the 14th majlis, this criticism was muted, but resumed with renewed vigour when his credentials were rejected.[51] At the Tudeh's first general conference after the 1944 election results, Pishihvari was conspicuous by his absence.[52]

The denial to Pishihvari of a place in the majlis has been regarded by several commentators as critical in his decision to break completely with the Tudeh and with the Iranian parliamentary system, and thereafter pursue his own independent and more radical policies.[53] The commencement of the most radical period of Pishihvari's activities, however, also coincided with the change in the tempo and direction of Soviet policy which followed the majlis' rejection of its oil demand. While Pishihvari's personal grievances may have contributed to his radicalism, just as important was the Soviet Union's perception of him as an ally who could assist in the furtherance of Soviet aims in Iran.

Pishihvari's background and previous relations with the Tudeh made it unlikely that the party would have given him its unqualified support, even though this might have assisted their campaign in Azerbaijan. When Pishihvari wrote, after the rejection of his credentials, that he was convinced of the 'impossibility of a constitutional solution for Iran', he was condemning the existing government, but also the Tudeh who were then trying to work with it.[54] Pishihvari's treatment by the Tudeh and his experience in the electoral campaign may have been partly behind his decision to pursue more radical policies and to upstage the Tudeh. Yet possibly more important than a desire for revenge were his close links with the Soviet Union. In distancing himself from the Tudeh, Pishihvari was also responding to Soviet pressures for a new initiative in Azerbaijan. The pattern of his activities points away from the conclusion that he was the disinterested reformer that some of his sympathisers claimed him to be.[55]

The majlis had in some ways played into Pishihvari's and into Soviet hands. In rejecting Pishihvari's credentials, in spurning the Soviet oil delegation, and alienating elements of Azerbaijan's political hierarchy, they had unwillingly provided the basis for a strong alliance of interests. With Soviet support the Azerbaijan Democrats assumed a threatening aspect. Curiously too, and not for the first time, the Tudeh secretly found themselves in agreement with some of their political opponents, at least as regards their attitude towards Pishihvari and the menace of separatism. From the Soviet viewpoint, the Tudeh had revealed its weakness as a party which could press for the achievement of Soviet goals in Iran. In Pishihvari the USSR perceived the opportunity to launch a new initiative, to create a new party with a different impetus and direction: one which would be closely bound to Soviet interests.

The Tudeh never gave its wholehearted support to the Azerbaijan Democrats. When the ADP broke loose from Tudeh dependence, the latter offered it conditional support, out of a sense of solidarity for democratic ideals and also from a shared sense of loyalty to the USSR. This however, was a path which many Tudeh members trod unwillingly. Relations between the two parties did improve during the ADP's year in power, as discussed in chapter 3, but the union was never a happy one. Beneath the superficial unity, divisions ran deep. The debate over deference to the USSR which was raised by the crisis in Azerbaijan exposed the rifts in the broad-based democratic platform which the Tudeh had sought to promote. The party's credibility and unity were seriously weakened by the events of 1944–7 and in them can be traced the origins of the subsequent split.

The continued existence of the ADP in exile cannot, as already suggested, be taken as indicative of a strong base of local support. The party remained, as it had always been, a tightly-knit, pro-Soviet party, focusing on sectarian grievances. The increasingly pro-Soviet focus of the Tudeh helped to bring the two parties closer together until they finally united in 1960. There have been no subsequent indications of any popular movement in support of autonomy, at least in Iranian Azerbaijan. The experience of the Mussadiq years, and again of the post-revolutionary period have served to demonstrate that there is no sense of 'unredeemed' nationalism in Azerbaijan, and that the Azerbaijanis, despite their natural affection for their region, their language and their customs, perceive themselves to be an integral part of the Iranian state in every sense.[56] In the early 1990s a question mark about Azerbaijan's future was raised by the situation in the Soviet Union and in particular in the neighbouring republic of Azerbaijan. Might Iran's Azerbaijanis, under certain conditions, consider an initiative from their Soviet counterparts to join forces in a 'greater Azerbaijan'? All the evidence so far suggests otherwise.[57]

3 The year of crisis: 1946

The new independent status of Azerbaijan was, for most Iranians, an unwelcome development, but it was hardly unexpected. Azerbaijan had been on the brink of crisis for almost a year following the USSR's angry reaction to the failure of its oil mission. Azerbaijan was not, of course, the only potential crisis area in Iran, as events in the coming year would prove. Yet Azerbaijan, or rather the entire Soviet zone, was unique in that the Iranian government had been obliged gradually to surrender its hold over the region. As a result of the threat from Azerbaijan there developed during 1946 a consensus among majlis members that a new prime minister be appointed who was regarded as acceptable by the USSR. If not, it was feared that Iran might risk losing its independence or territorial integrity. The result of this consensus, albeit only a temporary one, was the appointment, in January 1946, of Ahmad Qavam.[1] To him fell the unenviable mission of delivering the country intact from the vicissitudes of the Second World War.

Qavam's statesmanship, his sense of timing, and his ability to stay in power against all odds for almost two years, made his premiership the most important of the decade. In it was exposed the decadence of British power in Iran and the unacceptability of the sort of regime favoured by the USSR. America became the beacon that would lead Iran towards an independent future.

The course and outcome of the Azerbaijan crisis, like its origins, cannot be understood in isolation from the activities of foreign powers in Iran. Without Soviet encouragement, the Azerbaijan Democrats could neither have launched their attack, nor sustained their resistance against Tehran; nor would the Tudeh party have been able to exercise so great an influence. Without British encouragement, the rebellion of the southern tribes (discussed later in this chapter), in itself a reaction to events in the north, would probably never have taken place. Without American intervention, the division of Iran into Soviet and British spheres of influence might have become permanent. There is, however, little meaning in discussing the possible range of outcomes had external conditions differed. Foreign interference has been a constant conditioning factor in Iranian history. Yet while the influence of foreign powers, dealt with more fully in the last three chapters of this book, is never far from the forefront of this discussion, the internal dimension is no less important or worthy of separate consideration.

It would be wrong to assume that Iran was a mere pawn of the great powers and was therefore incapable of independent action. The American ambassador, Allen, once complained that Iranians were 'so accustomed to outside interference they resemble a man who has been in prison a long time and is afraid to go out in the sunlight'.[2] Yet the country's long experience of foreign intervention had produced a breed of politicians who showed a certain adeptness in manipulating the interests of foreign powers while retaining a surprising degree of independence. Ahmad Qavam was one such example. During his term in office (1945–7) he was able to extricate the country, united and independent, from its wartime entanglements and obligations. In view of the obstacles in his path, this was no mean achievement.

Qavam advocated friendly relations with Britain, the USA and the USSR, but he wished to achieve a more equal balance between them, a policy he described as 'positive equilibrium'. He was equally insistent however, on the need to maintain Iran's territorial integrity and independence: a state which Britain, the USSR and the USA all solemnly agreed to uphold, but which all, at some stage, were ready to compromise. Qavam was a skilful, if devious politican: 'The old style Persian grandee, in the Persian tradition . . . Justice must be cajoled by special inducements to perform her duties.'[3] Yet his style of statesmanship was precisely what was called for, a weaker man would not have survived the combined weight of internal and external pressures.

The Democrats in power: January–June 1946

With the opening of the Azerbaijan national parliament on 12 December and the final surrender of the Iranian gendarmerie led by General Darakhshani, open resistance to the ADP ended. The party's swift and little resisted takeover was accompanied by a feeling of euphoria. The slogan 'The nation is with us!' captured this early mood.[4] Observers were impressed by the organisation of the new administration. On a visit to Tabriz after the Democrat takeover, the US press attaché found calm and efficiency, although he thought it impossible to judge the state of public opinion because of the 'recent terrorising of the city'. On the basis of its reports from Tabriz, the Foreign Office thought that 'politically and militarily Azerbaijan was in the bag'.[5] Yet at the same time there were a number of obvious contradictions within the Democrat regime. Some of these were already evident in the contrast between the radical reform programme on the one hand, and its need

54

to present a moderate image to secure national and international support on the other.

Within the province, there was a call for 'business as usual'. The bazaar was encouraged to carry on trading to preserve an atmosphere of normalcy, and to avoid adding further economic disruption to that already caused by the breaking off of trade relations with the rest of the country. It was also hoped that foreign powers might enter into trade relations with the new regime. Perhaps not surprisingly, the only country willing to continue trading with Azerbaijan was the USSR. As the latter's terms of trade proved to be almost invariably unfavourable, the province was soon threatened with serious economic problems.[6]

With respect to their relations with Tehran, the Democrats also tried to present a moderate image. While calling for an 'autonomous Azerbaijan', they also insisted that they had no desire to separate the province from Iran, assurances that were repeated in the Tudeh press.[7] Evidence of this desire, as Pishihvari told the American vice-consul, was the absence of a foreign minister in the Democrat cabinet.[8] The party could not, however, shrug off its revolutionary associations so easily and the attempt to present a more acceptable image failed to convince most observers. Moreover, the obvious contradictions of the regime were only accentuated by its own press statements: 'The world must recognise our autonomy. Five million Azerbaijanis will not remain in slavery. They want to be masters in their own house without threatening Persian unity and independence.'[9]

By the beginning of 1946, Prime Minister Hakimi had shown himself to be without a policy as far as Azerbaijan was concerned. Even after the autonomous governments were formed, he still insisted that he could not accept any independent government in Azerbaijan and would use force to put down the rebellion. In a response to a Soviet note which described the recent events in Azerbaijan as merely a question of securing 'democratic rights', Hakimi denounced the Azerbaijan movement as a contravention of constitutional law in a country where 'democracy was already established'. He also accused the Soviet Union of consistently hindering Persian forces from restoring security in the north.[10] In Tehran there was widespread opposition to Azerbaijan developments from such diverse elements as the members of the religious community and Azerbaijanis living in the capital, yet the government failed to formulate an effective strategy to deal with the crisis.[11]

While majlis deputies feared that Hakimi's attitude would provoke a further Soviet reaction, the situation in early 1946 became particularly tense with speculation that the Democrat rebellion might soon spread. While rumours of an imminent 'march on Tehran' were undoubtedly exaggerated,[12] there was evidence of parallel activities in other areas in the Soviet zone. In Khurasan and Gilan, there were rumours of Soviet troop movements. In Mashad, there were reports of the arrival of large numbers of *muhajirin*, believed to have played an important role in the Azerbaijan uprising, while Soviet loudspeakers broadcast speeches extolling Azerbaijan's independence. In Mazandaran, some towns had been seized by Democrat supporters, and a report from Rasht claimed the local Tudeh branch was preparing a proclamation to announce the creation of an independent 'Tabaristan'.[13]

The anxiety of the majlis was heightened by the news that the Moscow Conference of Foreign Ministers had failed to make any progress on the Iranian question. At about this time there was a general move in favour of Qavam, who had already publicised his intention to 'appease the Soviet Union' if he was appointed prime minister.[14] In the panic created by events in Azerbaijan, certain deputies had already suggested the repealing of the 1944 oil law and the removal of Sayyid Ziya supporters from their posts, policies with which Qavam was known to sympathise, and a growing number of deputies were now ready to pledge him their support.[15] Conservatives may still privately have believed that force was the best way of dealing with the northern rebels, but they also recognised the folly of further provoking the USSR, and were ready to concede that some conciliatory gestures were called for to overcome the present impasse. The left, both inside and outside the Tudeh party, insisted that the government was to blame for the state of affairs in Azerbaijan: 'Those who accuse the Democrats of treason, are also condemning the authorities who have done nothing for the people and govern the country with force and repression.'[16]

As the criticism against Hakimi mounted, only the Shah seemed reluctant to let him go, fearful of the consequences of reappointing his old enemy, Qavam. Hakimi clung to power a little while longer, agreeing to dismiss a few of his most unpopular colleagues, and offering to go to Moscow to negotiate directly with the USSR.[17] The Soviet government, however, let it be known that Hakimi would not be welcome in Moscow.[18] The mortal blow to his administration was then delivered over his attitude towards British proposals calling for a Tripartite Commission on Iran presented to the Moscow conference. It was enough that Hakimi had even contemplated the British plan, with its provisions for the holding of elections for provincial councils and legitimising the official use of minority languages.[19] For many Iranians the Commission idea smacked of an allied trusteeship and a corresponding loss of Iranian sovereignty and independence.

Hakimi's cabinet modified the British proposals, limiting the role of provincial councils, removing the clause on minority languages, adding the condition that two Iranians should be placed on the commission, and insisting that 'all recommendations should fall within the framework of the Constitution'.[20] These modifications, which, for different reasons, were unacceptable both to Britain and the USSR failed to silence Hakimi's critics. Mussadiq led the majlis opposition with a fiery speech on 10 January calling for Hakimi's resignation and the appointment of a prime minister who would conduct a non-aligned foreign policy.[21]

The news from the north weakened Hakimi's position still further. The Democrats had consolidated their hold over the province and were now insisting on a total revision of earlier constitutional provisions for the election of provincial councils. *Azerbaijan* attacked the old system as out of date and called for changes including the introduction of universal suffrage. Both the elections to the Azerbaijan majlis and the forthcoming municipal elections were carried out on the basis of the extended franchise.[22]

Plans were also underway for the reorganisation of the Azerbaijan militia. The ragged band of Democrat volunteers or *fida'iyan*, who, with Soviet assistance, had effected the military takeover in the province, were now to form the basis of a 'national army'. Recruitment started in December, and in January Biriya urged officers and men of the dismantled Iranian garrison to take advantage of a general amnesty and join the people's army under 'significantly improved conditions'.[23] Among the thirty or so officers were some Iranian army deserters, including those who had participated in the Mashad mutiny, as well as officers of the Soviet army. Pishihvari had always stressed the importance of an organised army to realise his goals. In an early demonstration of the Democrats' military might, an orderly parade of some 2,000 footsoldiers and 50 mounted troops paraded the streets of Tabriz in early January.[24]

In the area of social and economic reforms the Democrats also appeared to be tackling an imposing amount of legislation. There were plans to asphalt roads and introduce a bus service; for educational reforms, including the introduction of 'political instruction' for government employees; for tax reforms and land redistribution.[25] According to one leftist Tehran newspaper the province had witnessed a 'definite improvement, prices are down, the trains are running and people are satisfied'.[26] Small gestures of defiance to Tehran stressed the province's independent status. Postage stamps were overprinted with the words 'Azerbaijan National Government, 21 Azar 1234', schools took down their once obligatory pictures of the Shah, even the hats used by the local police no longer bore the old badges with the 'lion and the sun' motif. A new flag appeared over government buildings, and Tabriz adopted Moscow time – half an hour behind Tehran.[27]

The early confidence of the Democrats helped to disguise some of the weaknesses of the new regime. A major problem was finance. The British consul in Tabriz thought that the lack of funds would prove to be a major obstacle in the implementation of the Democrat reform programme.[28] It was not clear how the ambitious projects listed above would be paid for. Another difficulty lay in relations with the Kurdish Democrats. During their visit to Baku, the Kurdish leaders had been told to work with Pishihvari, but had since shown a growing reluctance to do so. They also claimed jurisdiction over a wide area which included Rezaieh, which was part of the territory claimed by the ADP.[29] There were also rumours of divisions among the Democrat leaders themselves. Biriya, who saw himself as the popular figure behind the Democrat movement, was annoyed that Pishihvari had assumed the dominant role in the party. After a poorly disguised quarrel between the two, *Azerbaijan* published an attack on 'little men in important positions who are doing the movement great harm'.[30]

These then were some of the early obstacles faced by the young Democrat regime. They were not however immediately apparent to outside observers. The activities of the provincial government, considerably bolstered by their own and Soviet propaganda, were decisive in finally convincing a majority of majlis deputies that action must soon be taken to conciliate the USSR. There was no longer any excuse for retaining Hakimi. He was unacceptable to the USSR and had aroused widespread public hostility over the Tripartite Commission question. He further annoyed Britain as well as the USSR by instructing Hasan Taqizadeh, Iran's ambassador in London, to lodge a complaint against Soviet interference at the United Nations Security Council. The complaint proved inconclusive since it was subsequently agreed to await the results of bilateral discussions between the two countries.[31] Nevertheless Hakimi's position was further weakened. As one deputy commented, the prime minister had failed to either solve the Azerbaijan problem, reform the administration, or to clarify his foreign policy. The Shah had no choice but to accept his resignation on 20 January. Six days later Qavam was elected prime minister by a majority of only one.[32]

As Qavam came to power, the mood in Iranian political circles was pessimistic. His arrival marked the beginning of a more positive approach, and introduced a new style of statesmanship. This style had some antecedents in the recent opposition to the Tripartite Commission: a refusal to be dictated to by outside powers, and an insistence that the country be allowed to settle its own affairs in its own way. This was what Qavam's very personal style of leadership intended to do. He formed a cabinet without the usual majority of royalist and pro-British representatives, and retained for himself the ministries of the interior and foreign affairs. Without giving the majlis time to consider his selection, Qavam left for Moscow to negotiate directly with his Soviet counterparts.[33]

Qavam's mission to Moscow lasted three weeks and achieved few obvious results. Molotov, still indignant at Iran's rebuff of the oil concession in 1944, wanted Azerbaijan to be granted full autonomy, and the USSR to be awarded a new oil concession before Soviet troops withdrew from Iran. Stalin was less hostile, but adamant that the Soviet Union could not be expected to withdraw its troops without some assurances from Iran. Qavam, for his part, offered certain concessions to the Azerbaijan regime, and on the oil question finally agreed that if Soviet troops did withdraw, he would hold elections and suggest that the new majlis consider the abrogation of the Mussadiq law. Despite Soviet pressure, Qavam gave no guarantees, and he returned empty handed to Tehran on 10 March.[34]

He found the majlis in a state of chaos. The continued presence of Soviet troops on Iranian soil, the imminent dissolution of the majlis, and the continuing defiance of the Azerbaijan regime were the main causes of concern. However, Qavam's cabinet, his style of policy making and his leanings to the left also alarmed some colleagues, particularly the pro-British and royalist deputies who now sought to prolong the life of the 14th majlis. They believed this move could prevent Qavam from becoming a 'virtual dictator'.[35] Qavam skilfully frustrated these efforts and the majlis was dissolved on 12 March as planned. As prime minister without a parliament, but with a cabinet of his own making, Qavam was in a particularly strong position, not only to deal with the Azerbaijan question as he wished but also to resume his own personal struggle with the Shah. Despite the continuing reservations of the conservatives, Qavam was not seriously challenged because, as the American ambassador insisted, he was the only man considered 'capable of handling the situation'.[36]

The day before the dissolution of the majlis, Qavam addressed a secret session of seventy deputies to reveal the outcome of his Moscow visit. He admitted that he had failed to reach agreement on the three key issues that affected Irano-Soviet relations: oil, evacuation of troops and Azerbaijan, but he claimed that Iran was now held in 'high regard' by the Soviet government, and that discussions would continue following the arrival of the new Soviet ambassador, Sadchikov, in Tehran.[37] The latter proved to be more accommodating than Stalin and Molotov, suggesting that Qavam's claim was not altogether unfounded. However, probably more important in changing Soviet attitudes was the fact that Iran had once more become the focus of international attention following a new appeal to the United Nations.[38] Ready to reach a compromise on Iran when faced with the weight of world opinion, the USSR agreed to withdraw its troops within six weeks. On 4 April an Irano-Soviet communiqué was signed also agreeing to the establishment of a joint Irano-Soviet oil company, subject to the approval of the 15th majlis, and accepting that Azerbaijan was an 'internal matter' to be dealt with by the Iranian government which 'taking into consideration the necessity of reforms and in accordance with existing laws would make arrangements with the people of Azerbaijan for a solution of the existing problems in a benevolent spirit'.[39]

Qavam had secured Soviet troop withdrawals, and had received an assurance of Soviet non-interference in Azerbaijan. In return, he had promised the USSR a 51 per cent share in a joint-stock company which would be set up to exploit Iran's northern oil reserves. This arrangement was similar to that discussed secretly by Bayat at the end of 1944.[40] With this agreement, he had satisfied Soviet demands without having to abrogate Mussadiq's law which had been directed against foreign concessions and did not specifically mention joint companies. The dividing line was thin, and many of Qavam's critics believed that the oil company would make permanent the USSR's economic and political influence in northern Iran. The oil agreement however, had not yet been finalised, and therein lay Qavam's great strength.

Qavam's skill in the Moscow and Tehran discussions lay in his ability to convince the Soviet government of his own good faith. The USSR assumed that the oil agreement would have an easy passage through the majlis, and Qavam endorsed this impression on different occasions when he spoke of a Soviet concession as a 'natural development' which was 'long overdue'.[41] Yet there was, of course, no guarantee that the new majlis would be favourable. Even if Qavam could carry his slender majority into the 15th majlis, his own supporters, once free from anxieties about Soviet policy in Azerbaijan, might not support the measure. Elections could not be held while Soviet troops were still in Iran, and the USSR had, in any case, committed itself to withdrawal. The Democrats could be relied on to support Soviet interests, but how long could they survive without Soviet support? The USSR had entrusted its future security in Iran to the uncertain alliance of Qavam, the Democrats and the Tudeh.

Once the joint communiqué had been signed, both sides moved to expedite the different clauses of the agreement: the USSR to complete troop evacuations and the Iranian government to negotiate with the Democrat regime. Anxious not to further alienate the USSR, Qavam agreed to drop Iran's case from the Security Council's forthcoming agenda.[42] Its subsequent retention was the result of American pressure. The Iranian left shared the indignation felt by the Soviet Union at this unilateral American action in the United Nations.[43] The USSR appeared nevertheless to abide by the agreement, and Qavam, by tactfully selecting a commission of his own supporters to report on the state of troop withdrawals, was able to avoid further antagonising the Soviet government.[44] Once a satisfactory report had been produced, the Security Council was obliged to let the matter rest.

Before turning to the Azerbaijan question, Qavam made further con-ciliatory gestures towards the left. These were designed to please the Soviet Union and improve his own position in his planned constitutional struggle with the Shah. Restrictions imposed on left-wing activities by Qavam's predecessors were lifted, while to the alarm and discomfiture of Britain, Qavam now proceeded to implement his earlier threats to dismiss prominent rightists. Sayyid Ziya, Hasan Arfa and Ali Dashti were among those arrested, charged with 'conspiracy and intrigue' against the government.[45] One of Qavam's own closest advisers, Muzaffar Firuz, was not only critical of Britain, but also well known for his pro-Soviet sympathies and his dislike of the monarchy.[46] Qavam's cabinet was still by no means leftist, but it did contain more than the usual number of anti-British and anti-royalist politicians.[47]

Qavam also showed tolerance to the Azerbaijan Democrats. Towards the end of April, he drew up a statement on Azerbaijan which included a list of concessions which the government was prepared to make to meet the wishes of the population 'in so far as was possible under its commitments to constitutional law'. These concessions gave the Azerbaijan provincial council the right to elect its own officials, with the exception of the governor general and the army and gendarmerie commanders; permitted the use of Azeri in government offices and the first five grades of primary school; revised the existing tax and budgetary arrangements; allowed the ADP organisations unrestricted freedom of action, and finally promised to consider an increase in the number of Azerbaijani deputies in the majlis.[48]

Dizzy at their own success, the Democrats were unimpressed by Qavam's offer. Pishihvari called it a 'decree from heaven' and complained that he had not been consulted. In particular he opposed any reform package that fell within the Iranian constitutional framework:

The fundamental laws of the constitution, 40 years old, worked out under reactionary authorities do not conform to today's world. The laws must conform to the spirit and will of the people. If Tehran wants to prove its goodwill . . . it should abandon its outmoded policies and choose a new political line which relates to the present era. It must account for itself to the nation.[49]

In an editorial article *Azerbaijan* warned that if their demands were not met, the people of Azerbaijan would bring down the government. Even a Tudeh representative was sent to Tabriz to advise the Azerbaijan majlis to accept Tehran's offer, to little apparent effect. 'Death but no retreat' had become a new party slogan.[50]

Talks continued in Tehran between government representatives and a three-man delegation from Azerbaijan led by Padigan, but progress was slow: 'The Azerbaijanis were willing to compromise on matters of form, such as the term "provincial council" to replace national assembly etc. . . . but they would only yield on the semblance of power, not on the realities, especially on the appointment of the Governor General or troop commander.'[51] The Democrats were clearly reluctant to surrender their hard won position. Until the six week deadline for the withdrawal of Soviet troops had expired they could afford to be intransigent. Another reason for delaying agreement with Tehran was the failure to work out any satisfactory arrangement with the Kurds. During April, delegations from Tabriz and Mahabad met and finally worked out the basis for joint cooperation in military and economic matters.[52] Finally, disagreements between the Democrats themselves may have affected negotiations with Tehran. Moderates like Pishihvari seemed willing to compromise, while hardliners, notably Biriya, were reluctant to surrender any of the party's early gains.[53]

When Qavam and Pishihvari met in May, one major obstacle to agreement still remained, the future of the Azerbaijan peoples' army which Qavam said should be totally disbanded. Qavam cleverly blamed his difficulties on the Shah. As he told the American ambassador, he was confident that he could 'make arrangements with Pishihvari', but the Shah had raised objections, and was insisting on 'sending three brigades of the Iranian army into Azerbaijan'.[54] The Soviet Union played little part in these negotiations. It was in Soviet interests that the two sides should come to terms, since agreement with Tabriz was a condition for the holding of elections, which would bring the USSR one step nearer to the ratification of their oil agreement.[55] The Tudeh, however, continued to press for further concessions. The Democrats' economic and social reform programme was one with which the party could easily sympathise. The period between the Irano-Soviet understanding in April, and Qavam's final agreement with the Democrats in June proved to be halcyon days for the Iranian left. The Tudeh and Democrat press called for Azerbaijan-style reforms throughout Iran: 'Here it is not just a question of Azerbaijan. The question is that freedom and democracy must reign throughout Iran. What upsets the Tehran reactionaries and the country's great landlords is that the people of Azerbaijan are striving to establish the rights of the people throughout Iran.'[56]

Before Qavam had been able to finalise his agreement with Tabriz, he was obliged to turn his attention elsewhere. Labour unrest in the southern oil fields resulted in a one-day strike against the Anglo-Iranian Oil Company (AIOC) at the end of April. This was followed by an elaborate MayDay parade and further sympathy strikes calling for better wages and conditions.[57] The Tudeh-supported action was well timed. With the deadline for Soviet troop withdrawals still a few weeks away, and with Azerbaijan still independent, the party was in a particularly strong position to put pressure on Qavam to make further concessions to the left.

Qavam had no intention of alienating the Tudeh or inviting Soviet wrath over southern developments. He also saw that his own position might be usefully served by rapping the knuckles of the British. He refused to send extra troops to the oil fields area to assist the AIOC police and local army garrison, a move which effectively forced the company to yield to certain worker demands. Inspired by this success the Tudeh organised a larger strike at the Agha Jari oil fields, which was followed by further concessions. Finally, after a potentially more serious strike in July, the British took action to check the unrest and were able to negate some of the strikers' early achievements. Qavam, however, appeared as the champion of Tudeh demands.[58]

Having thus regained the initiative in the south, Qavam took further steps to strengthen his position before continuing his negotiations with the north. By introducing some attractive reforms of his own, Qavam hoped to steal the initiative from the Tudeh and the Azerbaijan Democrats. In March he had established a 'supreme economic council' designed to regenerate the economy, implement social reforms and develop a five-year programme for the municipalities. In May he announced that a land reform bill would also be drawn up before the next elections. In view of the Democrats' own plans to introduce such reforms, the latter proposal, as one of his own ministers suggested, was probably 'window dressing' designed to bolster Qavam's position.[59] The same thinking, directed as much against the Tudeh as the Democrats, lay behind Qavam's labour law, of May 1946. This piece of legislation established a 48-hour working week, limited overtime to four hours daily and laid down guidelines for dispute settlement.[60]

In June, having weathered the oil strike, witnessed the final evacuation of Soviet forces and shown his own reforming colours, Qavam returned to his thorniest problem: Azerbaijan. Firuz was sent to Tabriz to start a new round of negotiations, and by the middle of the month a revised agreement was produced. This satisfied the Democrats, because it appeared to detract little from the province's autonomous status. It was also accepted in Tehran because, by postponing decisions on the most contentious issues, it left open the possibility of Azerbaijan's future return to central government control. On paper, the Democrats had done well. Although their provincial assembly would disappear, and Pishihvari had to drop his title of prime minister, the new 'provincial council of Azerbaijan' would have wide autonomous powers, and Javid, formerly minister of the interior, was to be appointed as governor general. The province also seemed set to enjoy virtual economic independence with 75 per cent of the province's revenues to be disposed of at the discretion of the council.[61]

Although it appeared generous, the June agreement was not markedly different in substance from Qavam's earlier statement on Azerbaijan, even if it was phrased in different terms. It was agreed that the Azerbaijani army would be incorporated into the Iranian army and a commission would be appointed to discuss its functions and the appointment of its commanders. Likewise the status of the local gendarmerie would also be made the subject of a special commission. The 15th majlis, when it convened, would consider the introduction of a new electoral law as well as the possibility of increasing the number of Azerbaijani deputies and the introduction of a new town councils law to be applied throughout Iran. Regarding the use of Azeri, Qavam's earlier statement was modified to allow teaching in both Persian and Azeri in secondary schools 'on the basis of the Ministry of Education's reforms and . . . of a programme drawn up in suitable form'. Other clauses dealt with lesser issues such as responsibility for road repairs, although a promise to complete the Mianih–Tabriz leg of the railway was significant in view of the poor existing links between Tabriz and the capital.

Pishihvari described the agreement with Tehran as 'the commencement of an historical revolution and of a process of transformation for Azerbaijan and the whole of Iran'.[62] Yet ultimately, it was Qavam who emerged as the victor from what *Kayhan* dubbed as the 'great agreement'.[63] Despite the apparent continuity between the Azerbaijan majlis and the provincial council, the composition of the latter was ultimately dependent on Tehran which reserved the right to confirm all appointments. With regard to the governor general, the government would merely 'ascertain' the views of the provincial council before making its choice. Qavam, in a tactical move, agreed to the appointment of Javid, known in any case as the most moderate of the Democrats,[64] but there was no guarantee that in the future either Qavam or his successors would again prove so accommodating. The very vagueness of the agreement, which as the Democrats admitted left 'four of five conditions outstanding' was almost certain to rebound to their disadvantage.[65]

Qavam had succeeded in convincing the Democrats and the Soviet Union of his own good faith, and his capacity to command a majority in the 15th majlis to carry through his proposals. Both of the latter believed that they had won important concessions. In reality they had been bought off with vague promises. Qavam's policies, however, did not earn him unqualified support in Tehran. The Shah opposed the June agreement. Referring to the clause which envisaged the incorporation of Azerbaijani recruits into the Persian army, he reportedly said that he would rather 'cut off his hand than "sign a decree conferring officers' ranks on a bunch of cut-throats, criminals and spies"'.[66] The American ambassador, despite some sympathy for Qavam, also felt that there was 'no cause for congratulations' in the agreement, and warned that Azerbaijan might soon 'take over'.[67] The signature of the Tabriz agreement had coincided with the period in which the Iranian left appeared dangerously powerful, and this helped to heighten tensions. Yet the Firuz–Pishihvari accord proved, in many respects, to be a turning point in the left's fortunes. From June the Democrats experienced an inexorable decline, a fate also shared by the Tudeh. However much his opponents may have disliked the fact, it was Qavam who presided over their demise.

After the excitement caused by the agreement with Tehran had subsided, the deficiencies of the Democrat regime became all the more apparent. Its relatively strong position, which had been artificially sustained by the tense national and international situation, was soon eroded. Of the problems already mentioned, perhaps the most serious was continuing financial embarrassment. After the initial severing of links with Tehran, Azerbaijan's finance minister, Ilhami, had embarked on a tax collection campaign which included measures more drastic than those attempted by the American financial advisor Millspaugh, and which had contributed to the latter's downfall. Even the arrears on Millspaugh's much criticised income tax were demanded, although those on low incomes were excluded.[68] Measures such as these met with resistance: 'Even in Azerbaijan, it seems there is a last ditch, and those who shed but scanty tears for their country are now prepared to shed anything rather than their toumans which the minister of finance is now avidly hunting.'[69]

In an attempt to further boost Democrat coffers, Pishihvari announced the takeover of the Tabriz branch of Bank Milli (the national bank). Following this much fêted move however, he revealed that the bank was trading with a deficit of 10 million toumans and ordered it to cease its private operations forthwith.[70] The same order was soon issued to other Tabriz banks, causing panic among investors. At the same time all banks were told to make cuts in staff and wages. Another group to feel the economic pinch were government workers. In January their salaries were paid in arrears, and in March it was proposed that a 'treasury note' be introduced in lieu of 30 per cent of their wages, which could be exchanged for goods in 'government shops'. Another move to reduce expenditure was the sacking of 'redundant' workers in official posts.[71] Thus far the Democrat promise of finding employment for all Azerbaijanis had not been realised.

The trade picture was depressingly similar. After the Democrat takeover, in November 1945, the bazaar, the nerve centre of Tabriz, was paralysed for a month. The breakdown in communications with the capital and the latter's effort to isolate the province meant that there was virtually no movement of goods between Azerbaijan and the rest of the country. The local government's ban on the sale of foodstuffs outside the province was a positive disincentive to sell. Merchants, too, could only dispatch their merchandise outside the province if they provided a written undertaking that the proceeds of their sales would be returned to Tabriz, where, according to the British consul, they would go straight into government funds in lieu of 'unpaid taxes'. These were not measures to endear the commercial sector to the new regime. There was no incentive to sell, while purchasing power was also limited by the raising of duties on all goods entering the province.[72] Such legislation, though designed to protect local industry and prevent 'exploitation' by Tehran, only helped to increase the province's economic difficulties.[73]

To offset economic hardship, the Azerbaijani leaders continued their efforts to enter into trade agreements with other countries, a policy that was linked to their desire to seek status internationally. Apart from the Soviet Union, however, foreign governments were most reluctant to enter into trade relations with Azerbaijan since this would also imply an acceptance of the province's autonomous status. The Democrats' links with the USSR were thus reinforced further. Another device to promote trade – the formation of a government trading organisation – also failed. Just as Azerbaijan's citizens were reluctant to show their commitment to the regime by paying up taxes, so too were merchants and investors unwilling to volunteer funds for the new trading scheme.[74]

The general economic climate also hampered the Democrats' efforts to rehabilitate industry. Although successful in reviving both the Pashminih and Khusravi factories by placing large government orders to provide boots and uniforms for the Azerbaijan army, the provincial government lacked the capital to prop up Tabriz factories indefinitely. Local industries, which had already suffered from the cancellation of Soviet war orders, were now also adversely affected by the new trade restrictions. The Tabriz work force, whose expectations had been raised by Tudeh and Democrat propaganda, was quickly disillusioned. Within months of its establishment, the provincial regime was forced to announce wage cuts in all major factories. Subsequently the old allowance system for providing workers with bread, charcoal and clothing was abolished, leaving them with only a reduced basic wage.[75]

On the agricultural front the situation appeared more promising. In January 1946 two bills were passed in fulfilment of Pishihvari's promise to pay 'special attention to landlord–peasant relations and to adjust such relations on a fair basis'.[76] The first related to the requisition of lands belonging to 'Azerbaijani exiles who carry out propaganda against the National Government, or any persons opposed to the freedom of Azerbaijan'; the second provided for the redistribution of state or public lands to existing tenants. Since the requisitioned estates now became public lands, there was a considerable amount of territory available for redistribution and most peasants received between 1 and 5 hectares. A further series of measures related to the provision of communal facilities and an increase in the sharecropper's portion of the harvest, and the setting up of 'village committees' to supervise these arrangements.[77]

Pishihvari's agrarian reforms were widely regarded as important and progressive measures by observers both inside and outside the country. Qavam's recognition of this fact inspired his decision to draft his own land reform bill. Peasant proprietorship would end the feudal tradition of absentee landlordism which had hindered technical and social progress in many rural areas. Many landowners owned up to 100 villages which they rarely visited, leaving their management to the corrupt and unpopular bailiffs and gendarmerie. Few landlords were willing to carry out even the most basic improvements, leading to the state of affairs described by Vice-Consul Wall:

In what is probably the most fertile province of the Iranian plateau, agriculture is shockingly backward and the land produces probably no more than half the food it could. Peasant proprietors could do no worse than the semi-serfs who have scratched it up hitherto.[78]

Despite the progressive nature of Pishihvari's agrarian reform programme, it was not one that could immediately pay dividends. Before any benefits could result, there was a need for a settled period where the reforms could be put into effect. No one was convinced by *Azerbaijan*'s claim of a 500 per cent increase in production by May.[79] On the contrary, there was evidence of an overall reduction in harvest yields for 1946. Wall thought the division of lands had not materially increased the area under cultivation. The peasants who suddenly found themselves independent landowners had little experience of farm management. Many of them were so poor that they could not afford to buy seeds for planting let alone the equipment needed to cultivate the land. Their landlords, who under the new arrangements were supposed to assist in these purchases, proved to be uncooperative. Both landlord and peasant alike opposed the new sharecropping law which obliged them to sell a share of their wheat crop (20 per cent and 70 per cent respectively) to the government at fixed prices. Many peasants believed that they had lost one landlord merely to acquire another, while a group of landlords sent a petition to the new governor general asking to amend the new regulations. Their protest was ignored. Nevertheless, the general unwillingness to comply with the new agrarian measures was a growing problem. Not only did the harvest suffer, but some farmers actually allowed crops to rot rather than to sell to government buyers at unfavourable prices.[80]

The Democrats fared better in their reforms of the public services. The newly elected Tabriz municipal council set to work at once with a programme to pave the streets, introduce a cheap and efficient bus service, develop a water and sewage system and improve the local railway network. The budget for 1946/7 (1325) placed high priority on communications, health, education and agriculture. The difficult economic conditions, however, made it impossible for the Democrats to realise all their ambitious schemes. One lasting achievement was the opening, in May 1946, of Tabriz University, whose funding, at least partially, had been provided for by the June agreement.[81]

The Democrats' plans to organise an efficient fighting force soon ran into difficulties. Pishihvari's promise of a 'great national army' with 'aeroplanes, cannons and all kinds of arms', which had caused such alarm in Tehran's political circles, never materialised.[82] The previously untrained *fida'iyan*, who according to Wall, were 'toughs on the make',[83] rejected discipline and training. Conscription was also unsuccessful. Despite Biriya's tireless efforts and the publicity given to the importance of an efficient army to defend the 'free country of Azerbaijan', call up notices appeared to have little impact on a population, which according to Pishihvari was 'ready to die' for the province.[84] In an attempt to give the army a more appealing image, Pishihvari also claimed that 'top Azerbaijani families' who had at first avoided conscription, were now putting their sons forward to train as officers.[85] However other reports suggested the contrary: conscription was intensely unpopular among all classes and most Azerbaijanis of military age tried to avoid it.[86]

The balance sheet of the provincial government's achievements, even before the June agreement was signed, revealed serious shortcomings. Lack of support, paradoxically both from the USSR and the government in Tehran, was a major obstacle in the implementation of the Democrats' reform programme. Their failure to raise living standards, and the need to pursue unpopular policies, contributed to their declining popularity. Relations with the Kurds remained unsettled. The latter disliked their forced subordination to the Azerbaijan regime which had been made explicit in the June 1946 agreement.[87] Finally, the divisions between the Democrat hierarchy now came out in the open. Biriya, who had already clashed with Pishihvari over certain cabinet appointments, now made clear his opposition to the agreement, insisting that 'nothing short of an autonomous Azerbaijan' should have been accepted. At the end of June, Biriya was implicated in an assassination plot against Pishihvari which led to thirty arrests. According to one US consular official, the only reason that Biriya was not himself 'purged' was because of his continuing popularity among the workers.[88] The June agreement had thus ended the state of euphoria which the Democrats had managed to sustain during their first six months in power.

The Democrats in decline: June–December 1946

With the Azerbaijan agreement behind him, Qavam sought to consolidate his own position and secure himself a solid majority in the 15th majlis. In late June he launched his own party, 'the Democratic Party of Iran', in a thinly disguised attempt to steal the reforming banner of the left. He also hoped to appeal to a broad section of public opinion, including some conservatives who might support his planned army and police reforms. The Democratic party of Iran also reaffirmed Qavam's desire to promote close relations with all 'friendly powers'.[89]

Qavam's party excited suspicions of both the left and the right. The former were particularly wary since the new party's creation coincided with an announcement by the Tudeh and Iran parties that they had formed a 'united front' to fight the 'reactionary and combatitive influences of imperialism'.[90] However confidence in Qavam's good intentions, bolstered by rumours that he was considering including some Tudeh members in his cabinet, silenced the opposition.[91] Conservatives remained sceptical of Qavam's move. Ready to welcome a new party to provide a more moderate alternative to the Tudeh, many believed that the prime minister had gone too far in his dealings with the Azerbaijan Democrats and the left, and was 'under the influence of the Russians'.[92] Their anxiety heightened when, after a cabinet reshuffle at the beginning of August, Qavam offered three posts to Tudeh members, while appointing his friend Firuz to the newly created post of minister of labour and propaganda.[93]

This last move also alarmed the British and the Americans. Yet Qavam's actions were intended to strengthen his own position rather than that of the Tudeh. At least this is what he implied when he told the British ambassador of his intention to sober the Tudeh with responsibility, and in remarks he made to the American ambassador about how the party could be better 'handled' from within the government. These assumptions were tested when Qavam sought Tudeh assistance to resolve a new industrial dispute in the oil fields.[94]

The labour troubles among Khuzistan's oil workers which had begun in April and had been temporarily defused by Qavam's conciliatory gestures and the promise of concessions by the AIOC, resumed in earnest in July. The Khuzistan Workers Union, dissatisfied with the AIOC's response to a new list of demands, ordered their workers to begin a new general strike on 14 July. Violence erupted when Arab oil workers, formed into an anti-Tudeh union, clashed with the strikers. This time the British coordinated efforts with the governor general of Khuzistan to restore order, while Qavam also cooperated by sending a battalion of troops to the province. Casualties numbered about 200.[95]

It was not Qavam's intention to alienate the Tudeh permanently but to utilise them to serve his own ends. He thus sent a government commission, headed by Firuz and including two Tudeh members, to investigate the strike and to end the deadlock between the strikers and the oil company. To the annoyance of the British, Firuz immediately called for a ceasefire, released imprisoned Tudeh members and started peace talks. Qavam's action had secured a peaceful conclusion to a violent and dangerous confrontation; the Tudeh ordered the Khuzistan workers to end the conflict.[96] Yet, by involving the party in the negotiations, Qavam helped to divide the Tudeh and undermine its position. As one of Qavam's colleagues told a British embassy official, there had been 'marked dissention' among the Tudeh hierarachy over Qavam's offer. In the long run too, the Tudeh's decision, which in some respects identified the party with the country's ruling elite, helped to undermine its image as the champion of the working class.[97]

Qavam's strategy to divide the left may have been successful, but it did not improve his relations with the conservatives, or the British. Azerbaijan was still, for all practical purposes, independent, and despite the Tudeh's temporary reversal in the oil fields strike, the party still looked as strong as ever. Britain's ambassador, John Le Rougetel, thought that the inclusion of the Tudeh in Qavam's cabinet 'rendered improbable any attempt by the new Democratic party of Iran to compete seriously with the Tudeh for influence'.[98] The Shah too, remained sceptical. Meanwhile, with the new Tudeh ministers implementing 'sweeping changes' including the dismissal of a number of officials and their replacement by party sympathisers, it seemed unlikely that Qavam's hope of moderates or anti-court conservatives being attracted to his party would be realised.[99]

The fears of the right proved to be greatly exaggerated. Qavam's alliance with the Tudeh was short lived; he succumbed to British pressures to recall Firuz from Khuzistan, a move which resulted in the prompt rearrest of Tudeh members and a subsequent negation of the strike's achievements; he prevaricated over the question of settling the outstanding items in the Azerbaijan agreement, and even spoke of seeking a 'final solution' to the Azerbaijan question.[100] Qavam also showed tolerance in his dealings with a widespread uprising against Tudeh influence in southern Iran, and finally started to release some prominent conservatives that he had arrested earlier in the year. Yet even these measures failed to rally support for Qavam's new party. This was perhaps because, as both the British and Americans concurred, the party attracted little support from 'prominent Persians', while Qavam's close association with Muzaffar Firuz was also seen as a serious deterrent.[101]

The extent to which Qavam's policies had failed to reassure his political opponents was demonstrated by a large-scale uprising of the southern tribes, together with the subsequent efforts of the right to undermine Tudeh influence. The uprising was the answer of Britain and the conservatives to the threat posed by the left; it also gave the Shah the opportunity to undermine his prime minister's policies. Even if Qavam, as he always insisted, was preparing to strike a blow against the Democrats and the Tudeh, the events in the south forced him to abandon his step-by-step approach and take immediate action. This enforced policy change was to his disadvantage since it lost him the support of his fellow travellers on the left while increasing the power of his right-wing opponents, who insisted on taking the credit for the new hard-line approach.

The origins of the tribal revolt lay in the resistance of Khuzistan's Arabs to the oil fields strike and subsequent developments. There was earlier evidence of tribal unrest in Kirman and Fars, directed against the Tudeh and the USSR, and influenced by developments in Azerbaijan,[102] but the government's handling of the strike was decisive in sparking off a fully fledged rebellion which threatened to unite the country's western and southwestern tribal groupings. Once the strike was over the Khuzistan Arabs wanted revenge and sent an appeal to the Arab League in Cairo for 'assistance in gaining autonomy'.[103] This move was soon followed by the announcement that a 'mutual defence pact' had been signed by the leaders of the Bakhtiari and Qashqa'i tribes. Although claiming loyalty to Tehran, the tribal leaders made clear their opposition to the government's recent policies and demanded 'cooperation in the suppression of local brigands' and joint action to be taken against 'mutual enemies'. They then announced their intention to seize Isfahan and Shiraz and destroy the local Tudeh organisations.[104]

Rumours of an impending tribal revolt reached Firuz who immediately left for Isfahan with the intention of crushing the movement before it had any chance of spreading. Addressing a local worker organisation on his arrival in Isfahan, Firuz denounced the recent 'plots and conspiracies' as an attack on the country's independence. He ordered the arrest of two Bakhtiari leaders, declared martial law in Shiraz, and sought evidence to prove that the whole tribal plot was inspired by Britain's consular representatives.[105]

Firuz failed to thwart the tribal chiefs' plans. At the end of August a 'southern manifesto' was issued which appealed for a mobilisation of local forces to resist the threat of 'communism and anarchy'. The manifesto played on popular anxieties, warning of the Tudeh's attitude towards religion and social tradition. Referring to the activities of the Tudeh minister of education, it described as 'intolerable' the fact that the education of the young should be in the hands of the communists. In Azerbaijan, the manifesto continued, the Tudeh were undermining the national integrity of Iran. Finally, in a direct attack against Qavam, the manifesto concluded: 'The head of the government is intimidated by foreign political activists and believes that Tudeh participation is necessary . . . we see their participation as open interference in Persia's foreign policy . . . the participation of anarchist leaders in the democratic and Moslem country of Persia is considered as a threat to independence and integrity.'[106]

The southern manifesto was not merely a statement by Iran's tribal leaders. It carried with it the hopes and fears of Qavam's political opponents. The uprising had created, as the Shah told the American ambassador, a 'decisive situation': Qavam must now take steps to reunite the country or watch it disintegrate.[107] For the Shah, the uprising could help further to damage his prime minister's prestige, and curb his pro-leftist policies. For Britain, it provided the excuse to check Tudeh influence in the oil fields, or alternatively to provide the means for establishing provincial autonomy in the southern provinces. If Azerbaijan was to be autonomous and pro-Soviet, why could Khuzistan and Fars not be autonomous and pro-British?[108]

Neither Britain nor the royalists thus showed particular dismay at southern developments. Nor, since they both hoped to gain something from the rebellion, did they show any great inclination to check it. The uprising, not surprisingly, spread. The Qashqa'is and Bakhtiaris were joined by the Arab tribes of the Gulf and other tribal elements of Fars. Bushihr and other coastal towns were taken over, and Shiraz was surrounded before talks were initiated between the governor generals of Fars and Kirman and the Qashqa'i leader Nasir Khan. The latter demanded the release of imprisoned Bakhtiari leaders, the removal of government officials from Fars and the dismissal of the Tudeh ministers in Qavam's cabinet.[109]

Qavam was quick to respond to the new challenge. He said publicly that the southern crisis was inspired by 'reactionaries' and called on all 'liberals and progressives' to rally around his government.[110] He appeared to accept the claims made by Firuz that Britain was involved in the southern uprising, but failed to take strong action and even appeared to show some sympathy to the demands of the tribal leaders. In a meeting with Nasir Khan in Tehran, Qavam refused to accede to the latter's demands that the present cabinet be dissolved or that a Qashqa'i chief be appointed commander of the local gendarmerie. He did agree however, to the replacement of the then military commander of Fars, a Firuz nominee, and to the establishment of town and provincial councils on the Azerbaijan model. Qavam had effectively offered the tribal leaders a modified version of the Azerbaijan settlement.[111]

Nasir Khan finally accepted Qavam's terms in mid-October, by which time the tribal alliance had also forced the surrender of government troops and Khurmuj and Kazirun. However, the uprising had been contained within the Fars region and the threat of further action by the Khuzistan Arabs or the western tribes of Kermanshah never materialised. Following new guarantees that Fars would be granted local autonomy, and a promise by the Shah to grant a general amnesty to all those involved, the tribal revolt was over.[112]

From the point of view of subsequent developments, it was not the settlement itself which was significant, but the political consequences of the tribal uprising. It gave Britain and the Iranian right the opportunity to reassert their influence. It also led to a decline in the fortunes of the left. Although Qavam had perhaps intended to deprive the Tudeh of their influence, his own position was also weakened. The need to strike a blow at the Tudeh and the Azerbaijan Democrats thus caused Qavam to lose an important element of support.

Even before his turn to the right, the Tudeh and Democrats had become suspicious of the prime minister's intentions. For the Tudeh, Qavam's administration did not prove to be a vehicle for radical reforms, and the early enthusiasm over participation in his government soon waned. Only a few days after the coalition cabinet had been formed, there were clashes between members of the Tudeh and Qavam's party during a parade to celebrate the anniversary of the Constitution on 5 August.[113] Further disagreements followed Qavam's attempt to implement his labour law. The Tudeh were indignant at the prime minister's statement that, under the new law, workers would be 'free to join any party or union they wished'. This implied that the Tudeh no longer had the monopoly of the working-class vote, and might be obliged to compete with the Democratic party of Iran for support. The Tudeh press called Qavam's intervention 'inopportune' and expressed the hope that his party would desist from further meddling in trade union affairs.[114] Unrepentant, Qavam refused to retract his statement, and a few days later gave a new order which forbade members of the army, police force or gendarmerie from joining any political party: a move directed against the Tudeh since the party had been trying to win support among junior officers and other ranks.[115]

Yet another bone of contention was Qavam's refusal to accept the Tudeh's offer to join a 'united front of democratic parties' to campaign in the forthcoming elections. Qavam did not reject the offer outright, he merely imposed a series of conditions for his party's affiliation which were unacceptable to the Tudeh, notably, that it should predominate in the alliance which would also accept his principle of 'friendly relations' with all foreign powers. Since the Tudeh were, not surprisingly, unwilling to accept these conditions, Qavam remained aloof from the united front widening the gap between himself and the communist party.[116] Finally, the Tudeh were irritated by Qavam's procrastination over reaching a settlement with Azerbaijan. Qavam had continued his dialogue with Pishihvari, but had still not conceded to any of the Democrats' outstanding demands. The Tudeh's presence in the cabinet had failed to bring the Azerbaijan affair to a satisfactory conclusion.

The tribal uprising and its settlement thus set the stage for the final showdown in the struggle between the Tudeh and Qavam. Tudeh leaders were worried by the nature of the rebellion, and by Qavam's sympathetic handling of it. The party also deplored the failure of the army to take effective measures to control the unrest.[117] Following the press announcement of the Fars agreement on 15 October the Tudeh protested that the cabinet had not been consulted. The next day, the Tudeh members failed to take their places at the scheduled cabinet meeting, giving as their reason, Qavam's decision to replace certain governor generals with candidates whom the Tudeh found unacceptable. Later *Rahbar* complained of Qavam's continued opposition to the Tudeh's union organisation and of his choice of an electoral committee which was composed entirely of his own supporters.[118]

Qavam's policies were enigmatic to the last. On 16 October, the day on which the Tudeh cabinet members failed to appear, he still attended the anniversary celebration to mark the party's foundation. Two days later, in their continued absence, he announced a cabinet reshuffle, dropping the Tudeh ministers, together with his controversial colleague, Firuz, who was later sent as ambassador to Moscow.[119] Qavam spoke of his impatience at what he called the 'irresponsible' behaviour of the Tudeh ministers, and claimed that their desire to promote their own interests had caused them to 'totally neglect' domestic policy.[120] He later told the American ambassador how he had hoped that Tudeh members would prove to be 'patriotic Iranians once they saw from the inside how the USSR treated Iran every day, but they continued to follow the Soviet line'.[121] Qavam appeared still to be in control of events, certainly that was the impression he wished to convey. However it is difficult to assess the extent to which his policy changes were influenced by outside pressures, notably from the Shah. There were rumours that the Shah had threatened to oust Qavam if he did not sack the Tudeh ministers, while it is unlikely that Qavam would have sacrificed Firuz willingly. The Shah took the credit for the latter move, saying later that he had only agreed to let Firuz go to Moscow because Iranian ambassadors were 'always treated like dogs by the Kremlin'.[122]

Soon after the dismissal of the Tudeh ministers, Qavam took the first steps towards dismantling the Azerbaijan provincial council. As was the case with the Tudeh party, the Azerbaijan Democrats had become increasingly disillusioned with the policies of the central government, and had begun to doubt Qavam's goodwill – that essential ingredient for ensuring their future security. Since the June accord the Democrats' problems had mounted, while all the issues left outstanding by the arrgement had evaded solution despite frequent passage of delegations between Tabriz and Tehran.

Economically the province faced immense difficulties. The decision to allot 75 per cent of its revenues to local expenditure was of little value while the province was in a state of economic depression. The provincial government's lifting of some of the severe trade and financial restrictions and the gradual resumption of trade with the rest of the country brought only little relief. Meanwhile, according to the American ambassador, 'reckless spending and lending' had continued.[123] A severe shortage of funds led to repeated requests for loans from the central government, while Pishihvari also demanded a sum of 15 million toumans which he said was owed to Azerbaijani investors by central banks.[124] To add to the province's financial difficulties, problems in implementing the Democrats' land reform programme meant that the province could expect no profits from the agricultural sector. At the end of August, Azerbaijan's governor general, Javid, left for Tehran at the head of a delegation whose priority was to obtain a substantial aid package from the government.[125]

Assistance from Tehran was all the more important in view of the USSR's failure to supply Azerbaijan with an economic lifeline. Rather than proffering assistance, the Soviet Union's own needs meant that its wartime policy of 'plundering Azerbaijan' continued. Wheat and livestock as well as manufactured goods continued to flow across the border. The Soviet government had promised to pay for these items by providing the Democrats with agricultural and other machinery, as well as supplies for the Democrat army. Apart from supplying light weapons to the Azerbaijani volunteers, however, the USSR appeared to make no contribution to the Democrats' increasingly precarious existence. 'One would seek in vain throughout Azerbaijan to find a single Soviet tractor, harvester or other piece of machinery', noted one US report.[126]

Economic problems were only one aspect of the Democrats' difficulties. A further obstacle, as Pishihvari himself admitted, was their failure to agree with the central government over the status of the army and gendarmerie. After the breakdown of another series of negotiations, Javid, on the eve of his departure for Tehran was told not to return without agreement on this vital issue.[127] The prospects were not good. In early September, Qavam took his first formal step to regaining control in the north when he announced that two battalions of gendarmes had left Tehran en route for Zanjan, to implement a new arrangement whereby the Zanjan gendarmerie would be composed of 300 *fida'is* and 300 gendarmes appointed by Tehran.[128] Meanwhile, sensing that the Democrats were already assuming a defensive position, local tribes, notably the Shahsavans, who had played a part in resisting the Democrat takeover, had already launched raids against Democrat strongholds in the region of Ardibil, obliging the provincial government to dispatch troops to restore order in the region.[129]

Despite the adverse circumstances, the Democrats still managed to keep up an impressive show of propaganda. Constitution day was celebrated in great style in Tabriz, with Pishihvari unveiling a bust of the local constitutional hero, Baqir Khan.[130] At about the same time, great publicity was given to the provincial council's approval of a labour law, similar to Qavam's earlier legislation, but with the added innovation that the Trade Union of Azerbaijan Workers – the official union of the Democrats – was granted equal status with the ministry of labour.[131] This move, designed to revive the flagging spirits of Azerbaijan's factory workers and to demonstrate the Democrats' continued reforming zeal, failed to disguise their failure in bringing about an industrial revival, or in retaining the support of the workers. The reality was cuts, shortages and growing popular apathy. Even the public works programme, which had helped to alleviate unemployment and produced some noticeable benefits to the province, had ground to a standstill. A further blow to Democrat popularity came with reports of its anti-Muslim attitude. In one incident in the holy month of Ramadan, a Democrat party member who spoke against religious observance in a mosque was stabbed to death. Shortly after, a local Muslim leader claimed that he and other influential Azerbaijanis who refused to join the Democrats would be 'liquidated'. The American consul told how the province's religious leaders believed that Azerbaijan 'was slipping away from Iran', that the 'work only for the USSR, and Islam is being eroded'.[132]

By the autumn of 1946 there were few weapons left in the Democrats' armoury. The support they had once enjoyed had been progressively undermined. Agreement with Tehran looked an increasingly distant goal. Javid's delegation celebrated the first anniversary of the ADP's foundation in Tehran with renewed demands for money and arms from the central government.[133] Qavam's goodwill had evaporated. As he confided to Allen, he was disappointed with the results of his conciliatory policy towards Azerbaijan, which had yielded 'no results', but merely encouraged demands from other areas.[134] For the Democrats, while support from Tehran looked increasingly improbable, the likelihood of Soviet assistance also seemed remote. The USSR of course wanted to see a favourable settlement of the Azerbaijan question, but it was more anxious to secure ratification of its oil agreement, and thus did not interfere in the negotiations between Tabriz and Tehran.

Qavam's announcement that electoral preparations would begin in early October was welcome to the left and the USSR, but failed in the long term to serve their interests, since like Qavam's earlier decision to appoint Tudeh ministers to his cabinet, it became a weapon in the hands of the right. Qavam insisted that he had only taken the decision to hold the elections when the end of the Fars and Azerbaijan rebellions was already in sight, implying that he was in total control of events.[135] By October, however, confidence in the prime minister's capabilities was fast waning. Anxiety at the presence of Tudeh members in the cabinet, whipped up by the right in the Fars rebellion, turned to general alarm with the news that the country was preparing to elect a new majlis while the writ of the central government was ineffective in the north and southwest of the country, while there were still 'communists in the cabinet' and the prime minister was talking of joining an alliance of progressive parties.[136] An article in *Kayhan* captured the national mood:

Foreign forces and internal corruption gnaw at the root of the nation. Rebel groups in the north and south depend on foreign powers. One requisitions the property of the people while the other plunders them. The central government, instead of sending troops to subdue both sides is begging from them. To hold elections now would be disastrous.[137]

In the short space of time which elapsed between the Shah issuing the decree calling for electoral preparations to begin and the cabinet reshuffle in the wake of the Fars agreement, there were rumours of a possible coup against Qavam. According to Allen, the US ambassador, a group of 'prominent Iranians' was contemplating the overthrow of Qavam and the establishment of a government favourable to the maintenance of Iranian independence against the designs of the USSR. The plan had the support of the Shah, the military and some conservatives; it also assumed the cooperation of Britain and the United States.[138]

Such a drastic measure proved to be unnecessary. After a few days of speculation, the Fars agreement was signed and the Tudeh ministers had disappeared. Qavam survived. The Shah insisted on taking all the credit for the policy changes. He said that Qavam had been threatened with arrest if he did not break his links with the Tudeh. The prime minister had only been allowed to remain in power because 'no one else was suitable' and, because he had been responsible for the present difficulties the country faced, he must therefore also take responsibility for resolving them. Qavam, of course gave a different version of events, attributing the changes to his own foresight and planning. As Allen perceptively observed: 'No two historians will probably agree on the exact circumstances which brought about the new cabinet.'[139]

The truth probably lay somewhere between the two versions. Qavam had not been able to ignore the pressures of the Shah and the Western allies, but he had not been as humbled and weakened as the Shah wished to imply. All major policy decisions still displayed his personal touch. The Fars settlement was a typically 'Qavamian' compromise, the dismissal of the Tudeh ministers could be attributed as much to Qavam as to the Shah, the negotiations with the Azerbaijan Democrats continued, and the possibility of an alliance with the Tudeh still remained open. Furthermore Qavam insisted on retaining good relations with the USSR. In a continuing gesture of defiance to his opponents, Qavam's party continued to imitate Tudeh language and tactics. Its celebration of its first hundred days was, according to Le Rougetel, a 'copy' of the Tudeh's earlier anniversary gathering. Meanwhile, Firuz on the eve of his departure for Moscow, gave a speech praising Soviet generosity to Iran, and expressed his confidence that Iran could continue to expect similar generosity in the future.[140]

Yet for all his defiance, Qavam had been seriously weakened by recent developments. He had also failed to still the national anxiety about the holding of elections during the state of uncertainty which still prevailed in the country. The absence of Tudeh members in the cabinet did not alleviate the spiral of tension produced by the events of the previous year. Protests against the electoral preparations continued, notably from among members of the religious and mercantile communities who now urged popular non-participation: 'In view of the abnormal state of the country, unrest, diminished sovereignty and lack of political freedom, elections could not be in the Persian interest or that of Islam: all brethren should abstain from taking part while circumstances remain unchanged.'[141]

Faced with the possibility of serious unrest unless he rapidly restored central government control throughout the country, Qavam, after a period of rumours and speculation, finally took action in late November, when he issued the following statement which was sent to all governor generals: 'In order to secure the order necessary for free voting, reliable security forces are to be dispatched from Tehran to every province. There must be enough security forces in all constituencies. Should the necessity arise, these will be reinforced by army units . . . This precaution will be taken in all parts of Iran without exception.' If the elections were obstructed, Qavam further warned, they would be invalidated.[142]

Qavam had maintained a dialogue with the Azerbaijan Democrats throughout October and early November. There were even reports that he had finally reached agreement with the Democrat delegation in Tehran. A draft of such an agreement was published in *Azerbaijan* on 22 November, and appeared to represent a considerable scaling down of the Democrats' demands. It contemplated the compensation of landlords who had been deprived of territory under the land reform bill, the complete evacuation of Democrat forces from Zanjan, and placed Azerbaijan's finances under the control of the central bank. Yet the agreement also made concessions to the Democrats on the reorganisation of the armed forces and gendarmerie, and promised to pay the arrears on salaries of government officials owing since the previous June.[143] Typically this 'final agreement' was never ratified; it was probably only intended to preserve the appearance of good relations until the decision to dispatch troops was made. As such it was unsuccessful. Even before this agreement was drafted, *Azad Millat* had warned that Qavam would 'soon act against Azerbaijan'. At the same time both the Azerbaijan and Kurdish Democrats joined the Tudeh's electoral coalition.[144]

The beginning of electoral preparations also finally removed the last traces of cooperation between Qavam and the Tudeh. Qavam had kept the possibility of an electoral alliance open, although the Tudeh was reluctant to accept his terms. The final rupture came in early November. Qavam announced that his party would compete on an independent platform.[145]

With the gulf between the two parties now publicly opened, there was no further reason for Qavam to delay his planned troop movements.

On 22 November, Zanjan was reoccupied by a battalion of gendarmes and martial law declared. The gendarmes then proceeded north, stopping at a small village about 20 miles outside Mianih. The details of the operation were left to the war minister, Ahmadi, while Qavam retired to his tea estates in Gilan, in order to be 'free from political visits and interviews'.[146]

Predictably the events in Zanjan were followed by attacks on Qavam in the Soviet, Tudeh and Azerbaijani press. *Rahbar* accused Qavam of having given way to the forces of 'reaction' and of playing the dangerous game of 'dollar and atomic diplomacy' by seeking assistance from the USA. *Azerbaijan* repeated reports from Zanjan which spoke of the killing of Democrat party members by the gendarmerie.[147] There was speculation of an imminent attack against Tabriz, and Democrat troops were sent to Mianih to meet the advancing government forces. In Tabriz, confusion reigned, and communications with the capital were broken off.[148]

At first the Azerbaijan Democrats attempted resistance. The press and radio insisted that the people would fight 'to the last drop of blood'.[149] There were rumours however that the Soviet government had told Pishihvari to settle his differences with Tehran, hence his acceptance of the terms of the draft agreement in November. Javid too bowed to the inevitable: on 3 December he gave orders that Azerbaijanis should complete the electoral forms in Farsi, thereby surrendering one of the ADP's most hard-won concessions.[150]

The Soviet Union showed its displeasure at developments in Azerbaijan, but apart from sending warnings to Tehran, it would do nothing to ensure the survival of the provincial regime. According to British embassy reports, two Soviet officials travelled from Tehran to Tabriz on 25 November, and told the Democrat leaders that they should not resist the entry of government troops.[151] Qavam, confident of American support in case of Soviet reprisals, proceeded undaunted with his plans to reoccupy Azerbaijan. Shabistari wrote to him insisting that it was unnecessary to send troops 'since the Azerbaijan fida'is were part of the regular forces'. Qavam replied that: 'the provincial council were not entitled to express views on this subject . . . Azerbaijan does not have special privileges . . . as the present forces there have not yet won public confidence, and are not yet organised in a regular manner, they cannot be regarded as adequate to maintain order during the elections'.[152] Qavam's new assertiveness was also evident in his replies to attacks in the Soviet and Tudeh press: Azerbaijan was either part of Iran or it was not 'if it was, then the proposed action was not their concern, if not, then the sooner it was known to the world the better'.[153]

Operations resumed on 10 December; Mianih was occupied and government forces proceeded to Tabriz. The following day *Azerbaijan* published its last article in favour of resistance, and the same afternoon, after receiving news of the fall of Mianih, Biriya distributed a circular expressing confidence in the good intentions of Qavam and telling the people of Azerbaijan to receive government troops with 'dignity' and avoid any further disturbances.[154] Javid then sent a telegram to Qavam to request the termination of hostilities, promising to facilitate the peaceful entry of government forces into Tabriz. On 12 December, as troops entered the provincial capital, Shabistari sent a further telegram promising loyalty to the Shah.[155]

Despite the orders of the Democrat leaders to cease resistance, there was some fighting, mainly around Mianih in the south, and Ardabil and Astara in the far northeast of the province, where the local tribes joined forces with government troops.[156] In Tabriz, little resistance was encountered, although the American consulate spoke of 'sporadic firing' from the area around the Democrat army barracks. Most of the Democrat leaders fled across the Soviet border; only Javid remained in Tabriz. Casualties were estimated to be 500, a figure which included not only those killed in the fighting, but suspected Democrat supporters who were victims of later violence.[157]

There was general rejoicing at the reoccupation of Tabriz. Few mourned the passing of the Democrat regime. Yet the return of central government control did little to improve the lot of the Azerbaijani population. The indiscriminate looting and killing carried out by government troops – which Qavam lamented but did nothing to prevent – the imposition of martial law and other repressive measures, caused US vice-consul Dooher to remark that Azerbaijan was being treated like 'a conquered foe rather than a part of Iran which had been separated from the mother country by foreign influence'. Following a visit to the province in February 1947, Dooher observed how the Iranian government had failed entirely to live up to its pledges of installing an enlightened and progressive regime in Azerbaijan.[158]

The case of the Kurdish Democrats was even more tragic. Consistently ignored by the Persian government and even by the Azerbaijanis themselves, who had finally despaired of reaching an accord with the independent Kurdish chiefs, Mahabad was occupied three days after Tabriz. The Kurds agreed not to resist the army and there was no confrontation. Nor did the Kurdish leaders flee the province but remained hoping to negotiate their status with the central government. Qazi Muhammad and others were arrested, and in March the following year, he and two other Kumalah leaders were publicly hanged.[159]

Qavam and the Shah had finally resolved the Kurdish and Azerbaijan uprisings with force. The Fars rebels, in contrast, had been pardoned.

Qavam's policies had turned full circle. At the beginning of 1946, he had pursued a policy of conciliation towards the USSR and the left as the best way of retaining Iran's independence. By the end of the year, the same goal had pushed him into the arms of the right and the USA.

Buoyed up by his success in Azerbaijan, Qavam started 1947 in a strong position. His party won electoral victories throughout the country, except notably in the areas under martial law, and Qavam looked set to enjoy a 'comfortable working majority' in the 15th majlis.[160] He won some acclaim for his projected seven-year development programme which he intended to present to the new majlis for its approval.[161] However there was little evidence of the old Qavam, the conciliator. He was now associated with repressive measures against the left, and in Azerbaijan, where he had promised to take 'special care' in the selection of officials, and personally assume the role of governor general until after the elections, when a new provincial council would be established, he agreed instead to the appointment of the conservative, Ali Mansur, distinguished for his career under Reza Shah.[162]

Qavam's move to the right had helped him to stay in power, but his position became increasingly difficult, for he could neither work with the Shah, nor seriously compete with him for power. The Shah's personal prestige had grown steadily since the end of 1946, as had that of the military, who with the successful operations in Azerbaijan finally recovered from the shame of 1941.[163] During the spring of 1947, the Shah negotiated an agreement with the American government which would permit Iran to purchase a substantial amount of surplus military material.[164] He also managed to generate public goodwill by making a personal visit to Azerbaijan in June.[165] Nevertheless, the continuing popularity of his prime minister was a source of concern. The Shah described Qavam's government as 'the most corrupt in Persian history', and told Allen of a new plan to remove him before the majlis convened, on charges of fraud, corruption and manipulation of the elections.[166] Once again however, the Shah hesitated at taking such a step, believing perhaps that many majlis members who had supported Qavam to secure positions for themselves might switch their allegiance once the majlis convened. Another reason for retaining Qavam was 'to make him handle his own mess over the petroleum question'. Thus when the 15th majlis opened on 17 July, Qavam was reappointed as prime minister, but in command of a fast diminishing majority.[167]

The convening of the majlis at once revealed the strength of Qavam's opponents, and the weaknesses within his own party. He survived barely long enough to present his new programme to the majlis in September. The prime minister spoke at length, reviewing his past achievements and promising a radical reform programme for the future.[168] It was already too late. His opponents only allowed Qavam to stay in power just long enough to preside over the debate on the Irano-Soviet oil agreement.

Qavam had already warned the Soviet government that the agreement, in its present form, might no longer be acceptable to the majlis, and he suggested revisions. The Soviet ambassador, Sadchikov, refused to amend the agreement and insisted that the original proposals should be submitted for ratification without delay. Following a long debate on 22 October, the majlis decisively rejected the agreement by 102 votes to 2. Qavam had not given the USSR a 'blank negative', it was agreed that if oil was discovered in northern Iran, the Iranian government might then enter into negotiations for its sale in the USSR. But the USSR at once showed its dissatisfaction with this offer and with the majlis decision, and Qavam now became the target of Soviet propaganda attacks.[169]

With this last issue remaining from the 'year of crisis' now resolved, Qavam's demise was rapid. Soviet pressure was not, in itself, responsible for his downfall, but it contributed to the impression that the prime minister was surrounded by hostile forces. His opponents gathered strength following the rejection of the oil agreement, and even some of Qavam's most loyal supporters deserted him. Following a split in his own party, Qavam resigned in December. Shortly after, he left the country for Switzerland.[170]

Qavam's sudden and ignominious demise could not disguise the achievements of his two-year term in office. He had secured Iran's political independence and territorial integrity, both of which had been seriously threatened as a consequence of the war and allied policies. He had not been able to do this however, without substantial American assistance – both moral and material. Moreover, in weakening and dividing the left and in alienating the right, Qavam had failed to provide an acceptable political alternative and therefore paved the way for the return of authoritarian rule. The Shah and the United States would prove to be a powerful alliance capable of resisting the most formidable of internal and external foes. That alliance, was at least in part, one of Qavam's own making.

4 The Soviet challenge

It seems reasonable to conclude, from the action of the Russians in Persia since August 1941 and from what we have seen of their policy elsewhere, that they intended from the beginning to utilise the presence of their troops to establish their influence in North Persia for good . . . From the moment when Soviet troops entered North Persia in August 1941, the Soviet authorities used every means to weaken the influence of the Persian Government in Azerbaijan by interference both in the civil administration and in the application of security measures, but the recalcitrance of a Persian Prime Minister, Mr. Sa'ed, and the unexpectedly early end of the war with Japan, gave Russia the choice between losing the chance to turn the occasion to profit or taking more overt action. In the end she chose overt action.[1]

So wrote Britain's ambassador to Iran, Sir Reader Bullard in March 1946, in an attempt to explain the purpose of Soviet policy in Iran since the start of the allied occupation. It was not an unfair assessment. Soviet actions in Iran during the war were clearly designed to secure permanent influence in the country and thereby revise the existing balance of forces, which since the 1920s had been hostile to Soviet interests.

Russia's interest in Iran, and interference in its affairs, have a long history. The fact that the two countries share a common border of 1,250 miles does much to explain Russia's repeated efforts to extend its influence southwards. By the twentieth century, defeat in war and one-sided treaties had substantially reduced Iranian territory in Russia's favour. What remained of Persia was regarded as an important buffer against the possible designs of external powers.[2]

Until the Revolution of 1905, Russia enjoyed an unassailable position in Iran. Indeed Tsar Nicholas II believed that the annexation of Persian territories would continue. As his minister of finance, Sergei Witte, declared: 'the entire northern part of Persia was intended, as if by nature to turn in the future, if not into part of the great Russian Empire, then in any case into a country under our complete protectorate'.[3] Only in 1907, in the wake of revolution and war with Japan, did a weakened Russia sign an agreement with Britain to establish zones of influence in Iran.

The Anglo-Russian Convention[4] was renounced shortly after the October

Revolution, and in 1918, Trotsky, as Peoples Commissar for Foreign Affairs, also repudiated all tsarist agreements and concessions relating to Iran.[5] This action did not end Russia's ambitions in Persia; the countries of the southern flank remained vital to the Soviet security equation. In this respect there was considerable continuity of policy before and after the 1917 revolution.[6] The problem of protecting Russia's borders, the need to promote trade, and rivalry with Britain still conditioned policy towards Iran. The Eastern question took on a new perspective, but the USSR's desire for influence in that part of the world did not disappear. Rather it was reinforced by the weakness and isolation of the new Soviet government.

The Persian offensive was thus resumed before even the last shots in the civil war had been fired. Now, however, it was harnessed to the rhetoric of the world revolution, in which it was believed that Persia would play a leading role. The state of unrest in Iran, and in particular the uprising in Gilan, raised great expectations: 'The Persian revolt [can] become the key to a general revolution . . . Owing to Persia's special geopolitical position, and because of the significance of its liberation for the East, it must be conquered politically first of all. This precious key to revolutions in the East must be in our hands . . .'[7]

The Gilan revolt was to provide a foretaste of the USSR's later and more ambitious attempt to influence events in Iran.[8] Yet the attempt to graft Russian communism on to what was essentially a local nationalist insurgency failed. The abandonment of the Gilan Republic, and the signing, in Moscow, of a 'friendship' treaty with Iran in February 1921,[9] was perceived at the time as the optimum means of maximising Soviet influence, taking into consideration domestic constraints and the threat of foreign intervention. Soviet policy would follow a similar pattern twenty-five years later when the USSR abandoned its support of the Azerbaijan regime. The Moscow Treaty demonstrated the continuity of tsarist and Soviet preoccupations: together with similar treaties signed with Afghanistan and Turkey it represented 'an entering wedge in the drive to undermine British interests in the Near East'.[10]

The Soviet government's efforts to woo the Iranians met with little permanent success. Notes were exchanged, conventions and treaties were signed, notably a further bilateral treaty in October 1927 guaranteeing Iranian neutrality, together with another important agreement giving the Soviet Union rights over south Caspian fisheries.[11] Yet the Soviet government failed to regain the influence in Iran once enjoyed by the Tsars, a picture which did not substantially change during the interwar period.[12] By the 1930s, much to Soviet chagrin, Iran was already developing important economic relations with Germany.[13]

The allied invasion of Iran in 1941 at last provided the USSR with an opportunity to improve its position *vis-à-vis* its important southern neigh-bour. Prior to the invasion, during its brief alliance with Hitler's Germany, the USSR had already marked out its interests in the region. One of Molotov's conditions for Soviet membership of the Four Power Pact was that 'the area south of Batum and Baku and in the general direction of the Persian Gulf be recognised as the centre of aspirations of the Soviet Union'.[14] The Germans, for their part, had already encouraged the USSR to adopt a more aggressive policy towards both Iran and Afghanistan, with the aim of weakening British influence there.[15]

The German invasion of the USSR obliged the latter temporarily to shelve its regional aspirations, but the Persian issue was kept very much alive because of the large numbers of Soviet troops on Iranian territory. There can be little doubt that the USSR intended to use this physical presence in Iran to exercise influence on the government in Tehran when an appropriate opportunity should arise. It is probably wrong to speak of a Soviet master plan at this stage, although certain American early Cold War warriors believed that such a plan did exist.[16] The pact with Germany did, of course, give rise to certain expectations. Certainly Stalin wished to retain the separate frontiers he had worked out with Hitler,[17] but reeling under the effects of the Nazi invasion, the Soviet government was hardly in a position to launch a new Persian initiative. Its policy appeared to be *ad hoc*, a response to local conditions and circumstances. As one British diplomat unkindly put it: 'Russia came to Iran without a policy and got in a mess.'[18] Nevertheless, the USSR's obvious desire to regain its traditional foothold in the country had already caused consternation among its allies. Churchill had already told General Wavell that his presence in Tehran would be 'helpful', and further counselled that Soviet influence in Iran be kept within 'reasonable bounds'.[19]

Two stages can be defined in the development of Soviet policy towards Iran. The first coincided with the period in which the USSR was too occupied with the war to seriously revive any long-term ambitions in Persia. In these years Soviet activities were limited to quiet probing, and what the British consul called 'passive obstructionism'.[20] The second stage followed the improvement in Soviet fortunes in war after the Stalingrad campaign. By 1944 there was a distinctly aggressive note in Soviet policy as demonstrated by its behaviour in the oil concession crisis.

Despite the obvious weakness of its position in Iran at the beginning of the war, there were grounds for Soviet optimism regarding its long-term prospects in Persia, in the event of an allied victory. On the one hand, there were the assurances given to Stalin by Churchill in 1941 that 'we would not seek any advantages for ourselves at the expense of any rightful Russian interest, during the war or at the end'.[21] On the other hand, the USSR's invocation of the 1921 Friendship Treaty, prior to its invasion of the northern provinces, was a particularly useful weapon in Soviet hands. Its fourth clause had special pertinence:

in the event third Powers, by means of armed intervention, shall attempt to implement a policy of aggrandizement of Persian territory as a base for military operations against Russia, in the event the frontiers of the Russian Soviet Federal Socialist Republic or of its allies are menaced and if, after a warning from the Russian Soviet government, the Persian government is unable to avert this menace, the Russian Soviet government shall have the right to advance its troops into Persian territory in order to take the necessary military action in self defence.[22]

Although the treaty also included an undertaking to withdraw once the danger was removed, its invocation had important implications. The Soviet move was accepted by Britain and the USA giving a legitimacy to Soviet actions, which could be extended from meeting the German threat to confronting 'hostile forces' within Iran itself. While the USSR found the Iranian government 'unfriendly' or subject to foreign influences, it could and did continue to justify intervention in the same way. By the same token, it was difficult for the USSR's allies to withdraw a right to which they had earlier acquiesced.[23]

As the occupation commenced, the USSR could thus feel cautiously optimistic about its position in Iran. Certainly the potential for Soviet influence was far greater than at any time during the interwar period. This fact could be partly but not wholly explained by the presence of Soviet troops. The existence of widespread popular unrest also played into Soviet hands. So too, curiously, did the prevailing pro-German sentiments of the local population. If, as the British consul claimed, Iranians were hoping for a German victory and showed 'jubilation' at the German advance in the Caucasus, there was every reason for the USSR to proceed with a strong hand.[24]

The Soviet occupation had, in fact, met with little resistance: the taking of Tabriz required one batallion and a dozen armoured cars, although some bombing was reported. The Soviet army met a Persian force of about 10,000 'in total shambles', which apparently had 'no idea why they were fighting'.[25] As already noted in chapter 1, the panic and mass departure of members of the local elite in the face of the Soviet invasion proved to be short lived. While the middle and upper classes tended to remain hostile to the USSR, particularly those who suffered from the Soviet policy of requisitioning, before long much of the local population had adapted themselves to the new conditions.[26]

The manner in which the USSR commenced the occupation of the northern provinces seemed to surprise both Iranians and the allies. Soviet policy was at first neither overtly aggressive nor interventionist. This fact obviously relieved the great apprehension felt regarding Soviet policy, and curiously may also have made it easier for the USSR later to press for greater gains. It also helped to correct some of the distorted images of life and politics in the USSR which had gained common currency in Iran. As the British military attaché commented:

> There has recently been a very noticeable change in the sentiments of the Persians towards Russia, closer contact with the Russians and experience of their methods has done much to modify the conception of Russia as a bogey and a savage . . . the admired sympathy for the lower class, advertised contentment with their own system, good relations between officers and men, magnificent morale, have all affected the preconceived notions of the Russian system.[27]

Despite, therefore, a legacy of mistrust of Russian troops, much of the initial fear and hostility of the USSR was soon dissipated. When questioned, the local population admitted that Soviet troops had behaved much better than expected.[28]

While the USSR's policy of 'non-intervention' in northern Iran was welcome to all parties, it was somewhat deceptive and may have encouraged a false sense of security regarding Soviet intentions. The pursuit of a policy of *laissez-faire*, in an area where conditions of unrest prevailed, and where the power of the central government was weak or non-existent, could be seen as a deliberate tactic to further strengthen the Soviet position at the expense of Iran. The British consul thought that the Soviet interpretation of little interference was narrow and prejudicial to the local community and economy, a feeling echoed by Ivor Pink, a Foreign Office official, who added that the Russians 'do nothing to keep the local Persian administration going and a great deal to hasten its tendency to disintegrate'.[29]

The state of semi-anarchy that existed in Azerbaijan reflected unfavourably on the central government, while providing a pretext for increasing Soviet interference on the grounds that the Iranians could not maintain the required levels of security. In this respect the Soviet position was assisted by the departure of leading government officials and the dismantling of the local police force as well as the general state of unrest. Communications between the province and capital, which had never been good, deteriorated rapidly in the prevailing confusion. In effect, a vacuum had been created as a result of the occupation into which the USSR could easily move.

Clearly it was not in Soviet interests to help restore order in Azerbaijan, a fact noted by the British consul.[30] On the contrary, there is evidence that the Soviet occupying forces at least passively encouraged a proliferation of anti-government activity and labour unrest which spread throughout the provincial capital. One observer accused the USSR of actively trying to 'win over' the Tabriz proletariat and of 'making advances' to Persian youth.[31] The Soviet government strongly denied that it was encouraging the formation of a local autonomous movement, but very early in the occupation there appeared to be a close identity of interests between the Russian troops on the one hand and those individuals or groups which had strong grievances against the central government on the other. Another provocative Soviet move was the organisation of a local security force consisting principally of Armenians and *muhajirin*. This was regarded with great hostility by the local population, and though soon disbanded, the creation of such force was perhaps indicative of the future trend of Soviet policy. As noted in chapter 1, both Armenians and *muhajirin* were prominent among the early protest groups in Azerbaijan, and were, for different reasons, closely linked to the USSR.[32]

While there can be little doubt that the USSR sought to exploit its position in Azerbaijan, the politicians in Tehran were also to blame for the deficiency of the administration and the general ineptitude of its officials. The central government, albeit partly for reasons beyond its control, was incapable of making good these deficiencies. The result was the consolidation of Soviet influence over the local administration. Taking advantage of Tehran's vacillatory policies and the vacuum created by the departure of local officials, the USSR started to fill in the gaps with their own candidates, and secure the removal of those government officials who remained: 'One by one the leading officials from Azerbaijan are being quietly removed from the scene. The process has penetrated down to the "chefs de cabinet" and section heads in the local administration.'[33] In the same way, by declaring that the government was unable to undertake the reforms necessary to restore the province to a sound footing, the USSR announced that it would take over this task. Even in the early days of the occupation, the Soviet government had discussed the introduction of a reform programme for Azerbaijan, including 'a minimum of self government'.[34] It thus became increasingly difficult for the central government to wield effective power in Azerbaijan, particularly since the USSR also imposed tight restrictions on the movement of Iranian troops in the province and consistently refused any increase in the police or gendarmerie quotas. Defending the latter decision, the Soviet consul general insisted that the Persian gendarmerie were 'ruthless' and made 'no effort' to keep order.[35]

Thus at the level of local administration, circumstances and Iranian policy helped to encourage Soviet intervention, which in turn reflected unfavourably on the central government. In the crucial area of food supplies for example, by withdrawing or releasing grain, the USSR could seriously embarrass Tehran's efforts to keep grain supplies flowing to different parts of the country. Control over the wheat harvest from the northern provinces – traditionally the granary of the country – was an important weapon in Soviet hands.[36] During the first year of the occupation, the USSR was able to promote the image of the Soviet zone as one of plenty by ensuring that the Soviet zone retained higher stocks of wheat than did the rest of the country. This policy soon failed as a propaganda tactic, however, when the excessive demands of the Red Army and the shortage of wheat in the Caucasian republics meant that more and more Iranian wheat was sent to the USSR.[37] Nevertheless, following a good harvest in 1942, the situation in Tabriz still compared favourably with that of Tehran, while in the southern zone near famine conditions were reported. By 1943, in view of the countrywide shortage of basic items, there were rumours, no doubt encouraged by the Russians, of the better living conditions in the Soviet zone.[38]

Throughout the war, the wheat question was a source of much controversy, both between Iran and the USSR and among the allies themselves. Meanwhile, subsequent harvests were affected by allied demands and hoarding as a result of the unwillingness of farmers to part with their grain at low prices. By the summer of 1943, rising prices and shortages led to bread riots in several major towns, including Tabriz.[39] Such riots proved to be to the USSR's advantage since they served to demonstrate further the failings of the central government while also mobilising local unrest: high prices and shortages were a sure way of securing a public response and generating dissatisfaction over prevailing conditions.

Food riots were only one manifestation of the growing popular unrest in Azerbaijan, and were part of a broader pattern of unrest that was spreading throughout the province. There existed in Azerbaijan, as noted in chapter 1, a reservoir of discontented elements, but these were neither united nor organised. The dramatic rise in incidents, protests and demonstrations that followed the occupation, however, reflected more than a spontaneous reaction to the release of central government authority. Soviet influence lent them direction and organisation that would otherwise have been lacking. The USSR was sympathetic to demands for provincial autonomy. It supported the Tudeh, both at the local and national level. In the USSR and the Tudeh, Azerbaijan's rebels found a forum for their variety of causes.

There can be little doubt that the proliferation of so called 'liberal' activities in Tabriz owed much to Soviet influence. The background of leading political agitators invariably showed close links with the USSR. Soviet compliance in the different popular demonstrations which took place was implicit, if only because they were allowed to proceed unhindered. The resuscitation of 'democratic' demands for greater provincial independence, with their precedent in Iran's recent constitutional history, could also be readily exploited. The USSR was able to mobilise popular support for the redress of long-held grievances against Tehran, such as the election of provincial councils and the use of the Azeri language. Many Azerbaijanis who were caught up in the wave of local protest against Tehran had little idea of the direction and purpose of Soviet policy, but saw the USSR and the Tudeh as the vehicles through which their desire for reforms could be achieved.

It is impossible to assess precisely the links between the Soviet occupying forces and the growth of popular unrest in Azerbaijan. Certainly the two were closely linked. At popular meetings and demonstrations, speakers invariably were effusive in their praise of the USSR.[40] If local leftist elements were not directly receiving Soviet aid, they at least looked to Moscow for encouragement. Conservative commentators insisted that the Soviet Union had 'assisted indirectly in the activities of local political clubs engaged in the inculcation of communistic theories', and named such groups as 'Today Azerbaijan', the 'Armenian Cultural Club' and the 'Dash Merchants' Club', which they claimed could 'build up a party which would be instrumental in demanding a greater share in local government or even to favour a political union with Soviet Azerbaijan'. An official at the American consulate in Tabriz believed that the USSR was exerting pressure locally through 'liberal' agitators, recently arrived from Baku.[41] For many observers, any doubts as to the Soviet position were removed with the inauguration, in November 1943, of the provincial branch of the Society of Friends of the Soviet Union, with its offices located prominently off the main street of Tabriz. The US consul thought it no coincidence that the appearance of the society coincided with local agitation provoked by the recall to the town of an unpopular governor general.[42]

Soviet encouragement of opposition groups in Azerbaijan was facilitated by the relatively good communications that existed between the Iranian province and the Soviet Union. Direct rail and road transport had long existed between Tabriz and Tbilisi and Baku, and other Soviet towns across the border, by means of a bridge across the Aras river. Until 1941, the journey between Tabriz and Tehran could be made only on slow roads. Even when the Tehran–Zanjan leg of the Trans-Iranian railway was completed, there still remained a 250 kilometre journey by road to Tabriz.[43] Tabriz enjoyed better communications with the USSR than it did with the Iranian capital, a fact which certainly assisted Soviet penetration in the northern provinces. Links between Iranian and Soviet Azerbaijan were further improved as a result of the war, which opened the border between the two countries, and encouraged a free flow of ideas, people and trade. A marriage of interests was quickly worked out between the local merchants and the Soviet Trade Agency. The latter preferred to deal directly with the local tradesmen and thus avoid the payment of import dues. This caused concern to the Iranian government and customs officials, but benefited some Azerbaijani merchants who could fix their own prices and increase profits.[44]

A lighter side to the USSR's efforts at cultural propaganda was the arrival of actors and musicians from the Soviet republics to perform in Azerbaijan's major towns, to demonstrate the livelier aspects of Soviet society, and to show, according to the American consul that 'the communists are not barbarians'.[45] Later the USSR tried unsuccessfully to promote religious contacts between the mullahs of Iranian and Soviet Azerbaijan.

While the USSR continued its efforts to woo the local population, it also attempted to isolate Azerbaijan, both from the rest of the country, and from foreign influence. These goals were achieved by the gradual removal of central government officials from the province, the promotion of Soviet candidates, and the limiting of the Iranian gendarmerie and troop presence, as well as the restrictions on the activities of British and American officials in the Soviet zone. A particular target were the American advisers: 'The Russians are annoyed that there should be an American consulate in a Soviet occupied area, and that an American should be on the spot directing food supply . . . the Russians want Azerbaijan for themselves.'[46] Another indicator of the USSR's desire to seal off its zone of influence came with the demand that Soviet supplies should be transported only as far as Zanjan and Qazvin rather than to the usual northerly points of departure, Pahlavi and Tabriz.[47]

The USSR's desire for complete freedom of action in Azerbaijan soon led outside observers to believe that the Soviet occupying forces were preparing for major changes in the province. As one historian has observed, any confidence in the assurances given by Stalin at the Tehran Conference could hardly have survived a careful study of Russian policy in the northern provinces.[48] Yet despite allied suspicions, little effort was made to censure Soviet activities. This was partly, of course, because of other pressing war concerns, and a desire to avoid provocation of the Soviet Union, but also because of the confidence inspired among the allies as a result of Stalin's signature of not only the Tripartite Agreement of 1942 but also the Declaration on Iran signed after the Tehran Conference at the end of 1943. From Britain's point of view, too close an examination of Soviet policy in Iran was unwelcome since it might invite similar scrutiny of its own activities in the south. Furthermore, both Britain and the USA were unwilling to risk alienating such an important ally as the USSR. As Churchill warned: 'grave issues depend upon preserving a good relationship with this tremendous army.[49]

There were then compelling reasons to avoid any confrontation with the USSR over Iran. It was only when allied victory looked secure and the USSR embarked on a more aggressive course in Iran that Britain and the USA considered taking action to check Soviet pretensions. Certainly, until the oil discussions late in 1944, the main source of opposition to Soviet policy was the Iranian government, which repeatedly showed its frustration and dismay at the lack of interest shown by the Western allies in checking Soviet designs.

While Soviet activities in the north continued to generate suspicion both inside and outside Iran, in Azerbaijan, much of the population appeared to have accepted the occupation and some even profited from it. Some members of the elite, including landowners and industrialists, said that they would favour a continued Soviet presence in the north if they could retain their present privileges. Among the lower classes, Soviet propaganda had also been effective. Workers and peasants alike believed that the USSR could bring them better living and working conditions, and showed their solidarity by turning out in large numbers in the May Day parades. Members of the left-wing intelligentsia likewise believed that the USSR could provide the model for much needed reforms.[50]

The left-wing press, which flourished in Tehran and Tabriz, also provided an excellent medium for Soviet propaganda. Although pro-Tudeh news-papers avoided open association with the USSR until the oil crisis of 1944, their content reflected strong Soviet influence. In Tabriz itself two pro-Soviet newspapers were circulated: *Vatan Yolinda*, published in Baku, which disseminated Soviet news, but made much of the links between Soviet and Iranian Azerbaijan, and *Kharvar-i Now*, published in Tabriz and subsidised by the USSR.[51]

Soviet activities during the early years of the occupation were thus successful in overcoming the hostility and prejudice of at least some of the population. For certain groups in Azerbaijani society, the presence of Soviet troops was therefore not wholly unwelcome. These groups may not have been representative of the population as a whole, but the potential for Soviet influence was evident. The increase in Soviet proselytism in Iran, and its particular success in the north was the subject of a US embassy report which found that:

Iran was ripe for socialist indoctrination . . . The Russians were at first regarded as exploiters and savages . . . Iranians would run for cover when the Russians approached, hide their women and goods in the certainty that Russia would abuse them. But Russia has played her cards well. Will they succeed in the second invasion of Iran with a philosophy of equality and brotherly love. Iranians are still poor and exploited. Communistic doctrine is spread by their good conduct – the word is that the Russians behave better than the British.[52]

By the end of 1943, the US consul believed that 'nothing could prevent a determined Soviet attempt to take over Azerbaijan'.[53]

For its part, the Soviet government could congratulate itself on a vastly improved position in Iran, particularly in terms of image, and on a successful propaganda campaign. Yet in terms of actual influence, which could be translated into durable gains, little had been achieved. A policy of mild subversion, the encouragement of a local opposition movement: what would these amount to once Soviet troops had been removed? An offer of military aid, made by Stalin to the Shah at the Tehran Conference, which might have brought the two countries closer together, had been turned down.[54] With the improvement in Soviet fortunes in the war after the winter of 1943, the government was able to pay greater attention to its longer term goals, in Iran and elsewhere, not only in ending the war, but in planning the peace that was to follow.[55] In Iran, 1944 proved to be a turning point for the USSR, bringing with it new opportunities for the pursuit of a more adventurous policy.

The move towards an active policy

The elections to the 14th majlis provided an opportunity both to test and expand Soviet influence in Iran. As discussed in chapter 1, despite Soviet propaganda in support of its preferred, largely Tudeh candidates, the party only managed to secure the election of eight members. This constituted an important pressure group for Soviet interests but was scarcely enough to change the complexion of the government. In Azerbaijan, the USSR's impact was greater: two Tudeh candidates were elected, together with a merchant with commercial ties to the USSR; another Tudeh member was elected to the northern Christian constituency. In general the seats won by Tudeh members were located in the northern provinces, indicating a link with the presence of Soviet forces. Nevertheless the overall pattern of results was a disappointment for the USSR.

Most Tabrizis, despite the barrage of propaganda to which they were subjected, did not even bother to vote. The victory of the Soviet-sponsored candidate, Pishihvari, and another Tudeh colleague, was short lived, since their credentials were rejected on the grounds that they had been elected because of Soviet pressures. A series of popular protests, in which Soviet influence was strongly implicated, followed this decision. In July, the newspaper *Kharvar-i Now* attacked the government's action, attributing it to the influence of Yazd deputy, Sayyid Ziya.[56] Such efforts were to no avail. The outcome of the elections only served to remind the USSR of the failure of its policies to secure a permanent foothold in Iran's affairs. When Soviet troops withdrew, under existing arrangements, Azerbaijan would return to its previous state and the USSR would be left with nothing to show for prolonged occupation of Iranian territory. With the end of the war in sight, the need for a new initiative became more urgent. It was the revelation that private negotiations had been taking place between the Persian government and American and British companies for the award of new oil concessions that provided the USSR with the opportunity to increase its pressure on the Persian government. The award of an oil concession now became the focus of Soviet policy.

The Soviet demand of 1944 was not without precedent. When Soviet forces had entered Iran in 1941, Stalin had raised the question of reviving Soviet rights to exploit oil in the Semnan region where an Irano-Soviet company had been established in 1925. However, the Kavir Khurian company, as it was known, had floundered through lack of capital and its activities lapsed. Stalin's desire to revive it in 1941 had a strategic function, since the USSR's actual need for external supplies of oil was debatable. On this occasion, the prime minister, Suhaili, was able to procrastinate over the Soviet demand by insisting that the Kavir Khurian project was covered by no bilateral treaty and the Iranian government had assumed it abandoned. He did however agree to enter 'friendly discussions' with the USSR on the question at a later, unspecified date.[57] It was not unreasonable of the Soviet government to resume such discussions in 1944, particularly in view of the precedent established by American and British companies.

A Soviet vice-commissar for foreign affairs, Sergei Kavtaradze, headed the delegation to Iran which arrived in September 1944. He told the Shah in an interview that the Soviet government was not satisfied with the present state of relations between the two countries and wanted extensive rights to explore for oil over a five-year period in the north of the country.[58] The Soviet official's visit was clearly prompted by the news of the possible British and American concessions, and when Kavtaradze met with a Persian refusal he was naturally indignant, and accused the Sa'id government of 'one-sided' policies and discrimination against the USSR.[59]

In theory, neither Iran nor its Western allies objected to a Soviet share in Persian oil, particularly in an area which was, for the latter, economically uninteresting. In practice, however, all had reasons to fear the political implications that a Soviet oil concession might bring. The Soviet initiative was thus blocked by the pro-Western government in Tehran. Sa'id's decision, apart from receiving a hostile reception in the Soviet and Tudeh press, also sparked off demonstrations in a number of major towns. The oil crisis forced Iran's press and politicians to demonstrate where their loyalties really lay.[60] The Freedom Front, as noted, supported the Soviet concession, although at the cost of losing some of its supporters. For the Tudeh, the Soviet move necessitated a drastic policy change, but the party showed that it could be depended upon to act in the interests of the USSR. The oil debate received identical treatment in the Soviet and Tudeh press.[61] While Soviet influence was not conspicuous in the popular demonstrations, the link between the two was indisputable, and before leaving the country,

Kavtaradze took the unprecedented step of appealing to the Iranian public to help end the dispute.[62]

If the aim of the Soviet Union in precipitating the oil crisis was to secure an oil concession and nothing more, then its policy was a complete failure. Soviet and Tudeh pressures helped to cause the collapse of the Sa'id government, but they did not bring the USSR any closer to realising its desired position in Iran. If the Soviet aim, however, was to embarrass the Iranian government and its allies, and to provide a show of strength, it was at least partly successful. Aside from the removal of Sa'id, the Soviet government had also helped to bring the whole question of oil into the public eye, generating a strong sense of nationalism, which ultimately spelt doom for all foreign concessions in Iran. Bullard had already predicted this scenario when he warned that the Iranian decision was 'something of a victory' for the USSR.[63]

A long view of the oil issue does not modify the conclusion that the USSR was still in a weak position in Iran. Although it has been argued to the contrary,[64] the possibility that the AIOC concession might at some future stage be threatened, particularly after the passage of Mussadiq's bill, was poor compensation for the USSR's failure to acquire its own concession. In support of this view, it should be noted that Mussadiq's decision did not, at the time, indicate a general move on the part of the government away from its Western alignment, in particular its growing American links. Nor was the agitation inside Iran by Soviet sympathisers enough to secure any improvement in the USSR's position. The Soviet government was obliged to recognise that it could not impose its will in Iran through normal diplomatic channels, or indeed through the activities of the Tudeh party. Perhaps the only option remaining to the Soviet Union lay in exploiting its position in Azerbaijan.

While Soviet forces remained in occupation of Iran's northern provinces, the Soviet government could continue to maintain pressure on Tehran. The failure of the oil negotiations at the end of 1944 thus provided the backdrop to the beginning of a more concerted offensive in Azerbaijan. Thenceforth the USSR showed reluctance in discussing the Iranian question as a whole, but particularly that of troop withdrawals, at any of the forthcoming allied conferences. Neither at Yalta in February 1945, Potsdam in July, nor at the London and Moscow Councils of Foreign Ministers in September and December would the USSR make any firm commitment about its position in Iran beyond stating that it would abide by the conditions of the Tripartite Treaty.[65] At Yalta, Stalin told the British foreign secretary, Eden: 'You should never talk to Molotov about Iran . . . Didn't you realise that he had a resounding diplomatic defeat there? He is very sore with Iran . . .'[66]

During the turbulent months of 1944 Soviet influence in Azerbaijan had grown steadily. The timing of the anti-government demonstrations in Tabriz showed how the USSR could wield its power in the province. If Soviet influence had failed to win votes in the elections, its propaganda was still effective in whipping up support among the population. What the USSR lacked in terms of sympathetic majlis deputies, it made up for with its predominance in the local administration. No one in Azerbaijan now raised their voices against the occupying forces. No opposition to the Soviet oil concession was heard. As both British and American sources concurred, local notables, tradesmen and even a member of the clergy had expressed their support.[67] One explanation for this attitude lay in the economic arguments behind the Soviet concession. One shopkeeper accused the government of disregarding the advantageous Soviet proposals which would give Iran a 50 per cent share of profits and help to improve the province's difficult economic situation.[68]

The oil crisis had led to a definite worsening of relations between the USSR and Iran. In Azerbaijan demonstrations went unchecked and the British consul noted the 'benevolent attitude' shown by the Soviet authorities towards anti-government unrest. Perhaps the most significant development arising from the crisis however, was the fact that the agitation for the Soviet concession was now being linked to the demand for provincial autonomy.[69] Soviet aims in Azerbaijan were still not clear, but the new impetus to the local autonomy movements gave an indication of their possible intentions. Although the Soviet government enjoyed better relations with Bayat than his predecessor, there was still no understanding between the two governments on the major questions which preoccupied the Iranians: the withdrawal of Soviet troops and the reestablishment of Tehran's authority in the northern provinces.

Other aspects of Soviet activities in Azerbaijan during this period included the opening of a school and hospital in Tabriz. The school, which opened in September 1944, and offered classes in Azeri and Russian, was reported to be a great success.[70] The USSR also started to publish a newspaper in Baku for distribution in Tabriz, *Dust-i Iran*, which was another source of Soviet propaganda. It was printed in Farsi, although the intermixing with words from the local Baku idiom at times rendered it unintelligible to the Persian reader. The Society of Friends continued to flourish, promoting Irano-Soviet cultural links, and in May 1945, it organised a visit to the USSR of a delegation from Tabriz which included teachers, newspaper editors and other professionals. The delegation visited Moscow and other Soviet towns including Baku where it took part in the 25th anniversary celebrations of Soviet Azerbaijan. In an address by a local communist party member, the visitors were told of the 'unbreakable ties of friendship' which bound together the peoples of the two neighbouring provinces of Iranian and Soviet Azerbaijan.[71]

The USSR's propaganda efforts did not neglect religion. In the summer of 1944, the Soviet vice-consul invited the leading mullahs of Tabriz to join their colleagues in Soviet Azerbaijan in a programme directed at 'all Azerbaijani Muslims'.[72] In March the following year, the British Public Relations Bureau in Tehran noted the opening of a new Soviet centre in Tabriz which laid special emphasis on the encouragement which the Soviet authorities were giving to the practice of the Muslim faith in the USSR.[73] Such efforts appear to have been remarkably unsuccessful. Most Iranians still regarded the USSR as a godless country, and no amount of propaganda could convince them otherwise.

On the labour front, Soviet activities continued to produce results. The Tudeh, after winning control of the local labour movement, attracted a growing number of supporters from among Tabriz factory workers. At the same time, according to the British consul, the USSR continued to focus its propaganda efforts on the exploitative relationship between landlord and peasant that existed in Iran.[74]

By early 1945, there were rumours that Soviet activities in Azerbaijan were directed towards the annexation of the Iranian province to the USSR. Fears over Soviet intentions were highlighted by the earlier announcement that the Supreme Soviet had decided to extend diplomatic representation to individual Soviet republics. This upgrading of their status, giving the republics full powers to enter into relations with foreign states, was seen in Iran as a propaganda move to demonstrate the importance which the Soviet government attached to its different cultural and ethnic groups, or even as a prelude to Soviet absorption of Azerbaijan.[75]

One Soviet Azerbaijani who was active in promoting links between the two Azerbaijans, and who regarded as inevitable the annexation of the Iranian province by the USSR, was the chairman of the communist party in Baku, Baqirov. Soon after the occupation started, Baqirov was reported as saying that the frontier between Soviet and Persian Azerbaijan no longer existed in a 'cultural or psychological' sense, and the day would come when 'the whole of Azerbaijan would be one'. He was later known to have held talks with some of the Democrat leaders, and following the collapse of the provincial regime told Pishihvari at a dinner in Baku that the Democrats' biggest mistake had been their failure to stress the importance of a union between the two Azerbaijans.[76]

While certain Soviet Azerbaijanis may have nurtured the idea of a united Azerbaijan, such a policy was probably not supported in Moscow, nor indeed among the majority of Iranian Azerbaijanis. Then, as today, the existence of a strong united Muslim republic on the Soviet border would have been fraught with dangers for the government.[77] Although certain Cold War historians have argued otherwise, Soviet policy was designed not to annex Iranian Azerbaijan, but to win local support and to place pressure on the government in Tehran.[78] The closer the links between the USSR and the province, the more effective would be Soviet pressures. Annexation would not, in any case, end Soviet security anxieties over Iran, nor was it the most effective way to secure influence over the country as a whole, unless accompanied by other political initiatives.[79] Thus while many Iranians and foreign observers continued to believe that annexation was the Soviet goal, 'more considered opinion', according to the American vice-consul in Tabriz, had reached the conclusion that:

the USSR had accorded support to liberal elements to safeguard Soviet interests by effecting a change in the reactionary Iranian government by building up a liberal majority . . . the increased liberal representation in the Majlis would facilitate a sympathetic attitude of the Iranian government to the USSR and meet the desire of the USSR to have only friendly states on the vast Soviet frontier.[80]

By the summer of 1945, the USSR and its supporters had already introduced changes in Azerbaijan which gave the province the appearance of virtual autonomy from Tehran. Nearly all posts in the local administration were occupied by candidates known to favour Soviet interests, or at least by those who would not dare to openly criticise the USSR; many were Soviet Azerbaijanis.[81] The Soviet consul generally openly promoted his own nominees. Soviet troops in Azerbaijan consistently resisted the sending of Iranian reinforcements to the province, thus thwarting any efforts by the central government to restore its power in the north. Noting these changes, the British embassy in Tehran warned of the 'tremendous efforts' being made by the USSR to obtain 'mastery of Persia', before the evacuation of allied troops.[82]

In the period between the rejection of the Soviet oil concession in the autumn of 1944, and the formation of Pishihvari's Azerbaijan Democratic party in the late summer of 1946, the USSR maintained steady and increasing pressure on the Persian government. The fall of Bayat in April 1945, and his replacement by Hakimi in May, and then Sadr in June, angered the Soviet Union since both reversed the trend of Bayat's more moderate policies. Especially singled out for Soviet and Tudeh hostility was Sayyid Ziya, who was believed to be at the centre of Iran's opposition to Soviet goals in Iran, and whom *Pravda* accused of trying to establish a right-wing dictatorship.[83] So too was Britain, and in particular the Anglo-Iranian Oil Company. As General Ahmadi, former war minister, was told by the Soviet ambassador early in 1945, the defeat of British influence was the USSR's 'primary' goal in Iran.[84]

By the summer of 1945 the Soviet media was maintaining a constant stream of propaganda against both the Iranian government and Great Britain, much of which was repeated in the Tudeh press. Moscow radio alleged that the Iranian government was facing a crisis brought about by the lack of changes and reforms since the days of Reza Shah, and that the main hope for democratic development lay in the Tudeh party, since all other democratic organisations were 'very weakly represented in the majlis, because the 1943–44 elections had been far from democratic'. *Kharvar-i Now* also attacked the Persian Ministry of Foreign Affairs, describing it as the most 'inefficient and weakest organisation of the government, directed by old families loyal to hated reactionary regimes and trained in the school of "one-sided foreign policy"'.[85]

While Moscow radio was speaking of the Tudeh as the main hope for Iran's future, the Soviet occupying forces in Azerbaijan were already paving the way for the dismemberment of the local party branch and its replacement by the Azerbaijan Democratic party. The Tudeh had shown its limitations as a party able to serve the furtherance of Soviet aims in the short term. It was not altogether abandoned, but merely harnessed to the new Soviet campaign which had Azerbaijan as its focus.

The precise role of the USSR in the creation of the Azerbaijan Democratic party is difficult to determine. Soviet occupying forces kept a low profile, but it was impossible to disguise the Democrats' dependence on the USSR's support and guidance. The decision to dissolve the Tudeh's local branch and to launch the new party could not have been made without Soviet assent.[86] Pishihvari, whose pro-Soviet background has already been noted, was a frequent visitor at the Soviet consulate.[87] In terms of practical aid, the USSR had been active in several ways. Firstly, Soviet forces did nothing to prevent the Democrat takeovers; on the contrary, they prevented the arrival of Iranian army reinforcements as the Azerbaijan and Kurdish Democrats took control over the provincial capitals.[88] Secondly, the Soviet government was believed to have brought in extra forces and Soviet Azerbaijanis from the region around Baku into Azerbaijan to strengthen its own and Democrat forces. Thirdly, Soviet arms had been distributed to Democrat sympathisers.[89]

The official position of the Soviet government towards the situation in Azerbaijan was to welcome the changes there as 'democratic developments', but to deny that they had played any part in them.[90] Prior to the ADP takeover however, the Soviet press had repeatedly criticised the Iranian government for its acts of repression against the Azerbaijani people. It was therefore entirely natural, argued *Pravda*, that the people of Azerbaijan should now be seeking their constitutional and democratic rights. The ADP was described as wholly representative of the Azerbaijani people, as a 'moderate' movement, guided by the Persian constitution, and aimed at 'safeguarding' Iran's independence.[91]

While also denying any involvement in developments in Azerbaijan, the Soviet military commander in Tabriz accused the Persian government of 'arming landlords' in the province and said that he would be 'forced to intervene' if the situation was allowed to continue. The USSR further argued that the introduction of Iranian troops to Azerbaijan would provoke further unrest in the province, and warned that any increase in the size of the Persian garrison in Tabriz would be seen as a threat to the USSR, and would be met by a similar increase in Soviet forces.[92] In the event the column of reinforcements dispatched by Tehran could proceed no further than Qazvin. The Soviet commander in chief sent a message to General Arfa, commanding Iranian troops, that any attempt to advance further would be regarded as an attack against the USSR.[93]

Once the Democrats had established control over the province, perhaps the clearest message of Soviet support for the new regime was the presence of the Soviet consul general at the Azerbaijan assembly's first meeting in December. Thenceforth, the Soviet press continued to give press coverage to events in Azerbaijan, and was consistent in its praise for the Democrat regime.[94]

At the Moscow Conference of Foreign Ministers at the end of 1945, Molotov refused even to discuss the Iranian question, repeating earlier assurances that he regarded existing treaties as binding. He described events in Azerbaijan as a 'natural phenomenon of post-war conditions'. Far from helping the Democratic movement, Molotov continued, the Red Army had been careful not to involve itself. He concluded that the whole matter was one of 'local national aspirations . . . of course if the movement had been hostile to the Russians, the Soviet government could not have played the part of passive onlooker'.[95]

Molotov's assurances about treaty obligations were unconvincing. In January 1946, he told Bevin of Stalin's continuing concerns about the security of Baku, where 'a man with a box of matches' could cause serious damage, and which he claimed was threatened by 'diversionary activities' from inside Iran.[96] It soon became apparent that the USSR was planning to retain some of its troops in the north for an indefinite period, at least until it was satisfied that Soviet interests were not threatened by 'hostile forces' within the country. As *Pravda* also noted, the retention of troops on Iranian soil was defined not only by the treaty of 1942, but also by that of 1921, which also permitted the presence of Soviet troops while certain conditions prevailed.[97]

The USSR's reluctance to withdraw its troops reflected its continuing frustrations regarding its position in Iran. No real progress had been made in improving relations with the Persian government. Only through exploiting the Azerbaijan crisis could the USSR hope to force concessions from Tehran. Until some satisfactory bilateral agreement had been achieved, Soviet troops would not be removed from the country. Even before the ADP had formally assumed control over Tabriz, the USSR had given some hints of what such a bilateral agreement might involve: an oil concession, air transport rights, and a port at Pahlavi.[98] Unconfirmed reports said that the USSR was already setting up an oil drilling rig just north of Tabriz.[99]

A Soviet oil concession, such as that rejected by the Iranian government in 1944, seemed to be the minimum price that Iranians must pay for an easing of Soviet pressure in Azerbaijan. The existence of the autonomous regimes placed the USSR in a strong position to secure fulfilment of its demands. There was a risk that its allies would protest against Soviet actions, but if an Irano-Soviet agreement could be signed quickly, and be presented to the world as a *fait accompli*, the chances of success seemed high. Molotov's opposition to Britain's proposed Tripartite Commission, which would have given the USSR certain leverage in Iranian affairs,[100] showed how he anticipated better results from bilateral negotiations with Iran. Although the Iranian government was most reluctant to accede to Soviet pressures, its desire to rid the country of foreign troops, together with the menacing attitude of the USSR, might have led to the granting of concessions, which in different circumstances would have been refused.

This then was the backdrop to a series of discussions between Iranian and Soviet officials. The appointment of Qavam as prime minister in January 1946 was welcomed by the Russians, and Stalin signalled his readiness to receive him in Moscow.[101] His predecessor, Hakimi, had been particularly disliked by the USSR, and his offer to go to Moscow for talks had been turned down.[102] Already accused of provoking armed clashes with the Democrats, Hakimi further infuriated the USSR by instructing the head of the Iranian delegation at the United Nations in London to write to the secretary general asking for an investigation of Soviet interference in Iran's internal affairs. Qavam had long been a favoured Soviet candidate, partly because of his independence from Britain and the United States, but also because, as a wealthy northern landowner with local interests to defend, he might be amenable to Soviet pressures. Qavam did not order the dropping of the Iranian question in the United Nations, but was willing to accede to the Soviet claim that bilateral negotiations were the most appropriate way to solve existing differences between the two countries, a decision which the Security Council then accepted.[103]

Despite Qavam's acceptability to Moscow, he was unwilling to acquiesce to Soviet demands regarding Azerbaijan autonomy or an oil concession. He told Stalin that the mere discussion of such questions could result in his impeachment by the majlis.[104] The Soviet leader was not impressed. He warned Qavam that evacuation of Soviet troops from northern Iran was dependent upon the reestablishment of order and security and on the Iranian government ending its 'discriminatory' attitude towards the USSR. Regarding the Azerbaijan issue, Qavam had been taken aside during a dinner at the Kremlin and warned by Stalin not to repeat the mistakes of the British, who had 'lost America' because they failed to introduce the necessary reforms in time, and were now about to lose India for the same reason.[105]

As discussed in chapter 3, Qavam's Moscow visit was inconclusive. The USSR did not withdraw its forces from Iran by the 2 March deadline. On that day, the Soviet press reported the decision that troops would remain in certain districts of northern Iran 'pending clarification of the situation'.[106] The question was resolved finally by a renewed Iranian appeal to the United Nations, coupled with strong American pressure. The USSR was greatly irritated at the Iranian question being brought once again before the United Nations forum, but were unwilling to risk further American displeasure. On 26 March, two days before the Security Council met, Gromyko pledged the complete evacuation of troops from Iran within a period of six weeks. The new Soviet ambassador to Iran, Ivan Sadchikov, subsequently signed an agreement with Qavam, which represented a substantial reduction of the USSR's earlier demands, particularly with respect to the Azerbaijan question. The Qavam–Sadchikov agreement[107] was clearly a compromise brought about by international pressures and Qavam's refusal to give in to Soviet bullying. Nevertheless, it did at first appear that the Iranians were to lose by the new arrangements which obliged them to accede to the Soviet demand for a majority share in a joint oil company. Moreover, when Soviet forces did finally withdraw from Iran in mid-May as agreed,[108] and the Azerbaijan and Kurdish regimes did not collapse, it seemed as though their very existence might make the oil concessions become a reality.

This was certainly the impression of the Soviet press when the Qavam–Sadchikov agreement was signed on 4 April.[109] The following day *Pravda* devoted most of its front page to the new understanding, which it claimed, opened a new era in Irano–Soviet relations.[110] For a few months at least the USSR had grounds for optimism that its long-term goals in Iran had at last been achieved. Qavam's conciliatory attitude, the continued existence of the Azerbaijan regime, which appeared temporarily strengthened by the June accord signed between Firuz and Pishihvari,[111] all seemed to indicate that the USSR's long-term goals in Iran had at last been achieved. As the British ambassador, Bullard, warned: 'We might soon have to face the unpleasant possibility that a government entirely subservient to the Soviet Union might soon be operating in Tehran.'[112]

The timing of the 15th majlis elections was critical to Soviet success. The

Irano-Soviet agreement stated that elections should be held within seven months, but clearly the sooner the elections were held, the better the chances of the new majlis approving the oil concession. While the autonomous regimes still existed in the north the USSR was in a strong position; should they collapse however, the future of the oil concession looked uncertain. With the benefit of hindsight, it seems that the Soviet government was unduly optimistic: on the one hand it placed too much faith in Qavam's good intentions; on the other it underestimated the USA's new commitment to Iran, and the capacity of the Iranian government to resist intimidation. Once its troops had withdrawn from Azerbaijan, the USSR proved unable to influence the subsequent course of events. Its only real weapon was propaganda, and this became less effective with every day that passed and Iran's friendship with the United States took on more concrete form.

The reversal in Soviet fortunes became apparent by the end of the summer of 1946. Qavam's invitation to the Tudeh to join his cabinet served neither the interests of the Tudeh nor the USSR. His agreement with the Democrats moreover, only hastened their demise, since Qavam had skilfully avoided or postponed decisions on all the issues on which the Democrats' continued existence depended. Although Qavam still appeared sympathetic to the USSR and the Tudeh, as witnessed by his continuing arrest of right-wing elements in the capital and his constant platitudes to the Soviet government, there was uncertainty as to his future intentions. This uncertainty was accentuated by the insecurity of Qavam's own position. There were rumours in Tehran of his possible removal by the Shah with the support of the army.[113]

Matters came to a head in the autumn. The oil fields strike and the southern tribal riots, together with the continuing state of uncertainty in Azerbaijan, revealed just how close to a state of anarchy the country had become. The new disturbances did not favour Soviet interests since the Iranian government's response was to move to the right. Gradually the concessions won by the left during earlier months were dismantled. The anti-Tudeh reaction produced by the oil fields strike inevitably had its consequences for the Azerbaijan Democrats as well. Before long Qavam would issue his final challenge to Azerbaijan. Yet he still continued to reassure the Soviet government, giving orders to commence the electoral campaign, and even discussing the grant of an air concession which would give the USSR control over the country's northern air routes.[114]

By November, Qavam's gestures to the USSR looked more and more like diversionary tactics. The Tudeh were out of the cabinet, talks with the ADP were deadlocked, the Soviet air concession had not been ratified, and finally Qavam had announced his intention to send troops and inspectors to all provinces to oversee the electoral process. Although the Soviet government advised strongly against such a move,[115] there was little it could do beyond returning its troops to Iranian territory – an option that was not seriously considered. There was a certain complacency in the Soviet government's attitude. It appeared to have misjudged the political climate in Persia, believing that Qavam would still secure majlis ratification of the oil concession, or even that the Azerbaijan regime had some chance of survival.[116] There can be no other explanation for the relatively mild manner with which the USSR received the news of the collapse of the Azerbaijan regime. The Soviet press commented on the events in Iran with a 'certain detachment'.[117] *Pravda* noted that the Persian government had been unable to 'oppose the forces of reaction', while the Soviet government let it be known that only 'moral support' could be offered to the Democrat regime.[118] Without Soviet backing, neither the Democrats in Azerbaijan, nor the Tudeh party in Tehran were strong enough to resist the new determination of the central government, now sure of American support.

The Soviet ambassador to Iran did, of course, try to dissuade Qavam from implementing his decision to send troops to Azerbaijan. On the last of several visits to the prime minister he warned that the USSR could not remain indifferent to 'disturbances created in the region of the Soviet frontier' and that it would 'revise its attitude towards Qavam personally if he persisted in the line he had adopted'.[119] Such threats, however, no longer carried great weight. Qavam believed, correctly, that with the oil agreement in hand, the USSR would abandon its interest in Azerbaijan, and would take no retaliatory measures. In the absence of Soviet forces in Iran, and with the security of American support, the majlis no longer felt intimidated by what could be no more than a war of words.

In retrospect, the USSR appeared to have handled the whole Azerbaijan affair very badly. Its new Iranian campaign had started well enough, with the launching of the ADP and the subsequent linking of concessions from the Iranian government with the question of troop withdrawals. The prospects for success seemed high: the presence of Soviet forces, the pressure on the Iranian government, and the feeling among the USSR's allies, at that time, that the USSR could not be denied an oil concession in a country where both Britain and the USA had similar interests. However, the USSR's mishandling of the Iranian crisis, the vital question of timing, in that developments in Azerbaijan coincided with the onset of the Cold War, and the resistance of both the Iranian and American governments, frustrated Soviet ambitions.

The USSR made the mistake of neglecting the Azerbaijan situation once it believed the oil concession to be secure. The Soviet government had encouraged the Democrats to sign the June agreement with Tehran,[120] an agreement that at the time had seemed generous, but which in fact left unresolved certain issues which worked to the disadvantage of the Democrat regime. If the USSR had been more insistent about the conditions of the agreement, the Democrats might have been provided with a stronger, more durable base. The USSR gave little of the practical help or advice that was essential for their survival, although it continued to praise the activities of the Democrat regime. Perhaps most important was the Soviet government's neglect of the province's economic difficulties. Azerbaijan was not an independent economic unit; on the contrary, it was closely integrated into the Iranian economy. It was therefore unrealistic to suppose that any 'autonomous' regime could survive for long without considerable external support. Even if the USSR merely wished to use the Azerbaijan regime as a lever of pressure on Tehran, it should have offered some assistance to the provincial government if the latter was to have any chance of surviving until the next elections. Of course there was no guarantee that, even with Soviet aid, the Azerbaijan Democrats could have survived a determined initiative by Tehran. However, the position of the Iranian government would certainly have been made more difficult.

The main Soviet contribution to the Democrats had been limited material support and a great deal of propaganda. The latter, apart from being effusive in its praise for the Tabriz regime, appeared to consist principally in attacking British activities in the south, where 'British agents' were linked to a range of reactionary activities, including keeping the region in a state of 'feudalist oppression'.[121] Such efforts, while embarrassing to Britain, and possibly helping to distract attention from events in Azerbaijan, did little to assist the Soviet position. Mere propaganda could not ensure the Democrats' survival. Nor would it persuade the Iranian government to accept the Soviet oil concession. Confronted with a hostile government in Tehran, assured of American support, the Soviet Union was left with few resources to protect its interests in Iran. Certainly the Tudeh and its beleaguered band of supporters could do little to secure the success of the Soviet campaign. The party's close affiliation with the USSR had lost it the chance of emerging as a broad-based democratic movement.

Pishihvari had been a willing Soviet tool throughout. Some of his colleagues had objected to following the Soviet line, particularly over the June agreement, and had wanted to press for more radical reforms. The USSR had stifled such initiatives, wishing to avoid prolonged debates between the Democrats and the central government which would have delayed even further the holding of elections. When Qavam announced his intention to send troops to Azerbaijan, Pishihvari, after conversations with the Soviet consul general, advised against resistance. Again, some of his colleagues appeared to oppose this decision.[122] The Azerbaijan Democrats, like their Gilani forebears some quarter of a century earlier, were sacrificed because of the Soviet desire to reach agreement with Tehran.

The most successful period of the Azerbaijan government's existence was undoubtedly during the early months when the Soviet Union was more committed in its support. Pishihvari had introduced wide-ranging reforms and the ADP enjoyed some popularity. In the early summer of 1946, the three-cornered partnership of the ADP, Tudeh and the USSR, appeared to be a strong one. Many believed that Soviet influence had come to Iran to stay. Yet even at the time of the Qavam–Sadchikov negotiations, and certainly by the time of the June agreement, cracks had begun to appear in the USSR's fragile edifice of influence in Iran. As time progressed these cracks widened. Before long it was clear that the Azerbaijan regime was an artificial creation with few roots in Iranian society. The establishment of the autonomous regimes in Azerbaijan was designed to secure the USSR's long-term interests in Iran. With this goal seemingly achieved, through the April agreement, the rationale of the Azerbaijan government simply ceased to exist. Although the USSR continued to offer its token support, the ADP had become dispensable. Lacking an independent base for its existence, its demise was rapid.

Following the collapse of the Azerbaijan provincial council in December 1946, the Soviet press carried little independent comment on the situation in Iran, merely reprinting articles from Iran's left-wing press. The USSR's failure to react to the collapse of Pishihvari could only have stemmed from their continuing confidence in Qavam and the belief that the oil agreement would give them an 'effective card of reentry into Persia'.[123] Nevertheless the Soviet border was opened to fleeing Democrats, and in December, *Pravda* reported on the brutal repression and killings of Democrat leaders and followers by the Iranian government.[124] Pishihvari died in 1947 in Soviet Azerbaijan, where the party continued its activities in exile.[125]

According to the British, following the province's recapture by the central government, the Soviet government kept Azerbaijan in a 'state of anxiety'.[126] Yet it is hard to see how this was sustained in view of the strict control which Tehran now exercised over Azerbaijan, and the total absence of Democrat or Soviet influence. However, from Moscow, Firuz, who had been an important ally to the USSR during the past year, insisted that the USSR would stop at nothing to secure the concession and even spoke of the possibility of Soviet troops returning.[127]

The Iranian government had little reason to fear Soviet wrath. With the USA now explicit in its support for Iran's actions,[128] including its decision to reject the Soviet concession, the Iranian government no longer felt intimidated by Soviet propaganda and new reports of troop concentrations on the Azerbaijani border. When the majlis did finally reject the proposed oil agreement with the USSR, there was inevitably a hostile Soviet reaction. In Tehran, the Soviet ambassador sent a series of hostile notes to Qavam, while from Moscow, *Pravda* insisted that the majlis decision had been made to please the USA and described the result as 'the triumph of dollar imperial-ism'.[129] As another Soviet commentator later recorded:

Under the pressure of the imperialist forces of the U.S.A., the external policy of Iran took on an anti-Soviet character . . . To please the American and English 'protectors', parliament on October 22, 1947, refused to ratify the agreement about the Soviet–Iranian Company for exploitation of oil in northern Iran.[130]

Qavam had tried to placate the USSR by suggesting that it could still buy northern oil at favourable prices.[131] He was accused of gross discrimination, and 'double crossing' the Soviet government, and a short war of nerves followed. Until the summer of 1948, the USSR was still protesting against Iran's unfriendly behaviour.[132] Yet, short of sending troops back to Iran – an option that was never seriously contemplated – it could do nothing. Despite its most concerted efforts since the 1917 Revolution, the USSR had failed to regain the influence in Iran once enjoyed by the Tsars. While Iran chose political and economic alignment with the Western powers, and the United States chose to defend it, Soviet influence was to be excluded, although limited economic links were later resumed. Until the Iranian revolution of 1979 Iran's anti-Soviet alignment was constant. Since the revolution the country has adhered strictly to a 'neither East nor West policy' from which there have been few gains for the USSR.[133]

The lesson of the Soviet experience in Iran during the Second World War and in the Cold War which followed was that there was no way to accommodate, at least equally, the interests of East and West in such a strategically sensitive country. The USSR's idea of influence in Iran amounted to the institution of a 'friendly government' along the lines of the communist governments that were established in Eastern Europe. Yet, however much Stalin may have wished it, Iran did not feature in the 'spheres of influence' agreement sketched out by Churchill and Stalin in Moscow.[134] A government in Tehran that was friendly to Soviet interests was anathema to both Britain and the USA. Iran, like Greece and Turkey, came to occupy a central stage in the Western crusade against communist expansion.

While there may have been moments in which its allies appeared ready to accept at least a limited expansion of Soviet influence in Iran, the difference in interpretation as to what such influence would entail, together with the gradual breakdown of the wartime alliance, led the USA, followed, albeit at times reluctantly by Britain, to retract earlier offers of a Soviet foothold in Iran. The USA's new interests in Iran, and its determination to defend it from Soviet pressures, obliged Moscow to modify its policies and reassess its postwar ambition, not only in Iran, but in the Near East as a whole. In the ensuing Cold War there were to be losses and gains for both sides. Iran ranks among the USSR's earliest losses in the conflict.

5 America: the origins of a policy

The Second World War witnessed a remarkable growth of American influence in Iran, a country which had not previously been considered central to its national interests. The crisis in Azerbaijan, and the continuing interference of the Soviet Union in Iran's affairs were central to defining the future policy of the United States, not only in Iran, but in the Middle East region as a whole. Events in Azerbaijan also helped to draw together the different threads of an emergent Cold War policy: one grounded on changing perceptions of its wartime allies and of the United States' own world role.[1]

Prior to the Second World War, American involvement in Iran had been limited to missionary activities and economic and financial links of an advisory and usually temporary nature. The formal inauguration of diplomatic relations was marked by a treaty of friendship and commerce in 1856,[2] but there were no subsequent developments of any great importance until 1911, when a team of American advisers led by Morgan Shuster arrived in Iran to help reorganise the financial system. Shuster's radical sympathies, and his insistence on the need for a competent military force under his command to collect taxes, soon ran into powerful opposing interests, and he was dismissed before the end of the year.[3] American interests in Iran in the First World War were limited to the distribution of food aid to alleviate the near famine conditions that prevailed.[4]

Despite the failure of the Shuster mission, Reza Khan wanted to strengthen links with the United States, in part to counterbalance British and Russian influence. Meanwhile, US companies had shown an interest in Iranian oil,[5] and in 1922 the prime minister, Ahmad Qavam, initiated discussions with American oil companies with a view to the granting of an oil concession in northern Iran, while also applying to the US government for technical assistance.[6] The oil discussions came to nothing, but the latter initiative led to the appointment of Arthur Millspaugh as director general of finances in the autumn of 1922. The Millspaugh mission, more successful than that of Shuster, or of his own later mission to Iran during the Second World War, survived its full four-year term, although it was not renewed.[7] As oil discussions continued intermittently during the interwar period,[8] the two countries also held talks on the restriction of the opium trade, and in 1928 a bilateral treaty was signed to regulate their growing commercial concerns.[9] Although some date the beginning of serious US interests in Persia from the Shuster mission,[10] Irano-US relations did not witness a real take off until the 1940s. As a memorandum by the US Department of Near Eastern Affairs noted in 1933, American interests in Iran still centred 'around the activities of the Presbyterian board of foreign missions and the question of the extent to which its medical and educational endeavours are permitted to go by the Persian government is one which arises from time to time'.[11] Nevertheless, the potential for expansion existed long before the Second World War pushed America to the forefront of Iranian affairs. This was reflected in the continuing desire of the Iranian government to promote links with third powers to offset the traditional Anglo-Russian rivalry in Iran, on the one hand, and by the USA's burgeoning economic interests on the other. The same memorandum concluded that Persia was 'a country of outstanding interest from the economic viewpoint today'. Oil was, of course, an important part of this picture. The development of US interests in Iran was closely related to a growing appreciation of Middle Eastern oil reserves. Although still without an Iranian concession, American oil companies, in spite of British resistance, had made an entrée into the Middle East, notably in Saudi Arabia, Bahrain, Kuwait and Iraq. Further discoveries of important oil fields on the Arabian peninsula stimulated interest in Iran with its own large reserves and strategic significance.[12]

The allied occupation of Iran in 1941 brought with it a dramatic expansion of US involvement in Iran. Aside from the physical presence of a growing number of American missions, advisers and troops to help manage the supply line to the USSR and provide assistance to the Iranian government, the United States was in the most advantageous position to extend its interests in Iran at the expense of its allies. US policy was without imperialist undertones, and Americans were considered more trustworthy by the Iranians who associated both Britain and the USSR with exploitative policies. It was hoped that the United States, as a 'third power', would serve as counterweight to the traditional Anglo-Russian rivalry in Iran.[13] Although the first Millspaugh mission had ended on a somewhat hostile note, when US troops first arrived in southern Iran late in 1941, the United States was regarded by Iran as a most desirable ally. Indeed the main reversal in an amicable, albeit limited relationship between the two countries during the early twentieth century had been Iran's decision temporarily to withdraw its representatives from the United States following the appearance of two articles in the American press which likened Reza Shah to a 'stable boy' formerly employed at the British legation.[14] This crisis was soon overcome, however, and America's good standing restored. With its prestige considerably augmented by its non-participation in the allied invasion, the stage was set for the United States to prospect in new fields of influence, an opportunity that became increasingly attractive as the war years unfolded.

America undecided: 1941–1945

As a non-participant in the allied invasion and occupation of Iran, the USA did not add its signature to the Tripartite Agreement, despite considerable pressure from the Iranian government that it should do so. Nevertheless, American influence was an important element in ensuring that the treaty was signed. Iran's complaints about the nature of the occupation had their effect, particularly since they coincided with American suspicions about the intentions of their allies.[15] The belief that the good offices of the US government might be used to improve relations between Iran and its allies led secretary of state, Cordell Hull, to urge that some form of joint statement be made. Thus President Roosevelt had written to Reza Shah shortly before the latter's abdication:

My government has noted the statements to the Iranian government by the British and Soviet governments that they have no designs on the territorial independence and integrity of Iran . . . My government has already sought information from the British and Soviet governments as to their immediate as well as long term plans and intentions, and has suggested to them the advisability of a public statement to all free peoples of the world reiterating the assurances already given to Your Majesty's Government.[16]

The USA attached great important to the strict application of the principles of the Atlantic Charter in the relationships between countries large and small. The situation in Iran was considered most appropriate for the application of such principles. Thus, while speaking of the need for a formal allied agreement, Cordell Hull also referred to the 'wholesome effect' that such a statement would have on the entire Muslim world, while 'offering hope to the peoples of small countries everywhere'.[17]

Despite this thinking, which underlay the US administration's early policy to Iran, it was not prepared to sign the Tripartite Agreement. The United States was reluctant to intervene in, or take responsibility for, the management of countries hitherto outside its sphere of influence. Acting secretary of state, Sumner Welles, considered that 'It would not only be inappropriate, but positively prejudicial, for this government – out of a clear sky so far as it was concerned – to make any public declaration concerning the independence and integrity of Iran.'[18] As the secretary of war also remarked in 1942, while discussing the possibility of sending a US military mission to Iran: 'Iran was an area for which the British have assumed strategic responsibility.'[19] There was undoubtedly a strong body of opinion in the US administration which wanted to avoid close association with either British or Soviet policy in Iran. In the case of Britain, this was not only because of what Bob Dixon, Bevin's principal private secretary, later called the 'American phobia about the British Empire', but also because of the unfavourable impression created by British behaviour in Iran. The State Department, for its part, had already noted Britain's unwillingness to use tact when dealing with Iranians, an opinion shared by the American minister in Tehran who frequently referred to the harm that was being done to the allied cause by British policies.[20] The distance that existed between America and its allies in Iran, may at first have served to limit the extension of US influence. Later, however, it supplied the justification for forging a more independent policy.

Although not bound by any formal alliance, relations between Iran and the United States developed steadily. In March 1942, Lend Lease assistance was extended to the Iranian government when President Roosevelt found the defence of Iran was 'vital to the defence of the United States'.[21] The US Persian Gulf Command, involved principally in directing supplies to the USSR via the Persian corridor, numbered 30,000 men at its peak. A vital role of the US forces was to ensure the smooth running of the Trans-Iranian railway which carried millions of tons of supplies to the USSR.[22] While Lend Lease assistance to Iran, and the Persian Gulf Command, over which General Donald H. Connolly assumed command in October 1942, were geared to the successful prosecution of the war effort, perhaps more significant in the establishment of US interests in Iran in the long term were the various advisory missions which arrived during the course of the same year. The missions were in response to both British and Persian represent-ations, and were ostensibly designed to 'improve relations with Iran and thereby aid the cause of the United Nations in the Middle East'.[23] They later provided the mechanism by which American influence in Iran could be made permanent.

In August 1942, Wallace Murray, who was then adviser on political relations in the Near Eastern Department, thought that the United States would soon be 'in the position of actually running Iran through an impressive body of American advisers'. He went on to list those who had already arrived, or were about to arrive:

General Greely, acting as Quartermaster General of the Iranian Army . . . Two first-class Army Officers have already proceeded to Iran to organize and run the gendarmerie of the country which will guarantee internal security. A competent police official in this country is about to be engaged to reorganise the police forces of Iran. The Public Health Service is finding us an official to head that service in Iran. A Director of Supply and Transportation is about to be engaged . . . Finally, a full-fledged Financial Mission, more ambitious even than the Millspaugh Mission of 1922–1927, is about to be assembled here and sent to Iran.[24]

By October of the same year, Colonel H. Norman Schwarzkopf had arrived in Iran to head the gendarmerie mission, Major General Clarence S. Ridley, former governor of the Panama Canal Zone, had replaced John Greely as adviser to the Iranian army, and Millspaugh had been named as the likely candidate to head the new financial mission. The latter took up his duties early the next year, together with Colonel L. Stephen Timmerman who was named as adviser to the Iranian Police Force.[25]

The initial scope of the US missions was limited, due in part to lack of resources. Nevertheless they represented an unprecedented increase of US involvement in Iran, and would provide the broad outlines of future policy. As Sumner Welles explained to President Roosevelt:

I believe that the work of these various missions will be of great benefit since the officers and experts we have sent to Iran will not only be able to exert considerable personal influence on public opinion in a sense favourable to the general cause of the United Nations, but they will also be able to assist in the rehabilitation of the country which would seem to be a fundamental requisite for the ultimate conversion of Iran into an active and willing partner on our side. I feel now more than ever that the United States Army Mission to work with the Iranian Army could in fact play an extremely important role in this work.[26]

Thus, as early as 1942, the State Department was moving towards the view that the United States would play an important role in Iran in the future, not merely in an advisory sense, or as a disinterested third power to check Anglo-Soviet ambitions, but as an active participant in the struggle for Persia. Of course the views of Welles did not, at this time, represent the views of the majority. Nevertheless, by establishing a solid foundation for US interests through the wartime missions, a new forward Iranian policy was already taking shape.

Apart from the USA's own growing interest in Iran, and its concern to uphold Atlantic Charter principles there, the administration was drawn deeper into the country by the evident fragility of the internal situation and by continuing doubts about the intentions of its allies. Lack of unity was an early hallmark of allied policy in Iran. Referring to the Gulf region in general, the US ambassador in Moscow noted that 'the most outstanding immediate impression gained is that of profound mutual jealousy between the United States of America, Britain and Russia'. Regarding Iran in particular, the US embassy in London lamented that events in Iran had belied 'hopes that America and Britain agree about Persia'.[27] At first American complaints focused on Britain's 'high handedness' in its dealings with Iranians, for example in the matter of the arrest of prominent Persians with suspected pro-German sympathies. Meanwhile the favouritism shown to British nominees for high government appointments caused Murray to remark that he was 'not at all surprised at Mr. Dreyfus' suspicions that the British are carrying on machinations to obtain a puppet government'.[28] Another disagreement arose over Britain's lack of consultation with the United States over the entry of British and Soviet troops into Tehran, which had not been provided for under the Tripartite Agreement.[29]

Difficulties in Anglo-US relations in Iran were exacerbated by the supply question, in particular that of maintaining adequate food supplies to the local population. Iran, in normal years, was self-sufficient in wheat, but the heavy demands of allied armies threatened to provoke serious shortages. There were disagreements between American and British officials over transport arrangements, as well as differences between British and Iranian officials over establishing local requirements. The US Legation in Tehran blamed local wheat shortages on British 'intransigence' and accused both allies of 'fiddling while Rome burns . . . no effort had been made to resolve a difficult and dangerous situation . . . it is quite clear that Iran's needs are of low priority'.[30]

The tense Anglo-American relationship in Iran was exacerbated by the mutual dislike of heads of the respective missions in Tehran. Bullard spoke of the numerous complaints he had received about the American minister, Louis Dreyfus, describing him as an extremely unhelpful man who 'hated Persia'. Dreyfus for his part, thought that the British legation regarded the American advisers with disfavour, and irritated the British by expressing sympathy with the Iranian 'feeling of bitterness' towards the Soviet Union and Britain, which had contributed to the 'general instability of a people grasping blindly at democratic processes'.[31]

This personal antipathy reflected a deeper problem: that of mutual hostility and jealousy between the two countries regarding their present and future interests, not only in Iran, but in the Middle East generally. Clearly the struggle for oil was an important factor behind this attitude, but Britain's arrogant belief in its superior understanding of Middle Eastern affairs was not only an irritant, but also a challenge to US policy makers. Even with regard to the US advisers, which the British government had been so anxious to secure, Bullard could not resist the mocking comment that, for Iran, the Americans 'represented the virtues of the Anglo Saxons, but not the disadvantages'.[32] Dreyfus himself ventured the view that 'the British have two factors in mind in supporting our program – first, that if given enough rope we might hang ourselves in Iran by making a failure of the adviser program, and second, to use us, as do the Iranians, as a buffer to counter the growing menace of Soviet domination of the country'.[33]

There was nevertheless something equally arrogant about the self-righteous attitude of the United States which was also offensive to Britain. The following remark by Dreyfus was typical:

The British missed their great opportunity by not encouraging the reestablishment of security immediately after their invasion of the country . . . I personally should describe British policy as more shortsighted than evil intentioned . . . I honestly feel that this legation has been a restraining and stabilising influence in the relations of the British with the Iranians.[34]

Britain found such references to US prestige in Iran particularly irksome. Alexander Cadogan, Britain's under-secretary of state for foreign affairs considered that the 'pathetic belief in American prestige' would be a handicap to policy making: 'The "prestige" depends on the expectation of benefits to come. But I suspect that when the Americans get down to handling affairs, they will enjoy a large measure of unpopularity.'[35]

Part of the problem, for the Americans at least, lay in their belief that considerations of empire still motivated British policies in Iran. They were already aware that there was not 'a complete meeting of minds' between the different departments of the British government, but there was a tendency to assume – not quite accurately – that India Office officials predominated in Iran. This belief provided yet another reason for the US administration to maintain a distance from Britain. Dreyfus went so far as to recommend that the United States should 'avoid joining Britain in representations for fear that we should thereby lower our own prestige and share to some extent the historical onus which is certain to attach to British action in Iran.'[36]

The differences in approach, as well as the element of competition in Anglo-US relations in Iran were to be important considerations in defining US policy objectives. Americans would gradually assume many of Britain's responsibilities in Iran and the Near and Middle East, but on their own terms. Although Iran had never been a colony as such, it may not have been far from Roosevelt's mind when he spoke of working to 'free peoples all over the world from backward colonial policy', or indeed from Hull's when he insisted that 'unless dependent peoples were assisted towards ultimate self-government and were given it . . . they would provide kernels of conflict'.[37] Such thinking, as well as the administration's positive dislike of certain British attitudes and policies, may well have pushed the United States towards greater involvement in Iran, and gave new direction and permanence to measures which might once have been regarded as temporary wartime expedients:

Our aims should be: first a short range objective of using Iran's strategic position for the prosecution of the war, and second, the maintenance of our high prestige for constructive use in the post war period . . . Iranians cannot be expected to cooperate fully and voluntarily with two powers regarded with suspicion and distrust and if they are to be converted from passive appendage to willing partner it will only be through US sympathy and assistance.[38]

American policy towards Iran was not therefore merely a response to the Soviet threat, although the latter was clearly decisive towards the end of the occupation, but also reflected its own growing interests in the region and its competitive and sometimes hostile relationship with Britain. Certainly, between 1941 and 1944 the US administration probably paid rather scant attention to Soviet activities in northern Iran. It shared Britain's concern about the possible outcome of the Soviet occupation, but concern would not be followed by action until the Soviet threat assumed far larger proportions, and coincided with the realisation of Soviet aspirations in other areas. Until such a qualitative change took place in US thinking, the administration was equally preoccupied with British policy in Iran.

The importance of preserving a good relationship with the USSR in Iran led the United States to at first adopt a cautious or even conciliatory policy towards its communist ally. Aware of the vital role which the Soviet Union was playing in the war, and fearful at the time of the threat of the USSR and Germany making a 'separate peace', both the United States and Britain were unwilling to object too strongly to some of the more undesirable aspects of the Soviet occupation of northern Iran. British government representatives sometimes worried that the USA would overcommit itself in accommodating the Soviet Union, to the extent that it might even reach an accord with Moscow from which Britain was excluded.[39] While British fears were probably exaggerated, it was nevertheless true that in Iran, as in other areas, the decisive issues of the war did not always see Britain and the United States aligned against the USSR. Yet if the Soviet Union wasted no opportunity to exploit allied divisions, the course of Soviet–US relations was far from smooth, and there was little real possibility that the American government would, in the long term, acquiesce to major Soviet demands in Iran.

One early obstacle to the establishment of a good US–Soviet understanding was the advisory missions. While Iran and Britain were agreed on the necessity and desirability of US advisers, the USSR viewed the growing number of US advisers with great suspicion. At the beginning of 1943, the Soviet ambassador in London asked the British minister of war about the need for US advisers and the extent of their powers. He advised the minister against allowing the USA to obtain a position of authority in Iran and assured him that Soviet advisers were, in any case, 'more efficient'.[40] The Soviet government was particularly annoyed to learn that Britain was to hand over the task of running the railway to the United States, particularly since its own requests for control of the northern part of the railway had been persistently ignored.[41] In an attempt to allay Soviet suspicions, Millspaugh made several unsuccessful requests to be granted an interview at the Soviet legation in Tehran, in order to explain the nature of the US missions.[42]

A particular point of contention was the presence in Azerbaijan of Rex Vivian, a member of the food advisory mission, who was in charge of ensuring the smooth distribution of food supplies to the south. As the US consul commented, the Russians were 'annoyed that there should be an American consulate in a Soviet occupied area and that an American should be on the spot directing food supply . . . The Russians want Azerbaijan for themselves.'[43]

During the wheat shortage Vivian calculated that the Soviet drain on Azerbaijan's wheat would mean that even the province's 3 million inhabitants would soon be without grain, to say nothing of the rest of the country. He argued that the agreement whereby large quantities of wheat were to be sent to the USSR should never have been signed; if implemented, it would cause 'famine' in Azerbaijan.[44] It was clear that Britain alone was not responsible for the food shortages, but that the USSR also bore a share of the responsibility. The US administration was also quick to perceive how Soviet officials in Azerbaijan might use their control over the province's wheat supply as a lever of pressure in their dealings with the central government.[45]

Soviet policy on the wheat question, and the hostility shown towards the US advisers, demonstrated some of the problems that the US government would face in sustaining amicable relations with the USSR in Iran. It also awakened American suspicions about the long-term aims of Soviet policy. US representatives in Azerbaijan had already observed the growing Soviet interference in local politics. Consul Kuniholm in Tabriz noted the quiet removal of leading Azerbaijani officials, and the 'intimidation' of local officials who cooperated with the American legation, and warned that Soviet government policy might lead to the 'complete loss of independence of the northern provinces'.[46] He deeply mistrusted Soviet propaganda, with its aim to 'curry favour' with the local population. Dreyfus went further, fearing that Soviet proselytism, with its philosophy of 'brotherly love and equality', might convert the local population to communism. In April 1943 he told the State Department that Soviet policy in Iran was 'positive and aggressive':

I have reported in a series of telegrams and dispatches in the last months the effort which is being made by the Russians to ensconce themselves securely in Iran, by means of astute propaganda, by socialist indoctrination, and by the good example of their forces and by a policy consisting of a strange mixture of kindness and strong arm methods.[47]

While recognising the need not to alienate the USSR, first-hand experience of Soviet methods only further convinced the United States of the desirability of designing an independent long-term policy:

If events run their course indefinitely, it seems that Russia or Britain or both will be led to take action which will seriously abridge, if not destroy, effective Iranian independence. The best hope is to strengthen Iran to a point at which she will be able to stand on her own feet, without foreign control and protection and to call on our associates to respect the Atlantic Charter. The United States is the only nation in a position to render effective aid to Iran, specifically through providing American advisers, technicians and financial and other material support. We can only restrain Britain and Russia.[48]

The need to restrain Britain and the USSR fitted in neatly with the American pursuit of self interest. Relative to Europe, Iran was, or course, still of low priority for US policy makers, but there was a growing body of opinion within the administration inspired by the work of men like Murray and Jenergan in the Near Eastern Department, of Dreyfus in Iran, and General Hurley, a close colleague of Roosevelt, who was sent on a fact-finding tour of the Middle East, which was working to encourage greater American involvement and participation in Iranian affairs. There were those, such as General Connolly, commander of the Persian Gulf Command, who doubted whether the United States had any justifiable interests in Iran, but they would soon come to represent the minority. Certainly, by the beginning of 1944, both Roosevelt and Hull were looking to a future in which a permanent basis would be laid for US interests in the Near East.[49]

The United States was, in general, held in high regard by Iranians, but Americans were not spared from Iranian criticism, nor was the path to greater US participation in Iran always smooth. The Millspaugh mission was an early target of Iranian hostility. The nature of its work, effectively to assume control over Iran's 'entire financial and economic structure', the extensive powers Millspaugh was granted to carry it out, together with his own overbearing attitude, meant that the mission soon became the centre of controversy. Millspaugh was disliked by the USSR and the Tudeh party, both suspicious of any US efforts to seek greater influence in Iran; he was opposed by nationalist politicians like Mussadiq, who were opposed to foreign control of Iran; he alarmed the Shah by his attempts to implement cuts in army spending; he enraged merchants by his efforts to crack down on black market trading; the wealthy classes in general opposed his attempt to introduce income tax, and finally he alienated the majlis because of his personal claims to power. As Dreyfus had accurately predicted, as soon as Millspaugh started to 'tread on the toes of the entrenched classes, who consider themselves "untouchables" the day of his supreme test will have come'. Although Millspaugh retained his special powers for over eighteen months, his main supporters were the British, Sayyid Ziya, and the Americans themselves. He probably would not have survived so long had it not been for the fear of the Shah and right-wing politicians that his removal might alienate their new, important ally.[50]

Millspaugh was not the only US adviser who was subject to Iranian criticism. Vivian, in Azerbaijan, also experienced difficulties in his efforts to organise grain collection and distribution.[51] However, these were relatively minor setbacks. Iran was not discouraged in its search for greater American support. The United States, for its part, undismayed by the opposition, blamed the unpopularity of their advisers on the corruption of the ruling elite:

There is evidence of a concerted and deep rooted campaign against our advisers. This springs undoubtedly from corrupt and selfish political elements who stand to lose personally with the institution of the kind of regime our advisers contemplate . . . I have suggested with the Department the necessity of adopting a strong line in dealing with the Iranians in this matter. Unless we can require that our advisers be supported and given powers, their efforts will fail and the whole program will fall to the ground. The result of such failure would be not only to let down the Iranians but as well to cripple our own prestige. Our policy should be firm but kind, forceful but friendly, insistent but considerate.[52]

Events in Iran continued to conspire in the direction of greater US participation. A state of political crisis and serious food riots in 1943 led Dreyfus to believe that Iran was heading for disaster 'unless a government strong enough to cope with the entrenched classes can be instituted'. He went on to suggest that such a government might consist of a 'trinity of power' including Millspaugh 'to make the necessary regulations', a strong prime minister to put them into effect, and a war minister like General Ahmadi to enforce them 'on pain of summary and capital punishment'.[53] Dreyfus's opinion was one increasingly shared by officials in Washington, notably Hull. He advocated a programme of 'positive action' in Iran, involving not only the continuing provision of advisers and technicians, and other financial and material support, but also in taking the lead in 'remedying internal difficulties', working as much as possible through American advisers 'freely employed' by the Iranian government, as well as lending 'timely diplomatic support to Iran, to prevent the development of a situation in which an open threat to Iranian integrity might be presented'.[54]

The Persian lobby was rewarded at the end of 1943 when Roosevelt added his name to the Declaration Concerning Iran, signed following the allied conference in Tehran. The Declaration recognised the assistance given by Iran during the prosecution of the war, and promised to supply economic aid to make good the heavy demands of military operations in the country. It also reaffirmed the commitment of the allies to uphold the independence, sovereignty and territorial integrity of Iran. The American decision to sign such a declaration in December 1943, when early in 1942 it had been considered impossible, was less a reflection of allied solidarity than it was a demonstration of the administration's conviction that the United States had a vital and permanent stake in Iran's future.

Early in 1944 Roosevelt captured the administration's changing mood:

I was rather thrilled with the idea of using Iran as an example of what we could do by an unselfish American policy. We could not take on a more difficult example than Iran. I would like however to have a try at it. The real difficulty is to get the right kind of American experts who would be loyal to their ideals, not fight among themselves and be absolutely honest financially . . . If we could get this policy started, it would become permanent if it succeeded as we hope during the first five or ten years. And incidentally the whole experiment need cost the tax payers of the United States very little money.[55]

An American commitment to Iran had been established within two years of the allied occupation. It was still not clear how far that commitment could go, or exactly which direction it would take, but an irreversible decision had been made. The weakness of the Iranian government, British and Soviet policy and a combination of idealism and self-interest had brought the United States to Iran; the decline of Britain, and the new threat posed by Soviet power ensured the consolidation of America's position.

The events surrounding the oil crisis of 1944 provided a greater sense of direction and purpose to US policy. The crisis itself, as discussed in chapter 1, was partly the result of growing US interests in Iran, as reflected in the renewed desire of American companies to participate in the exploitation of Iran's oil reserves. Its outcome, however, was to be important in redefining the position of the United States with regard to its allies. The perception of the USSR as the main enemy in Iran would underlie future action designed to break communist influence – a pattern that was followed in other countries such as Greece and Turkey – which reached its crescendo during the struggle for Azerbaijan.

The approach made by Iranian government representatives to the US oil industry, early in 1943, was a reflection of the high standing that the United States enjoyed inside Iran, as well as of the Iranian government's desire to consolidate further links between the two countries. Despite the mutual recriminations over the adviser programme, American prestige in Iran was undiminished, and in February 1943, Iran's commercial attaché in Washington approached the Standard Oil Company of New Jersey to sound out their interest in an Iranian oil concession. After some hesitation, talks between Iran and the Standard Vacuum Company – a company operated by Standard Oil and Socony Vacuum – commenced in September. Meanwhile, a British company had also expressed interest in a similar concession, followed soon after by another US company, Sinclair Oil.[56]

Discussions on the subject of a new American or British concession continued intermittently for one year. They produced no concrete results yet gave rise to anxieties for all interested parties. The State Department feared that an oil concession might lose the United States its reputation as a disinterested power. The Irano-American discussions caused suspicion in British circles and resulted in heated exchanges between Churchill and Roosevelt as to who was trying to 'horn in' on the other's oil interests.[57] The Iranians acted with great caution, unwilling lightly to hand over so great a prize. The Russians, furious at their exclusion, helped to precipitate a new political crisis in Iran.[58] For the United States, which promptly acquiesced to Sa'id's decision to postpone all oil discussions until after the war, the oil debates and their consequences speeded the decision to make a positive commitment to Iran's independence.

It was not a Soviet oil concession as such to which the United States objected. On the contrary, the Americans had already informed the USSR that they were exclusively interested in a southern oil concession, and did not oppose Soviet ambitions in the north. They did however object to the manner in which the USSR had attempted to secure its concession, in particular its threats against the Iranian government when it failed in this aim. They were also alarmed by the visible effects of the Soviet propaganda machine which was immediately set to work once the Persian government's decision was made public.[59]

Fears about the long-term consequences of the Soviet occupation of Iran in the wake of the oil crisis produced a significant hardening of US attitudes, particularly since the perceived threat to Iran coincided with revelations about the USSR's policy intentions elsewhere, notably in Eastern Europe. They also prompted efforts to improve Anglo-US relations. The Soviet threat, coupled with the mutual suspicions of the two powers, in particular the sparring between Churchill and Roosevelt over oil, led to high level talks to resolve 'common problems'. In April 1944, acting secretary of state, Edward Stettinius, undertook a mission to London with the purpose of establishing that 'there was a general community of aims and outlook between the Foreign Office and State Department in Middle Eastern questions'.[60] More immediately, oil talks started which led to a preliminary agreement over petroleum in August. The agreement was never ratified, largely because of opposition by American companies, but the discussions served their purpose in contributing to an improved climate in Anglo-US relations in the Middle East. As a result of the Stettinius mission, the two countries also agreed to coordinate efforts to encourage allied collaboration over Iran. As Britain's ambassador to Iran, Reader Bullard, noted rather smugly in the wake of the oil crisis, the new fear of Soviet penetration in the Balkans and the Middle East, the latter at least partly the result of the oil crisis, would make Wallace Murray more willing to cooperate with Britain.[61]

This new found rapport between Britain and the United States in Iran was a reflection of the need to close ranks in the face of a common enemy and to coordinate allied war efforts. It did not remove America's suspicions of British policy. Even in 1945, after the end of formal hostilities in the war, the US administration still felt that

Iran may become a threat to allied solidarity and international security unless there can be achieved a reconciliation of British and Soviet interest and the stabilisation of Iran's internal affairs. The United States will try to impress on the British and Soviet governments the multilateral nature of their obligations to Iran.[62]

No formal commitment to Iran had been made, beyond the general assurances of the Allied Declaration, nevertheless the steady growth of US involvement in Iran, which took place during the allied occupation, provided the foundations of future policy: the State Department was moving towards the position where it would fight Soviet claims.[63]

A number of personalities had been important in urging the administration to take a more active role in Iranian affairs. The work of Dreyfus, in Tehran, was crucial, as was that of his two successors, Leyland Morris and Wallace Murray. From Moscow, Kennan, an architect of the policy known as 'containment', supplied his interpretation of Soviet conduct.[64] The Near Eastern Department, headed first by Murray, then by Loy Henderson, was also tireless in its efforts to secure greater US participation in the region. Roosevelt and his two secretaries of state, Hull and Stettinius, had gone some way in preparing the ground for their successors, but Roosevelt would not declare Cold War on Russia – especially not over Iran. He acknowledged the Soviet threat, but still hoped to combat it with the weapons that were the products of his own idealism: the Atlantic Charter, the United Nations, or, in the specific case of Iran, he had devised an allied trusteeship scheme.[65] Truman and Brynes however, had fewer illusions about the Soviet Union. No immediate offer of aid to Iran was made, beyond that already contemplated in the Allied Declaration or the existing advisory programmes, but Roosevelt's successors were soon converted into firm opponents of Stalin's postwar aims. In Eastern Europe it was already too late, in Iran it was not.

It fell then to Truman to revise American views of the 'strange alliance', which had served so well for the purposes of fighting the war but which collapsed in preparing for the peace that was to follow. He was suited to the task, being more comfortable with Cold War stereotypes. On the eve of the Azerbaijan Democrats takeover in Tabriz, the president could find much to sympathise with in Murray's views of Soviet policy:

Ultimately I think its principal aim is to establish in power in Tehran a popular government like Groza in Rumania, led by men of Soviet influence amenable to Soviet demands . . . However much we may deplore conditions in Iran, a cure administered by a minority group under Russian direction would be worse than the disease for the United States, the Iranians and world peace.[66]

This impression, which would soon be shared and encouraged by Robert Rossow, the young and influential American vice-consul in Tabriz, set the scene for a new series of American commitments. The vision of a Soviet dominated Iran – and possibly Greece and Turkey as well – became an obsession with US policy makers. The basis for an extension of US influence in Iran had been laid. Despite the demise of the Millspaugh mission early in 1945, following criticism of his attempts to dismiss the governor of the National Bank,[67] US power and prestige had continued to grow apace. The Iranian government looked increasingly to the United States for a way out of its present difficulties. In May 1944 a reciprocal trade treaty was ratified, and in November the following year an agreement to regulate US air transport services to Iran was signed.[68] Meanwhile, the door to a future agreement on oil remained open, or so at least the administration believed. Although the left-wing press periodically criticised US policy, Britain still bore the brunt of such attacks.[69] Aside from the Tudeh, and the parliamentary liberals – consisting mainly of Azerbaijani aristocrats and Mussadiq supporters, most majlis deputies favoured the establishment of closer ties with the United States. Even Qavam, despite his appeasement of the USSR, took the greatest care not to alienate such an important ally. His ability to defy successfully Soviet ambitions rested, in no small degree, on the knowledge that he could count on American support.

America committed: 1946–1947

'In early 1946', wrote Truman, 'Russian activities in Iran threatened the peace of the world.'[70] The failure of the USSR to respect those clauses of the Tripartite Agreement relating to withdrawal of its troops from Iran, and their interference in the northern provinces, were decisive in establishing America's commitment to defend Iran against Soviet pressures. Support for Iran in the United Nations in the spring of 1946 represented a turning point in US policy, for it marked the transition from a passive to an active policy. At Yalta, Roosevelt had not yet abandoned the idea of an allied trusteeship of Iran. By March 1946, with Soviet troops still occupying northern Iran, both Britain and the USA were talking of the possibility of war with the USSR over Iran.[71] To understand the changes that had taken place in American thinking, reference must be made not only to the Soviet threat, or to the change in US leadership, but to the complete breakdown of wartime allied accords over Europe. The development of US policy toward Iran in 1946 can only be understood within the framework of the contemporary world scene in which mutual misunderstanding, and rival claims to different parts of the world by the two emerging superpowers, dictated a revision of policies in Europe and the Near and Far East.

The creation of the Azerbaijan Democratic party, despite the alarm it caused, was not for the United States so decisive an event as was the failure of the USSR to withdraw its troops from Iran. While Murray tended to regard Soviet activities in northern Iran and Eastern Europe in the same light, he perhaps still hoped that the USSR would respect the March deadline for evacuation of its forces. The Soviet position in northern Iran was not, in any case, comparable to that of Eastern Europe. Yet if Stalin seriously intended to implement his threat to impose his own social system on every territory occupied by the Red Army, could that not also include the Soviet zone of occupation in Iran?[72]

Despite Murray's deep suspicions of the motives behind Soviet action, US policy remained cautious, awaiting further developments. Regarding the Azerbaijan Democrats, Murray thought that they aimed 'to strike a mid-course between the reactionary landlord class and the extremists of the Tudeh'. Meanwhile, Samuel Ebling, Tabriz consul, declared himself to be rather impressed with the Democrat leaders, and described Pishihvari and Shabistari as 'astute executives whose qualifications compare favourably with those demonstrated by many Majlis deputies'.[73] Although politicians in Tehran contested this view and insisted that Soviet policy in northern Iran was designed to create a permanent zone of influence there, the United States preferred to wait before taking action, and dispatched the embassy press attaché, Cuyler Young, to report on the local situation.

Young confirmed some of the rumours that had already been circulating in Tehran: the Soviet Union had distributed rifles to the Democrats, and had prevented Iranian reinforcements from arriving in Azerbaijan. He did not consider the regime either communist or separatist, but he noted that party propaganda was developing along 'communistic lines'. One change he regarded as significant was a change in local headwear. The previously fashionable European felt hat, the obligatory headgear under Reza Shah, had given way in Azerbaijan to the cloth cap.[74]

These and other similar observations, by American as well as Iranian commentators, did not take long to convince the United States that it was dealing with a Soviet inspired rebellion in Azerbaijan. The word 'communist' soon came to replace 'democrat' in US reporting of northern events; pro-Soviet parties in Iran, or in any part of the world, were regarded as highly dangerous. US policy makers were ready to share the attitude of the Iranian elite towards the Azerbaijan Democrats: that their position was entirely dependent on Soviet support.[75] *The New York Times* had already implanted the idea in the minds of its readers that Azerbaijan was a kingdom where the pro-Soviet Tudeh party reigned supreme, and humble citizens could not take a public bath or catch a bus without showing their Tudeh membership card.[76]

The changing US attitude towards the Iranian question became apparent after the Moscow Conference, which took place at the end of 1945. At Yalta and Potsdam, British and Iranian pressure had not convinced the Americans of the need for a strong stand against the USSR. There were, at least when Roosevelt was alive, hopes of a broad general agreement with the USSR, and the Iranian question was not considered important enough to risk damaging allied agreement in other areas. The United States, like Britain, agreed in principle to an advancement of the date for allied troop withdrawals from Iran, and US troops were the first to withdraw from the country in January 1946.[77] However, until Stalin's intentions in Iran became clear, Truman and Brynes had been willing to accept Molotov's informal guarantees that the USSR would abide by its treaty obligations. Even during the Moscow Conference, Brynes, to the consternation of Britain, still seemed set on reaching some agreement with the USSR, as Kennan remarked: 'he doesn't much care what. The realities behind this agreement, since they concern only such problems as Koreans, Rumanians and Iranians, about whom he knows nothing, do not concern him.'[78]

British Foreign Secretary, Ernest Bevin, who was hoping for American support to put pressure on Molotov over Soviet activities in Iran, Turkey and Greece, was dismayed by what he called Brynes 'equivocal, rather low-key policy'. As soon as the latter saw that the Iranian question was likely to postpone discussion of other issues he proposed that it be dropped from the formal agenda of the conference.[79] President Truman however, was unhappy at Brynes' action, and with the results of the conference which had produced 'not a word to suggest that the Russians might be willing to change their ways in Iran – where the situation was rapidly becoming serious – or anywhere else'. On his return from Moscow, Brynes was reprimanded for being 'too soft on the Russians', and was soon brought into line with the President's new way of thinking:

There isn't a doubt in my mind that Russia intends an invasion of Turkey and the seizure of the Black Sea Straits to the Mediterranean. Unless Russia is faced with an iron fist and strong language, another war is in the making. Only one language do they understand: 'how many divisions have you?' I do not think we should play compromise any longer. We should refuse to recognise Romania and Bulgaria until they comply with our requirements; we should let our position on Iran be known in no uncertain terms . . . Then we should insist on the return of our ships from Russia and force a settlement of the lend-lease debt of Russia. I'm tired of babying the Soviets.[80]

These sentiments, expressed in January of 1946, paved the way for decisive US action in Iran when the Soviet Union failed to withdraw its troops in March. The USSR's attitude towards the Iranian attempt to raise the question of 'Soviet interference' in the United Nations, and to Bevin's proposals for a Tripartite Commission, together with its continuing support for the Azerbaijan regime, and the intransigence shown towards the Iranian prime minister during his visit to Moscow, all demonstrated the USSR's obvious reluctance to abide by its treaty obligations. It therefore came as no surprise when Iran's ambassador to Washington, Husain Ala, sent a note to Brynes on 5 March asking the United States to send a protest to Moscow about the Soviet Union's breach of good faith in failing to withdraw its forces from northern Iran by 2 March. The note also stated that: 'In accordance with information received from well-informed quarters, the Soviet government is making the evacuation of Iran depend on the acceptance by the Persian government of certain very important demands, whereas the withdrawal of foreign allied forces at the end of the war has always been considered unconditional.'[81] On the same day Brynes also dispatched a note to Moscow warning that the United States could not 'remain indifferent' to Soviet actions'.[82]

The United States had decided to check Soviet ambitions in Iran. Stalin had called Truman's bluff. He had hoped to retain his troops in the north of Iran to maintain pressure on the government in Tehran and thereby work out an agreement favourable to Soviet interests. Treaty obligations, however, were a subject about which the United States had become inflexible, particularly where American interests were so intimately involved. At stake was not merely the future of Iran, and possibly Greece and Turkey as well, but the entire network of US interests in the Middle East.[83] The United States shared British fears that a Soviet-controlled Iran might lead to control of the vast oil wealth of the region, a prospect that was as intolerable to Truman as it was to Attlee and Bevin. The 'giant pincers movement' that threatened the Mediterranean and the Near East had to be checked.[84] In moving to defend Iran from Soviet designs, however, Truman took care that his actions should wear the UN cloak of respectability, and honour the principles of the Atlantic Charter. US policy made explicit its rejection of any great power arrangements to work out new spheres of influence in Iran. To the American mind, Iran was in need of protection from both Soviet and British imperialism.

Brynes' note to Molotov marked the beginning of the end of the USSR's postwar aspirations in Iran. It was not perhaps appreciated at the time, but the USSR would not risk a confrontation with the United States over the Near East. The extent of the Soviet defeat did not become apparent until the autumn of 1947, when the Iranian majlis finally rejected the Soviet oil agreement, but America's triumph was already evident in the manner in which the Iranian case was conducted in the United Nations. The United States had effectively won its 'first diplomatic victory in the Cold War'.[85]

The Soviet Union did not respond to the US note, thus helping to remove any lingering doubts in the State Department as to whether its actions had been justified. The coincidence of the US warning to Moscow, Churchill's 'iron curtain' speech at Fulton, and reports of new Soviet troop movements in both Azerbaijan and Bulgaria – seen as threatening moves against Iran and Turkey – were timely in convincing the US public of Stalin's global designs.[86] While *The New York Times* bore the front page news that Soviet troops were advancing on Tehran, Truman sent Averell Harriman to London as ambassador, announcing dramatically: 'It is important. We may be at war with the Soviet Union over Iran.'[87]

One US official who was instrumental in generating tension in Washington about Soviet moves in Iran was Robert Rossow, who replaced Samuel Ebling at the Tabriz consulate in early 1946. Ebling represented the old school with respect to US perceptions of Soviet policy. He thought some of the Democrats' goals to be moderate, and generally tried to 'get on' with the Russians. Rossow, on the other hand, soon gave up any attempt to befriend the Democrats, and produced reports about Soviet activities that were daily more alarmist. Although young and inexperienced at the time of his appointment, Rossow soon earned high regard in Washington, largely, it seems, because he told the administration what it wanted to hear. Rossow considered the Democrats to be aggressive and pro-Soviet. He described the 'sinister' activities of the 'Society of Friends of Soviet Azerbaijan' which sought to foster the union of the two nationalities.[88] It was during the critical weeks of March 1946, however, that Rossow, in his most dramatic style, reported the arrival of fresh Soviet troops, tanks and other heavy weapons in Azerbaijan, while 'columns' of Democrat forces were preparing to march east towards Rasht, Pahlavi and Tehran. This was 'no ordinary reshuffling of troops', insisted Rossow, 'but full-scale combat deployment'.[89]

Rossow's evidence both of the arrival of Soviet reinforcements and of the Democrats proposed 'march on Tehran' was not substantiated by other sources. It was based on his own personal observations including night sorties to the countryside around Tabriz, and studies of lorry tyre tracks and horse droppings. It seems remarkable, in retrospect, that such boy scout style reports could have created such an impact in Washington, and indeed helped to provide the justification for the US policy change in Iran. Rossow's analysis, furthermore, did not limit itself to Iran alone. He linked the extra deployment of Soviet troops in Azerbaijan to the broader Soviet aim of the 'reduction of Turkey'.[90] In short, Rossow helped to provide the State Department with the sort of information it needed to justify launching a counter offensive to check Soviet pretensions in the Near East.

Rossow's reports and the hostile tone of the Soviet press provided the backdrop to Iran's new UN appeal. Prime Minister Qavam had returned from Moscow, having failed to reach any agreement with the USSR, although he announced that bilateral talks would continue on the arrival of the new Soviet ambassador. Given the nature of the USSR's demands, however, the US administration believed that the Iranian government could not resist Soviet pressure alone.[91] Since Qavam also favoured the UN appeal, as it would improve his bargaining position with the USSR, the United States and Iran appeared to be acting in complete accord when Ala brought the dispute to the attention of the world organisation on 18 March. When it was subsequently proposed that the item be placed on the Security Council's agenda on 25 March, the Soviet representative, Andrei Gromyko, objected on the grounds that bilateral talks were already underway, and asked for a postponement until 10 April. The Americans refused.[92] On the one hand, Truman believed that the Iranian government was too weak to save itself, on the other, he was determined that the United States alone should call the tune in the United Nations.

The UN appeal proved decisive in obliging the USSR to reach an agreement with Tehran. Whether this would have been achieved without the intervention of the United Nations is a matter for conjecture. Certainly Qavam's position was strengthened by the Iranian appeal, and the US insistence that the Iranian question be retained on the Security Council's agenda. The US administration had effectively forced the USSR rapidly to conclude its bilateral negotiations with the Iranian government, or risk the censure of the world organisation. It was certainly no coincidence that on 26 March, as the Security Council met to consider Iran's case, Gromyko announced that a broad general agreement had been reached between the two countries.[93]

The timing of the Soviet announcement prompted speculation that Truman had sent a personal message to Stalin threatening US action if the USSR did not withdraw its troops from Iran. The President, in his memoirs, spoke of a 'blunt message' to Stalin.[94] Whether or not Truman did send an ultimatum, and the question has been the subject of lively debate,[95] the Soviet Union was still under considerable pressure to act before the Security Council meeting.

The Irano-Soviet agreement in itself had little to do with the United Nations but was the result of a compromise between the two parties. Brynes described it as 'not bad' but in reference to the formation of the Irano-Soviet oil company confessed his regret that Iran had been forced to 'pay a bribe for what was hers by right'.[96] Gromyko hoped that the mere existence of the agreement would lead to the immediate withdrawal of the Iranian case from the Security Council's agenda, but here again he was disappointed. Deprived of the possibility of presiding over the Qavam–Sadchikov negotiations in the UN forum, the United States was insistent that the organisation should at least endorse them and ensure their proper implementation. Thus when approving the agreement, on 4 April, the Security Council agreed to defer further action on the Iranian question until 6 May, pending reports on the state of Soviet troop withdrawals to be made to the Council by both Iran and the USSR. As the US representative at the United Nations remarked, the latter decision left the way open for the Council to consider 'at any time, as the first item on its agenda, reports from any member of the Security Council on developments which may retard or threaten the prompt withdrawal of Soviet troops from Iran'.[97] Subsequent representations to overrule this decision by Gromyko and Qavam himself – the latter faced with intense Soviet pressure – were resisted by US secretary of state, Stettinius, who insisted that 'the retention of the matter on the agenda did not infringe on the sovereign rights or independence of Iran', nor did it 'interfere with the agreements already reached'.[98] US action over the Iranian case, which caused even Secretary General Trygve Lie to express his concern, was unprecedented.[99] The US government had effectively taken unilateral action in refusing to allow the Iranian case to be dropped even after both parties to the dispute had so requested.

US policy in the spring of 1946 had been decisive in ensuring that the USSR did not evade its obligations in Iran. It was no coincidence that this show of strength in Iran was followed by the dispatching of the battleship *Missouri* to Istanbul in a gesture of solidarity towards Greece and Turkey.[100] Curiously, however, despite the restrictions placed on Soviet activities in Iran, the Irano-Soviet agreement did not at first appear to be a triumph for the United Nations as the Americans implied. On the contrary, the USSR appeared to regard it as something of a victory for Soviet interests. As some historians have suggested, the most important factor in securing Soviet troop withdrawals was 'the belief on the part of the Russians that Qavam had been won over'.[101] However, as discussed in chapter 4, the Soviet victory, if it can be so described, was an ephemeral one, dependent on Qavam's goodwill and his unstable alliance with the Tudeh and Azerbaijan Democrats. The American victory proved the more durable one, and the question to be asked here is whether the USSR, had it been dissatisfied with the bilateral negotiations, would have risked conflict with the United States over Iran. The answer is almost certainly no. No doubt it was gratifying to the USSR to have obtained what it thought was a major concession from Iran, but there is no evidence to suggest that it was willing to fight for it. The United States had effectively taken the lead in the race for Persia; neither Britain nor the USSR would wield their power again in quite the same way.

American assistance to check Soviet pretensions in Iran had been earnestly sought by the British government, but the United Nations appeal once again illustrated the conflicting and competitive elements of the Anglo-American relationship, while also reminding Britain of the new limits of her power. Britain would not have chosen the UN route as the best means of checking Soviet power in Iran. As discussed in chapter 6, Bevin had opposed the UN appeal in January, when Iran's Prime Minister Hakimi had first tried to appeal against Soviet interference.[102] In March, Britain followed the US lead, but played only a secondary part in the UN discussions. Britain was worried about the international exposure that its own oil concession might receive as a result of the discussion of the USSR's proposed joint company. In seeking American aid, the protection of Britain's traditional interests in the Near East was uppermost in the minds of British policy makers. In the United States however, perceptions were different. For the Americans too, oil and, in particular, the desire for an Iranian concession and the defence of American oil interests in the region, were key elements in the Iranian crisis. Brynes however, took care to remind Murray in Tehran that he should avoid any discussion of oil; American policy should not be seen to be based on the same principles as that of Britain or the USSR: 'no one should obtain a false impression that our determination to carry out our obligations under the Charter and the Iran Declaration has been influenced in the slightest by a selfish interest on our part in Iranian petroleum'.[103]

Thus, not for the first time, the United States found itself at odds with Britain over Iran. It was felt, on this occasion, moreover, that the Iranian crisis was responsible for a decline of British influence and prestige in the region. An incident in March 1946, when a member of the Bakhtiari tribe came to the US embassy in Tehran with a message from Sayyid Ziya asking for America's 'advice', led Murray to comment:

This call seems clearly to emphasise the decline of British prestige and leadership in Iran. I find it rather a startling development that sees the traditional British deputies coming to me to ask what to do. This coupled with the apparent total lack of a strong British policy in the crisis has given Iranians the impression that Britain has given up and is no longer interested in Iran. I realize that Britain may have been quiescent, feeling that strong positive action by the US government alone may have been the best for solving Irano-Soviet difficulties . . . whatever the motivation there has certainly been a loss of British prestige.[104]

Murray also thought that Bullard's departure from Iran in March and his replacement the following month by John Le Rougetel, a man with 'no area experience', could only heighten the impression that Britain had lost interest. Perhaps the most significant aspect of these developments from the US viewpoint was the danger that Bullard's departure, or the decline of British influence generally, might lead to a vacuum in Iran, which must be filled by the United States. Otherwise the threat of a Soviet dominated Iran might become a reality.

This threat was made more acute by Qavam's conciliatory attitude towards the USSR. His loosening of restrictions against the left, and his own faintheartedness in pursuing the Iranian appeal in the United Nations to its final conclusion, led to a revision of attitudes towards him personally, which coincided with the crystallisation of the administration's policy of containment. When Qavam was voted prime minister, he had been generally welcomed as the only person capable of handling the present situation,[105] but support for him wavered as he continued his policy of appeasement of the USSR. There was evidence that even during the spring of 1946 the US administration was already looking to the group around the Shah for a replacement to Qavam. As early as 1944, Leland Morris, then ambassador, spoke of the 'good impression' he had received from the Shah, and suggested that 'the strengthening of his hand would be one of the roads out of the internal political dilemma in which the country finds itself. One thing is certain, that the weakness at the top which is apparent here must be eliminated either through the hand of the Shah or by the rise of a strong individual.'[106] The possibility of promoting the Shah and his entourage, and the consequent sacrifice of Iran's short-lived effort at parliamentary democracy, was clearly an option held in reserve by US policy makers. Certainly, during 1946, the State Department seemed increasingly unsure that Qavam could be that 'strong individual', and there was growing pessimism as to his ability to conduct Iran's affairs in a way that matched America's growing interests in the region. Ultimately it appeared that the administration, like the Iranian right, thought that Qavam was a 'good instrument to steer Iran through dangerous waters', and were ready to let Qavam deal with the Azerbaijan question, the Tudeh and Iran's complex relations with the USSR.[107] But when these tasks had been accomplished, the Shah, having built up his own support base at Qavam's expense, was encouraged to seek absolute power for himself. America's role in this process cannot be underestimated, for the army, on which the Shah depended for his success, was improved and strengthened under the auspices of the US advisory missions.

The process by which the United States would come to favour the Shah over other Iranian politicians could be observed in the handling of the Iranian case at the United Nations. Husain Ala, close to the Shah, and strongly anti-Soviet, appeared to pursue policies quite at variance with the orders he had received from Tehran. In doing this, he had tacit US approval. Qavam declared himself to be greatly upset by Ala's tactics, particularly when the latter continued to support the retention of the Iranian case on the Security Council's agenda after Qavam himself had ordered it to be withdrawn. Despite the confusion over the different messages that were relayed between Tehran and New York, Ala had clearly acted far beyond his brief, and made no secret of his disagreement with Qavam on this crucial issue.[108] Qavam subsequently tried to recall Ala, but was prevented from doing so at the request of the US. Murray in particular believed that Iran's case at the UN would be seriously weakened by Ala's removal at this juncture.[109]

Apart from its support of Ala, the US administration made clear its dislike of some of Qavam's own colleagues, notably Muzaffar Firuz. The latter was described by one member of the Near Eastern Department as 'an unscrupulous phoney' who 'owed money to the US Treasury'. Ala, for his part, declared that Firuz was responsible for undermining Qavam's efforts to counter Soviet influence. According to Ala, Firuz took the attitude that resistance to the USSR was useless and that Iran must award further concessions because 'our head is in the bear's mouth'.[110] Doubts about Qavam increased after the signature of the Firuz–Pishihvari accord in June, and the subsequent decision to give cabinet positions to members of the Tudeh party. If such was to be the pattern of Qavam's policy making and political alliances, the United States clearly preferred Iran to be ruled by the Shah than to allow the perilous experiment in parliamentary democracy to continue.

The move against Qavam, nonetheless, was a gradual one. The United States recognised Qavam's skills as a negotiator and diplomat, and while worried by Qavam's conciliatory policies towards the USSR and the left, took comfort in his aristocratic background and his own confidence in his abilities. Also in Qavam's favour was his friendly attitude towards the United States, in particular his support for the continuation of the advisory missions. The missions, once regarded as temporary expedients, had already begun to assume an air of permanence. As Secretary of State Brynes remarked, in a memorandum on the subject, their continuation was now 'considered to be in the national interests of the United States. Strengthening of Iran's internal security forces by the American missions contributes to the stabilisation of Iran and thereby, to its reconstruction as a sound member of the international community.'[111]

At the end of 1945, both the gendarmerie mission and the military mission had been extended, while plans were underway for the establishment of a permanent postwar military mission to Iran. This was finally established by an agreement signed in October 1947, when the US army mission or AMISH became the official military mission to the Iranian army under General Robert W. Grow, replacing the more limited mission under General Ridley.[112] Behind all these activities there lay a clear message of US policy intentions as Brynes memorandum continued:

By increasing the ability of the Iranian government to maintain order and security, it is hoped to remove any pretext of British or Soviet intervention in Iran's internal affairs, and accordingly, to remove such a future threat to allied solidarity and international security. The stabilisation of Iran, moreover, will serve to lay a sound foundation for the development of American commercial, petroleum and aviation interests in the Middle East.

By the summer of 1946, with the decision to renew the US missions and the successful intervention of the UN in the Iranian crisis, the United States had already moved ahead in the race for Persia. British power was unmistakably on the decline: faced with the alternative of Soviet or American influence, Britain naturally chose the latter. Attlee and Bevin looked increasingly to the United States to assume Britain's responsibilities in the region – a role that the Americans were now willing to take on, though not always in the manner the British might have intended.

Meanwhile, the situation in Iran continued to favour greater American involvement, especially since the Soviet threat was still very much alive. The continued existence of the Azerbaijan and Kurdish regimes, and the strength of the Tudeh, were all evidence of the extent to which the USSR could still influence Iranian affairs, while the potential for still greater influence in the future lay in the possible ratification of the Irano-Soviet oil agreement. The Azerbaijan regime, in particular, encouraged both Soviet and Tudeh pretensions, and was regarded as highly destabilising to the country. Having survived the evacuation of Soviet troops it now looked as though force would be needed to bring the province back under Tehran's control. What was now called for, according to US policy makers, was a policy of sustained pressure on the Iranian government combined with American advice and encouragement in the appropriate quarters.

The decision to continue the military mission to Iran was important in helping the Iranian government to deal with internal threats. The ability of Qavam and the Shah to respond to the crisis in the north and south depended, in large part, on an efficient and loyal army. Hence the US role could be decisive. In supporting the army, however, the United States was also helping the Shah, for the army was still his own personal domain. This consequence of extending the army mission was certainly not unwelcome to the US government. Certainly, in all important respects, the American understanding of the Iranian situation coincided more closely with that of the Shah and his supporters than with the enigmatic and vacillatory policies of Qavam.

This trend, as noted, was reinforced by George Allen, the new US ambassador to Iran, who had arrived in April 1946. Allen urged the Shah to refrain from intervention in government affairs during the present crisis. Qavam, he thought, should take full responsibility for policy, and hence the blame for its results. This was good advice for the Shah, and he followed it.

He had, so he admitted, 'interfered' in the discussion between Qavam and Sadchikov in March to prevent his prime minister from 'giving away more than he should', but in the future he would let Qavam 'have his own way'.[113]

The steady growth of its involvement in Iran during the war was to have at least one unwelcome side effect for the United States: a decline in prestige. As US policy became less disinterested, there were rumblings of discontent, not only from the Iranian left, but also from nationalist and independent groups who had previously spared their venom for Britain and the USSR. As America started to assume, at least in part, Britain's former role, comparisons were inevitably drawn between the foreign policies of the two countries. After the UN appeal, Allen received several comments from majlis deputies about the decline of US prestige 'because of the Iranian conviction that American policy followed that of Britain'.[114] The Roosevelt line, and his personal reputation during the war, had helped to sustain American popularity; his demise weakened it, and his successors were not regarded with the same respect.

Popularity was not, of course, a necessary condition for the growth of US involvement in Iran, and assistance was now urgently solicited by both the Shah and Qavam. Meanwhile, the US administration was increasingly disturbed by the continuing political unrest in the country. Until Qavam announced his decision to dispatch troops to supervise the elections, the idea that Azerbaijan, Fars, or even the whole of Iran might soon be lost to the USSR gained certain currency in American political circles. Allen predicted in June 1946 that Azerbaijan would 'take over' the rest of the country, and that Britain would intensify its efforts to secure its hold over the south.[115] Rossow, from Tabriz, also thought that the June agreement with Azerbaijan, and the entry of the Tudeh ministers into Qavam's cabinet, made imminent the possibility that Iran would fall under Soviet domination. The coincidence of Iran's troubles with the crisis in Turkey led to greater pressure on the Iranian government to take stronger measures. In some respects, as Bruce Kuniholm has pointed out, Iran 'served as a model' for the United States in its future dealings with the USSR.[116]

Qavam's attitude continued to puzzle policy makers. He appeared to have accepted the existing status quo in the north, and had acquiesced in the domination of the Azerbaijan army by 'Soviet officers'. Yet at the same time he told Allen that he was 'considering action' in Azerbaijan, and asked what support Iran could expect from the United Nations if the USSR continued to support Azerbaijani separatism. Allen reasoned that Qavam might have been correct in assuming that the Tudeh could be 'better handled' inside the government, and noted approvingly that the Tudeh had not become entrenched in Iran.[117]

Matters were finally brought to a head with the southern tribal uprising.

The United States was not directly involved in this, although its timing was fortuitous in prompting the US to show Iran a further gesture of support. Most American commentators believed that Britain was in some way implicated in the rebellion, although Allen also thought it might be part of a plan by Qavam to strengthen his own party.[118] With a show of hostility towards Britain, and in controlling the tribes, Qavam might similarly force a settlement with Pishihvari. With this course of events the United States could sympathise; it was also a plan of action advocated by the Shah. The latter told Allen that the southern uprising had created a 'decisive situation' which would oblige Qavam to take his choice between a policy to reunite the country or to watch it disintegrate.[119]

Although both the Shah and Qavam were anxious to demonstrate their ability to take the initiative in resolving the new crisis, the United States once again showed its preference for the Shah's style of policy making. Allen shared the Shah's secret satisfaction at 'seeing developments take place in the south which he had predicted would result from Qavam's appeasement in the north', and also agreed that the new situation 'might provide an excuse to get rid of Qavam'. Qavam had, Allen considered, lost prestige by his 'failed policy', and the Shah, with the army on his side, could now take the initiative in forming an 'honest government'.[120]

While the events in southern Iran further demonstrated the US tendency to lean towards the Shah, they also helped to widen the gap between America and Britain. Many Iranians believed erroneously that the United States was simply following in Britain's footsteps, yet the Americans sympathised neither with Britain's involvement in the southern tribal uprising, nor with its tendency to 'look with a certain complacency on the loss of Azerbaijan', provided its position in the south was secure.[121] The United States might have approved of some of the consequences of the tribal rebellion, but the fact that it might have been prompted by secret meetings between tribal leaders and British consular officials was distasteful to the administration, which urged Britain to deny complicity in the rebellion and bring a swift end to the whole affair.[122] Equally unpalatable to the United States was the idea that Britain was using its influence in the southern provinces to secure autonomy on the Azerbaijan model should the country succumb to Soviet and Tudeh influence.

In 1946, Allen observed that Britain 'seemed ready to envisage the severance of Azerbaijan from the rest of Iran, and wanted a "definite frontier" to be drawn between Iran and the USSR'. The agitation in the south could be seen as a way to achieve this. Britain's idea, he suggested, was 'to cut off the rotten part of the apple rather than let it infect the remainder'. Whether or not this was Britain's intention, the United States was clearly opposed to any such division of the country: 'American policy must be to support Iran's independence and integrity, whatever the pros and cons.'[123]

British activities and Qavam's ambivalent position prompted the United States to take further action. Acheson, then acting secretary of state, considered that Qavam's policy of 'friendship and conciliation' towards the USSR had gone too far.[124] The Shah, in contrast, appeared to mirror US interests and concerns. Naturally the Shah was aware of the advantages of his position, and did not fail to exploit it wherever possible. He repeatedly expressed doubts and anxieties to Allen about Qavam's policies, and presented himself and the military as the only alternative source of power. He played the communist card effectively, and also seemed to have convinced the administration that he alone could defend US interests in Iran. At a time when Truman was poised to launch his new doctrine to check the global spread of communism, the Shah warned that Iran would be unable to resist Soviet propaganda without an economic development programme to raise the standard of living.[125]

Not to be outdone, however, Qavam also sought to turn America's new resolve towards his own ends. At the end of September, he directly asked Allen about the possibility of American aid. He declared himself to be disappointed with his policy of conciliation towards Azerbaijan, which, he said, had merely encouraged demands from other areas. He announced his intention to introduce changes based on 'an insistence of Iranian sovereignty' without sacrificing his planned economic reforms. To succeed in his goal, 'major assistance' was essential, and Qavam suggested that financial credits and the provision of military supplies would be a beginning.[126]

When presented with these requests, the administration proposed the extension of credits to Iran to be put towards the purchase of surplus military equipment. In this way the Iranian army would be strengthened in its efforts to restore central government control. Allen refused to consider Qavam's requests for combat military equipment and a credit of $250 million; a figure of $10 million was all the United States could offer Iran at this stage. Combat equipment was out of the question having been denied 'even to China and Latin America'. When Qavam asked why the United States, unlike Britain and the USSR, would not sell arms abroad, Allen reminded him that American policy, based on the 'founding principles of the United Nations', frowned on the 'pre-war practice' where small nations depended for their arms on 'direct approaches to a friendly government'. Another reason, he added, was 'the general feeling among the American public was that such traffic was, in principle, an undesirable type of commerce'.[127]

The raising of the aid question coincided with strong pressure on Qavam, by both the Shah and the United States, to take immediate action to restore order and national unity and to end his association with the Tudeh. Qavam had started negotiations with the Fars rebels, announced his intention to take measures against Azerbaijan and expressed his dissatisfaction with his Tudeh colleagues, but so far had taken no definite action on these questions which were now of utmost concern to US policy makers. Furthermore, he still spoke of maintaining friendly relations with the USSR, referred to the oil agreement as a certainty, and agreed to a Soviet monopoly over Iran's northern airways.[128] Finally, he acquiesced to Soviet and Tudeh pressures in announcing the beginning of the electoral campaign, and still had not altogether discarded the possibility of joining an alliance with the Tudeh.

Allen reasoned that the proposed aviation agreement might be seen as Qavam's peace offering to the USSR, on the eve of the sacrifice of the Pishihvari regime. Nevertheless, the US ambassador still considered that the concession would represent a 'severe blow to Iranian airways, in which there is substantial American interest'.[129] The announcement regarding elections created a state of near panic in US circles. There were rumours that the administration was ready to support the Shah's plan to overthrow Qavam. Ala, still at his Washington post, became the administration's close confidante during this period. The 'seriousness of the situation in Iran' prompted a long meeting between Ala, Acheson and Minor at the State Department. Ala echoed the prevailing US anxieties over the Iranian crisis: Azerbaijan was 'entirely under Soviet influence', the southern tribes had displayed a 'normal and natural reaction' against Soviet infiltration and Tudeh domination of the government, and the whole problem dated back to the 'original sin' of Soviet aggression in northern Iran; the country was at a crossroads, and the next moves were vital in determining its future destiny. Ala said that Qavam had tried to follow a patriotic course to protect Iran's independence, but was under serious Soviet pressure and had received no help from other powers. With American help and encouragement things would change. Otherwise, warned Ala, the elections would return to the majlis 'a solid block of Soviet dominated deputies from Azerbaijan and possibly from other northern areas as well', which would give the Russians 'virtual control of the central government and all that that entails'.[130]

Ala verbalised the State Department's fears, and the meeting provided the final impetus to action. Acheson assured Ala of the 'very close interest' with which the United States was following the present course of events in Iran. He pointed out how, only recently, Allen had told Qavam of the dangers in the proposed aviation agreement. Acheson was unsure about such 'definite American interferences' as asking Qavam not to hold elections, but thought it appropriate instead to offer him 'assurances of American interest and support, so that he might feel strengthened to take whatever action he might feel suitable in the circumstances to protect Iran's sovereignty'. At the end of the meeting, Acheson told Ala that he wanted him to take away the impression that the US government was sincerely interested in Iran and wanted to 'be of assistance at this critical time'.[131]

A few days later, the State Department issued a statement calling on Qavam to postpone the elections.[132] The Shah hoped the Americans would go further, and invited them to support a plan to overthrow Qavam and set up a new government free of Soviet influence. This was 1946, however, and the United States would not go so far as to approve a *coup d'état* by the Shah against his own prime minister. Allen thought the government should change 'through constitutional means. I had reached the conclusion myself that the present government of Iran was leading the country on a path which would result in the loss of independence, and I knew which course I would take if I were an Iranian . . . but they must decide for themselves.'[133]

Clearly the United States favoured a change of government. Shortly before the cabinet change in mid-October, a tacit agreement to remove Qavam appeared to have been reached between the Shah and the United States, as well as Britain. Yet Qavam survived. He came to an agreement with the Fars rebels and ousted the Tudeh ministers. As Allen wrote to Minor: 'The feeling that Qavam was helpless in the face of Soviet and Tudeh pressures had led to the belief that he could no longer take the initiative, but a fortunate coincidence made the shift of policy possible without the necessity of eliminating Qavam, who for all his faults and weaknesses is the best man for Prime Minister at the moment.'[134]

Allen later reasoned that the Shah had been right to give Qavam 'another chance'. He would bear the brunt of the hostile attacks against the government which now appeared daily in the Soviet and Tudeh press; the Shah, on the other hand, could 'reserve his power for future use'.[135] Moreover, a constitutional crisis, such as might have been provoked by Qavam's resignation, had been avoided.

Qavam remained in power, but was under increasing pressure. Criticised for his electoral procedure and his slowness in taking action in the northern provinces, and mistrusted for his ambiguous political stance, Qavam was warned by Allen that he could not expect the United States to support Iranian integrity indefinitely unless Tehran showed 'at least as much interest as we do'.[136] The reoccupation of Zanjan was welcomed 'as a start', and when plans proceeded for the reoccupation of Azerbaijan more US support was forthcoming. It is not clear exactly what the United States offered Qavam in terms of pratical aid and encouragement at this stage. Both, however, appear to have been requisites for Qavam's decision to give the final order to advance on Tabriz. Of the US role in the operation, the following is known.

On 19 November Allen was told by the Shah of 'a plan concerning Azerbaijan'.[137] Three days later Acheson prepared a statement setting out the administration's views on the Iranian situation. The statement included an American pledge to support Iran's independence, 'not only by words, but also by appropriate military acts'; it proposed the sale of 'non-aggression' military material to assist Iran in maintaining internal order; the maintenance and prolongation of the American military missions; the intensification of an 'informational and cultural programme' between the two countries, and assistance in obtaining an Exim Bank loan for Iran.[138] Two days later Qavam told Allen of the details of his plan to reoccupy Azerbaijan, and on 27 November, Allen told the newspaper *Ittila'at* that

It is the well known policy of the United States government to favour the maintenance of Iranian sovereignty . . . The announced intention of the Persian government to send its security forces to all parts of Iran, including such areas that are not, at present, under Tehran's control, seems to me to be an entirely normal and proper decision.[139]

Following Soviet pressure to reverse his decision to send troops to the northern provinces, Qavam looked to the United States for assurances of support should it be necessary to notify the Security Council of fresh developments in the Irano-Soviet dispute. Support was forthcoming. In response to an urgent cable from Allen,[140] Acheson indicated his approval of a possible UN appeal, and for taking other 'appropriate measures':

We do not see how valid elections can be held in Azerbaijan, so long as that province is not under the control of the central government . . . You can assure Qavam that this government will give its unqualified support to Iran and any other power the independence and integrity of which is threatened by external forces . . . provided it shows determination to maintain independence and freedom of action.[141]

With these guarantees, Qavam expedited his proposed measures against Azerbaijan. The weakening of his personal position that resulted from this action was, therefore, at least in part, the deliberate result of US policy. In December, Qavam and the United States were the targets of hostile attacks appearing in the left-wing press. Qavam, wrote *Azerbaijan*, had offered his services for 'American dollars', while the United States had 'incited the reactionaries to civil war'. In its final issue before the collapse of the Democrat regime, the newspaper condemned

the government formed by the enemies of the people . . . which stretched out its ignoble hand to foreigners, especially the Americans, who are planning to make Iran a colony, and who want to keep the Iranians lower than the negroes, who in America are treated and insulted worse than animals . . . [Qavam] wants to sell Iran to the Americans.[142]

The feeling in US circles was that the retaking of Azerbaijan had been a highly popular move, brought about through enlightened US policy and the prestige and influence of the United Nations. Allen referred to the Shah's 'fulsome and even embarrassing tribute to our help', and boasted of the credit which he had received from different Iranian sources for saving the country's independence.[143] The US consul in Tabriz, F. Lester Sutton, spoke of the 'striking evidence of change':

People everywhere looked relieved. When they saw the American flag on the car they smiled and waved. One droshky driver nearly fell out of his carriage doffing his cap and bowing low. As we passed the main streets where large numbers of people had gathered, they cheered and applauded. I could not help remembering how I had driven down these same streets only a few days before and had seen the same people stare at me sullenly, as if they wondered how I dared to be there. Now even the air seemed free and the tension had gone.[144]

The consul urged the administration not to waste the opportunity provided by its present popularity in Iran. Describing Allen as a popular hero, and claiming that an American 'could be elected to the Majlis', Sutton continued: 'To the people here we symbolise the strength of the United Nations and the championship of the rights of small nations.' Now was the time, he claimed, for America to act on the national mood and solidify its commitment to Iran's future; otherwise there would be other Pishehvaris:

The ease with which foreign control has been foisted on Persians in the past, not only gives a blue-print for action, it weakens the will of the people who must resist. In the face of what appears to be their fate there is less and less patriotism and more and more 'En sh'allah'. Against this prospect, there can be counted two powerful and unpredictable forces. One is the influence which other nations, and the United Nations, can exert on the preservation of Iranian integrity. The other is the industry with which Iran itself meets the task of governing its own realm and leaving no soil on which the seed of dissention may fall. It has been one of the favourable expressions of America that the price of freedom is eternal vigilance. Perhaps for our new role in international affairs we shall find that this too is an idea that can be exported.[145]

Armed with this idealistic vision, the stage was set for new US commitments, not only in Iran, but in other far-flung corners of the globe, wherever communism was seen to be on the march. The US perception of the Soviet threat in Iran thus made an important contribution to the formulation of the policy known as containment. Aid to Greece and Turkey under the Truman Doctrine bore a direct relation to events in Iran. The fact that Iran did not immediately receive such a substantial aid package did not lessen its importance in the US national security equation. The Iranian domino had withstood the Soviet challenge, but the Greek and Turkish ones were still believed to be in danger. In recognition of its new commitment to Iran, the US administration finally formalised its earlier offer by awarding Iran a $25 million credit for the purchase of military supplies in June 1947.[146] In the autumn of the same year, when the new majlis had finally convened, and

Qavam faced strong Soviet pressure to secure the passage of the oil agreement, the United States once again made clear its support for Iran. US policy, Allen told Qavam, was based on the same considerations that had prevailed during the Azerbaijan crisis: namely, that America would defend Iranian sovereignty and freedom of choice against external pressures.[147]

Qavam's passing from power was not regretted by the United States. In retrospect he had served his purpose well. During his twenty-two months in power Soviet and British pretensions in Iran had been checked, the communist party had been weakened and Iran's national integrity secured. Of course, the US administration, like the Shah, believed that its policy had also been important in securing these goals, yet despite the disparagement of Qavam, it was impossible to deny his personal contribution to securing Iran's independence. This consideration, however, was not enough to justify his retention. Qavam, like Mussadiq, was regarded by the United States as a clever, but unreliable brand of Iranian nationalist who was ready to flirt with communism if it suited his immediate goals. Such a leader was out of keeping with the American view of issues in a Cold War world, where, as the new US ambassador, John Wiley, wrote to the secretary of state, the difference between US and Soviet policy was 'the difference between black and white, and everyone should recognise it'.[148] Hence the United States felt ideologically more comfortable with the Shah, who was unequivocal in his anti-Sovietism and his admiration of the United States.

The foundations of American policy towards Iran had been laid during the Second World War. It has been argued that US policy in Iran did not take off until the Mussadiq period.[149] An examination of US policy during and immediately after the war, however, shows how important moves towards defining an Iranian policy had already been made by 1946. The United States had come to Iran in 1942 with an idealistic vision of bringing its influence to bear on a part of the world disfigured by old great power rivalries. A marriage between principles and interests was quickly effected as the United States came to appreciate the strategic and economic importance of the region in which they were now so intimately involved. Faced with the threat of Soviet influence in Iran and a parallel decline of British power, US intervention was soon to become a reality. By 1946 it was clear who were to be the losers and the winners in the struggle for Persia. In deciding to 'take on' Iran – the expression was Roosevelt's – the United States also helped to determine the course of Iran's future development. Of the political possibilities that had presented themselves during America's wartime involvement in Iran, only that of the Shah–military alliance had any enduring appeal, and seemed able to offer the security and stability which was required in a world defined by Cold War concerns. In winning Persia the United States had also helped restore the monarchy to power.

6 British power in Iran

The motives for the British occupation of Iran in 1941 were not only the German threat but reflected also the historical importance of the country to Britain's overseas interests. Trade routes, British India and its security, and later the exploitation of Iran's oil by British companies, marked the country as one of the most important outside Britain's formal empire.[1] Until 1941, Russia was seen as the greatest threat to Britain in Persia. When Germany, albeit briefly, supplanted the Russian threat, the security of India and Britain's southern oil fields remained the principal concern. The enemy was different, and Britain and the Soviet Union joined forces with the United States to overthrow the Nazi menace. Once the German threat was removed, however, Britain, like the USSR, sought to consolidate its position in Iran. Yet by 1945 the world had changed. British power had been diminished, and the USSR, though stronger, was now contained by a more formidable rival: the United States.

Between the two world wars British interests were predominant in Persia. This position, which reversed the status quo of the previous century, had been won more by default than good management, since it reflected the weakness of the new Soviet regime. Since the end of the nineteenth century, Britain had been looking for ways to reach an accommodation with Russia. This became possible after 1905, when a common concern for the growth of German power, which led to the remaking of the European alliances prior to the First World War, and the debilitation of Russia following the war with Japan and the revolution of 1905, led the two rivals to settle their differences in the Anglo-Russian Convention of 1907. The Convention not only established the division of Persia into Russian and British spheres of influence, but also attempted to reconcile the differences between the two powers in Tibet and Afghanistan.[2]

With the convention soon null and void as a result of the events of 1917, the British immediately tried to take advantage of their position by signing a bilateral agreement with the pro-British government in Tehran led by Vusuq al-Daulih. The Anglo-Persian Agreement of August 1919 attempted to realise the dream of the foreign secretary, Lord Curzon, to secure Iran 'as a buffer to protect British India and as a pillar of British influence in the Middle East'.[3] As such the treaty was regarded as unacceptable both by a majority of Iranians and foreign powers alike who thought it would reduce Iran to the status of a British protectorate.[4] The agreement was never ratified by the majlis, and on the advent to power of Reza Khan it was formally rejected. It remained, nevertheless, at least in Persian minds, as a point of reference, if not a statement of intent of British ambitions in the country.

The rejection of the Anglo-Iranian treaty did little to diminish British power in Iran. Reza Khan, at least in part, owned his swift rise to power to British support.[5] While he later moved to a position of greater independence and attempted to maintain a distance from all foreign powers, Britain was able to reap the fruits of its Persian connection virtually uncontested until the growth of German interests in Iran during the 1930s. Although there existed no formal treaty between the two countries, Britain exercised considerable influence in Iran through the Anglo-Iranian Oil Company (AIOC), over which the British government acquired a majority interest in 1914.[6] Persia was no longer an outpost on the road to India, but held what was perhaps Britain's greatest single external asset.

As the predominant power in Iran before the outbreak of the Second World War, Britain was the main architect of the invasion and occupation. It was Britain, therefore, who was primarily responsible for the serious internal upheaval which followed these developments. At the same time British policy helped to set in motion the process which led to the preponderance of US power in Iran, shifting the traditional great power rivalry to that of the two emerging superpowers. To some extent this change was unavoidable. The decline of British power in the region was inevitable, although its progress was undoubtedly speeded by the debilitating consequences of the war. Britain also, not unnaturally, looked to the United States to sustain its traditional influence in the area. Yet in terms of the development of the Cold War in Iran, British policy was crucial. Iran's political development, too, was profoundly influenced by the allied occupation. The negative effects of the war on Iran's economy, society and political life could have been alleviated by a more sympathetic treatment of the country during the war. In this respect, Britain, more than any other power, had an obligation to ensure that the Persian way of life should proceed with a minimum of disruption. Few observers could confidently state that this obligation was met.

One striking impression which emerges from a study of British policy in Iran in this period is the very low esteem in which the Iranian government and public were held by Britain. This attitude, which had its origins in the relations between the two powers since the end of the nineteenth century, was used both to justify the allied invasion of Iran and to dismiss its consequences. Apart from an attitude of contempt towards Persian officialdom, a new venom was added to Britain's relations with Iran as a result of the latter's developing relationship with Germany. Britain's attitude towards Irano-German relations was understandable, but unjustifiable. Iran's German links were not dictated by any pro-Nazi sentiments but by economic consider-ations and by Iran's desire to break away from the domination of Britain and Russia.

The extent to which Britain took this dislike of the Iranian government was reflected in various policy statements at the time of the occupation, of which the following, by Viscount Halifax, secretary of state for foreign affairs, is a good example: 'The result of the dual occupation might be the disappearance of the Iranian government, perhaps temporarily, perhaps forever. But I cannot say that their conduct has been of such a kind as to impose any deep obligations on us . . .'[7]

Similarly, while most observers acknowledged that the 1907 'spheres of influence' between Britain and Russia had been highly unpopular,[8] and caused considerable damage to Britain's image in Iran, it was decided that an agreement with Russia as to respective spheres of influence 'was essential'. The secretary of state for India, Leo Amery, openly declared himself in favour of such a scheme, as he told Halifax in the summer of 1940: 'The question I would put to you . . . is whether we should not deliberately do a deal with Russia over Iran as Grey did in 1907 (or Ribbentrop over Poland in 1939), encouraging her to do what she likes in the north, so long as she recognises our interests in the south.'[9] Halifax did not oppose the scheme, thinking it 'quite possible that we may be able to come to some agreement with (Russia) along the lines suggested'.[10] Although these plans were interrupted by the short-lived union between the USSR and Germany, they were soon revived following the German attack on the USSR in the summer of 1941. There were those who wondered if such drastic invasion measures were necessary, including both the British and Soviet ambassadors in Tehran. The intervention of Winston Churchill, with the strong support of the India Office, was however, decisive: 'We mean to get the Germans in our hands, even if we have to come to Tehran and invite the Russians there too.'[11] The allied advance swept not only the Germans before it, but the Shah as well. Both sides bombed Iranian targets, despite the acknowledged feeble-ness of the Iranian resistance.[12] The allies then settled into their respective zones, recreating the post-1907 atmosphere which had engendered so much Persian hostility and mistrust. Not surprisingly the Persians took little comfort in the Tripartite Agreement, with its promise to respect Iranian independence and territorial integrity. These then were the unpromising auspices under which the Anglo-Soviet occupation commenced.[13]

The degree of German influence in Iran, which provided the immediate justification of the occupation, has been exaggerated by historians and contemporary Western commentators, largely to provide a rationale for allied policy. While there was undoubtedly a high degree of German economic penetration in Iran – by the spring of 1940, Germany was Iran's most important trading partner[14] – there was no evidence that the country was harbouring 'Nazi fifth columns', or that it was the 'focal point for German intrigue in the Middle East'.[15] Iran's German links, and the Shah's reluctance to lose them, cannot explain the extreme course of action taken by the allies. As many Iranians rightly suspected, the British government found in the German issue a useful pretext for securing other aims in Iran. These included 'establishing a line of communication for helping the Russians', harnessing the Iranian economy to the allied war effort, and, linked to this, maintaining the flow of petroleum products from Abadan.[16] Such goals necessitated a subservient Persian administration, and since Reza Shah was unlikely to comply with allied demands, the British sought to remove him.

The destabilising effects of the allied invasion, the division of Iran into spheres of influence and the disruption of its economy, were all compounded by the decision to replace the Shah. Although the British had initially welcomed the advent of Reza Khan, relations between the two countries had become increasingly strained during his reign. The Shah's growing independence, his attempt to shake off British influence, his attitude towards the AIOC concession, and finally his links with Germany, all contributed towards the Foreign Office decision that 'the greatest benefit would be drawn from the elimination of the Shah'.[17] It was generally agreed that the Shah's son, Crown Prince Muhammad Reza should replace him, although Eden thought that 'if Reza Shah lost his grip he would be replaced by some general', and Amery favoured 'my friend Prince Hassan', the younger brother of the last Qajar monarch.[18]

The allied invasion of Iran met with a brief show of resistance, which lent greater intensity to Britain's anti-Shah campaign. Shortly before allied troops entered the capital in September 1941, and following a violent propaganda campaign against him, largely conducted through the BBC's World Service Broadcasts, the Shah quietly left the country on a British ship. He was taken first to Mauritius, then, against his wishes, to South Africa, where he died in 1944.[19] The British subsequently explained the Shah's removal as the result of his failure to respond satisfactorily to a series of Anglo-Soviet notes demanding the expulsion of Germans from the country.

There is little doubt that many Iranians were happy to see the Shah go. Nevertheless the manner of his departure and the fact that it was brought about by external forces, did not augur well for Iran's political stability. The sudden demolition of the Shah produced a chain of political consequences for which the country was unprepared. On the one hand, the Shah's ignominious departure and the pathetic showing of his army contributed to a sense of national humiliation and defeat. On the other, the increased measure of political freedom brought about by the allied occupation was deprived of many of its positive aspects precisely because it was brought about by external rather than internal forces. The flurried formation of political groupings, as described in chapter 1, that followed Reza Shah's demise took place in a somewhat artificial atmosphere defined by the exigencies of the occupation and allied war concerns. Not surprisingly, some of the new groups created merely mirrored the interests of one or other of the allied powers. Despite the range of democratic possibilities apparently opened up by the new degree of political freedom in the country, the circumstances of the allied occupation were hardly those in which democracy could easily thrive.

Iran's importance to the allied war effort made a certain degree of disruption inevitable. Yet this was allowed to reach dangerously high levels at least partly because of British policies and attitudes. Noting the widespread dislocation produced by the occupation, the American minister lamented that the British had 'missed their great opportunity by not encouraging the reestablishment of security immediately after their invasion of the country'.[20] There were a number of arbitrary arrests, and the rounding up of pro-German suspects.[21] Many Iranians, who knew little about the Nazi threat to Europe, deeply resented British activities, and were reluctant to cooperate with the allied occupation. The British, for their part, complained and criticised, but made little effort to secure Persian compliance with what were necessarily unpopular measures. The belief, as expressed by one British official, that Iran had only a thin 'veneer of civilisation', and that its people were 'capable of any brutality unless deterred by fear of the consequences' had gained certain acceptance in Whitehall.[22]

Britain's attitude towards Iran was linked to its policy towards the USSR. The benevolence shown towards Soviet policies reflected, in part, Britain's low opinion of Iranians, who, it was felt, were responsible for many of the problems they faced. Of course, the tendency to disregard the effects of the Soviet occupation of northern Iran also resulted from the great importance attached to Soviet cooperation in the war, and the accompanying belief that the price for such participation was the toleration of activities that in other circumstances would be unacceptable. The British government thus declared itself to be generally satisfied with the early conditions of the occupation and even considered that if Bolshevism did come to Iran it would be the fault of the Persians themselves.[23] Even when Britain grew increasingly wary of Soviet policy in Iran, the tendency towards *laissez faire* continued: 'So long as the Russians don't interfere with our sphere in Persia, we shall have to put up with those goings on in their sphere provided that their actions do not embarrass us politically or interfere with supplies.'[24]

In short, British policy during the early months of the occupation paid only minimal attention to the internal needs of Iran while also failing to provide a basis of genuine cooperation between the allies and the Iranian government. This was not provided by the Tripartite Treaty, signed in January 1942, which the Iranians had reluctantly accepted. Britain and the USSR paid scant attention to the sixth and seventh clauses of the treaty, in which, *inter alia*, they undertook 'not to adopt an attitude which is prejudicial to the territorial integrity, sovereignty or political independence of Iran . . . [and] to use their best endeavours to safeguard the economic existence of the Iranian people against the privations and difficulties arising as a result of the present war'.[25]

British policy in Iran was, of course, conditioned by its other more pressing war concerns and an accompanying reluctance to take on the extra responsibility and cost of administering extensive areas of the country. Moreover, the British government did not wish to probe too closely into Soviet activities in the north for fear that its own position in the south might be subject to similar scrutiny. To deal with this problem it was suggested in 1941 that Britain and the USSR should form a joint commission to deal with the problems arising from the wartime administration of Iran, an idea from which developed Bevin's later proposals for a tripartite commission.[26] Such schemes, however, which were unpopular among Iranians, while also raising American suspicions, ultimately failed. As a result Britain remained without a policy to effectively meet Iran's needs during the occupation, an oversight that was to have important consequences for allied policies.

British ascendency in Iran: the last years, 1942–1945

The first post-Reza Shah governments in Iran reflected clearly the predominance of British interests in Iran and accorded with Churchill's desire for a 'friendly government' in Tehran.[27] Of the ten different administrations during the period of the occupation, at least six were headed by prime ministers who openly sympathised with Britain.[28] Muhammad Ali Furughi, who had presided over Reza Shah's departure, was unmistakably a British candidate. One of his first tasks in office had been to give a eulogistic account of British policy in Iran, which, as the Foreign Office indicated, should be 'written from the British viewpoint, but so as to appeal to Iranians'.[29]

Britain's links with the various wartime cabinets notwithstanding, the Foreign Office view of the Iranian ruling class remained critical, if not contemptuous. Each successive administration was criticised for its failure to command stable majorities, its lack of reforming vigour or merely for its corruption and apathy. The British minister in Iran, later ambassador, Reader Bullard, perpetuated the popular notion that the Iranian elite was 'selfish and slothful' and 'impervious to change'; in the Iranian character he could find 'no civil virtues'.[30] Yet curiously, this attitude towards Iranians was accompanied by a great concern about Britain's image in Iran. Bullard was piqued by the relative popularity both of the United States and even the USSR, believing that all sensible and intelligent Persians should understand that their best interests lay with Britain. If British policies were unpopular, it was because Persians did not know what was good for them. Assumptions like these contributed to a further poisoning of Anglo-Persian relations. Iranians, not surprisingly, continued to place the blame for their misfortunes on Britain.

Concern about Britain's popularity did not result in any effective policy to reduce the alienation felt by Iranians towards the occupying forces. Britain was neither able nor willing to offer substantial aid and advice to the Persian government, and looked increasingly to the United States to fulfil this role. Britain's reduced capacity as the war continued meant that it was the Americans who reaped the benefit from any popularity engendered by the different assistance programmes. Moreover, in the one area where Britain did attempt to exercise its authority – the southern provinces – its efforts met with further hostility and suspicion.

Iran's southern provinces, notably Khuzistan and Fars to the west, containing Britain's important petroleum interests and commanding an important position over the Persian Gulf, and Baluchistan to the east, at the gateway of British India, had remained the focus of Britain's Persian policy. While desirous of maintaining its influence in Tehran, it was only in the south that Britain felt that more should be done 'to assist the Persian authorities and re-establish and maintain the administration'. This effort would include various attempts to 'gain the confidence of the tribes', whom it was felt might continue to support British interests in Iran even if the central government did not.[31] The revival of old tribal rivalries, a dominant feature of politics and society in the pre-Pahlavi period, was held in reserve as a possible policy option, although some, like Bullard, opposed it. He felt it 'undesirable to encourage the tribes . . . the object is to get the civil administration running, and we cannot have one policy at the centre and another in the tribal areas'.[32]

Bullard's position on the tribal question was just one example of a basic problem which coloured Britain's dealings with Iran: the tendency for both individuals and departments to diverge over policy, to the extent that it sometimes seemed as if Britain had two or more conflicting policies with regard to Iran. Some such differences had already emerged over the question of how to respond to the German threat in Iran, although they had a longer history. Part of the problem was India, and the assumption by the India Office that it alone had the required wisdom to direct Iranian policy.

Throughout the nineteenth and early twentieth century there had been 'endless wrangles between London and officials in India over policy',[33] and while the rivalry had to some extent subsided in the interwar period, it had by no means disappeared. As the American minister in Iran commented, the British legation was 'still staffed by officials of Indian civil service background who traditionally conduct their own policy with regard to Iran, almost independently of the Foreign Office'.[34] Bullard himself had not risen through the ranks of the Indian civil service, as was the case with other consular representatives in Iran. Yet Bullard, at times, also displayed an independence of thought which placed him at odds with the Foreign Office. Similarly, Bevin and Attlee found themselves at odds over Iran, alongside a range of other foreign policy issues, when Labour came to power in 1945.[35] The impression that Britain had two foreign policies in Iran was therefore perpetuated. Certainly, British policy appeared to suffer from a lack of clarity and consistency. This could not but have a detrimental effect on the prosecution of allied war aims in Iran. The India factor certainly affected Britain's relations with the United States, which distanced itself from what it regarded as Britain's imperialist approach to policy making in Iran.[36]

The political impact of the occupation was matched by changes to Iran's economy brought about by its enforced role in the allied war effort.[37] Iran's wheat fed allied armies, her communications network was given over almost completely to the transport of troops and supplies, her oil supplies and industrial output were directed to meet the allies' wartime needs. It was perhaps unavoidable that Iran's economy should be harnessed towards the war effort, but it must be asked whether such extensive disruption was necessary. Britain, like the USSR, paid scant attention to the economic consequences of its policies. Persians went short of basic items including wheat, kerosene and sugar, while all private transport was requisitioned. The rial was devalued by over 100 per cent, and, following an acute currency shortage at the end of 1942, the British pressed for the introduction of a currency bill which increased the money supply fourfold.[38] In addition, 60 per cent of Iran's annual trade surplus with Britain was frozen for the duration of the war. In the words of one Iranian writer, allied economic policies were 'a case of armed robbery against a desperately weak and poor nation'.[39]

In 1939, Iran had suffered from inflation, but this increased dramatically during the war: between 1941 and 1944 wholesale prices rose by nearly 400 per cent, the cost of living index by 600 per cent.[40] The deepening economic crisis was injurious to both Iranians and the allied war effort, yet Britain failed to take preventative measures. When shortages of basic items became a major problem, Britain's response was to blame Iranians for 'hoarding, obstructionism and smuggling'.[41] When Churchill suggested that Britain might start to import its own food requirements, the Foreign Office insisted that this was 'impossible', and that Britain had 'already imported food for civilian needs'.[42] Later a central body was created to coordinate allied food purchases and an American adviser contracted, but this was after a year of privation which generated much illwill among Iranians. The Americans were shocked by Britain's attitude. Bullard had even criticised the US food adviser, Joseph Sheridan, for unduly raising Persian hopes before his departure for Iran by saying that he was 'convinced that allied governments would not let Persia suffer from lack of food'. Certainly, in Iran at least, the Middle East Supply Centre failed in its goal of keeping the region 'fed and happy'.[43]

Britain's record in Iran during the early part of the occupation was not a happy one. Its position of influence in Iran meant that British initiatives were crucial in managing allied relations and treating Persian problems sympathetically. While Bullard made much of Britain's wartime achievements in Iran, including the extension of the railway network, the construction of roads and the building of 'no fewer than 29 modern aerodromes',[44] these were not gratuitous acts, but designed to facilitate the passage of war supplies. Britain's indifference to the long-term effects of the occupation had serious consequences, and contributed to a decline of British power in Iran. Persians were increasingly alienated from Britain, the Americans kept a distance, and Soviet policy makers could pursue their goals with impunity.

Part of Britain's problem lay in its unwillingness, or inability, to take on the responsibility for running Iran's affairs during the war. In view of this it was surprising that it did not encourage independent initiatives by the Persian administration. Yet, having opened the Pandora's box of political possibilities, the British did nothing to encourage this development. On the contrary, the Foreign Office and its representatives in Iran tended to ridicule Iran's capacity for independent government, constantly criticising the majlis, the politicians and their parties, whether or not these were pro-British in their orientation. A report by Bullard on majlis 'intrigues' led the Foreign Office to comment that 'Persia was not ripe for democracy . . . unless the Majlis is sat on, it becomes a nuisance.'[45] Press freedom was deemed to be equally inappropriate for Iran. Newspapers of all political colours flourished in post-occupation Iran, but they too came to be regarded as an impediment to allied operations. Even before the end of 1941 the Foreign Office had decided that Iran was 'too underdeveloped and irresponsible' to enjoy freedom of speech.[46] Although effective measures were never taken, the suppression of newspapers hostile to Britain became a cause for increasing concern.

British unease at the new political trends emerging in Iran placed the very existence of the majlis in question. Although both Prime Minister Furughi, and his successor Ali Suhaili, enjoyed British backing, neither had proved capable of 'controlling' the majlis. It was therefore suggested that the majlis be suspended altogether, or at least 'fettered'.[47] This idea had many supporters in the Foreign Office, but was never put into practice. Despite its many imperfections, and obvious unwieldiness, the majlis survived. The British, at times, seemed to barely tolerate its existence, and bypassed its activities wherever possible, continuing to promote their own candidates for high posts. As the State Department was not slow to observe, the British were far more active in promoting their interests in Tehran than were the USSR, at least, in the early stages of the occupation. Dreyfus also noted how Britain tended to favour a 'weak disorganised government, as opposed to a strong nationalist one'.[48]

Political instability in Tehran was but one of many causes of concern for Britain. Further alarm caused by serious food riots in the capital at the end of 1942, led to revived discussions over using its influence among the southern tribes to consolidate its interests in the south. It was rumoured that General Wilson, commander in chief in the Middle East, was subsidising the activities of Nasir Khan and the Qashqa'i tribe. He had reportedly said that this was the best way of protecting the supply route: 'If you don't fight and don't bribe, what do you do?'[49] No formal agreement on assistance to the tribes was ever reached. Bullard, as noted, was firmly opposed (as was Bevin when he became foreign secretary), and described Nasir Khan as a notorious anti-British intriguer.[50]

Apart from Britain's connection with the southern tribes, it had no special links with a political party or grouping that could be compared to those of the USSR with the Tudeh. The British tended to support individuals rather than parties. One controversial individual who did receive British support was Sayyid Ziya al-Din Tabataba'i, who had been closely associated with the British in 1921 when with Reza Khan he led the *coup d'état* against Ahmad Shah which ended the Qajar dynasty. Later banished by Reza Khan himself, Sayyid Ziya retained his British links. He returned to Iran from a long period in exile in the autumn of 1943 and set up his own political party, the National Will, whose mouthpiece was the *Ra'd-i Imruz* newspaper. Sayyid Ziya was both anti-communist and anti-monarchist, having been forced into exile by the Pahlavis. Elected as member for Yazd in 1944, he generally associated himself with the anti-Soviet factions in the majlis. The Foreign Office insisted that it had not offered direct support to Sayyid Ziya, but the Tudeh and the USSR were convinced that he was a British tool and he was subject to their fiercest propaganda attacks. In the intense political activity of 1944, Sayyid Ziya's presence seemed to herald an imminent power struggle between Britain and the USSR.[51]

Curiously perhaps, this struggle never materialised. While the British became increasingly concerned about the growth of Soviet influence in Iran, this concern was directed towards the preservation of British interests in the country rather than the exclusion of those of the USSR. For Britain the consolidation of its own position in southern Iran was not incompatible with a Soviet sphere of influence in the north. Regardless of the constraints imposed on the allies by the Tripartite Agreement and the Allied Declaration on Iran, the British regarded the extension of Soviet interests in Iran as inevitable. The problem, as Churchill had already observed, was to keep those interests within bounds. Yet Britain would never share the US sense of a crusading mission against the spread of Soviet influence in Iran. In Britain it was widely felt that the USSR had somehow earned a stake in Persia, be it through historical links, security considerations, or even as a reward for the war effort.

Soviet vulnerability over its common border with Iran was also understood. The security of India, together with Iran's oil fields were, after all, British priorities in Iran. The proximity of Baku to the Iranian border was 'almost as dangerous as the proximity of Leningrad to the old Finnish and Baltic frontiers', and in the event of an allied victory, the Foreign Office recognised that 'Russia would wish to safeguard its frontiers from the dangers of future attacks by incorporating into the USSR those areas of Finland, the Baltic and Rumania seized before the German invasion, but also a similar belt of territory in Persian Azerbaijan to ensure the safety of the Caucasian oil fields.'[52]

The main conclusion to be drawn from the above is that Britain did not oppose certain Soviet war aims in Iran, provided, of course, that these did not clash with Britain's own aims. It would have been counterproductive and even dangerous to do so, considering the nature of Britain's own interests in the country. Although the prospect horrified Persians, it seems clear that the British were prepared to accept a permanent return to the spheres of influence arrangement provided for by the 1907 convention, for 'only by recognising Russian dominance in the north could the central and southern provinces be preserved as fields for British economic enterprise and a belt of neutral territory to protect her position in the Persian Gulf.'[53] In defence of this position, the Foreign Office reasoned, no doubt correctly, that 'in practice, we shall be unable to prevent the Russians from doing what they like in North Persia'. The Persians should be convinced that resistance was useless: 'we should incur Persian illwill for opposing what we cannot prevent'.[54] The Persians, naturally, did not see things in the same light; Britain's attitude continued to cause misunderstanding and resentment. It also damaged British relations with the United States. For the latter, British policy in Iran could not be married with Atlantic Charter principles.

One example of Britain's desire to accommodate Soviet interests in Iran was Bullard's idea of introducing a form of local self-government through the establishment of provincial councils. Although Britain had initially favoured a joint allied commission as the best means of handling local problems, and was sceptical of the USSR's talk of local autonomy for the northern provinces, Bullard broached the question of local government to the Shah and Suhaili in 1943.[55]

For Britain such decentralisation had an obvious appeal. Local government would provide all provinces with a measure of autonomy, meaning effectively that through its representatives in the south Britain could ensure that its interests were protected. Likewise, by promoting its own candidates in the north, the USSR could acquire the influence it desired, but within a defined area. Britain would also, at least to some extent, be protected from a possibly hostile government in Tehran. Since provincial councils were also provided for under the 1907 constitution, it was hoped that the proposals would be acceptable to the Persians.

This British effort to please everyone was, not surprisingly, a failure. Bullard's proposals received a sympathetic hearing from the Shah and Suhaili who 'seemed to favour some degree of decentralisation and . . . to realise that a spontaneous grant of local councils to all the provinces might perhaps forestall a demand from Tabriz or Kurdish areas for still wider concessions'.[56] No action was taken, however, and although Bullard continued to raise the issue with every subsequent prime minister, he received no positive response that could be translated into action. Even when Bevin took up the matter in late 1945, after Kurdish and Azerbaijani autonomy had become a reality, Iran still prevaricated over the local government proposals which were part of his draft Tripartite Commission scheme.[57] What Britain had failed to recognise, or at least accept, was that one of the central planks of Iranian government policy since the early twentieth century was precisely to oppose any form of decentralisation which was seen as a threat to national integrity. Few Persians in leading positions would have wished to see the British proposals implemented.

The local government idea was doomed to fail. It also did nothing to improve British prestige in Iran. It smacked far too strongly of self-interest and confirmed the already prevalent suspicion that Britain wanted to conciliate the USSR. Persian leaders declared themselves to be very disappointed at the fainthearted British support for Iran in the face of Soviet pressures. Bullard's riposte was typical. He 'deprecated the tendency, noticeable in many Persians, even the Minister of Foreign Affairs, to try to draw in His Majesty's Government to every difference between Russia and Persia'.[58] Likewise, when the Persian prime minister produced a long list of complaints against the USSR for British consideration, the Foreign Office made clear its unwillingness to take up the issues raised with Moscow, except one item regarding the question of unpaid customs dues. The British government was not willing to interfere in Soviet activities in northern Iran. As one Foreign Office specialist reasoned:

If the allies win the war, we will owe the Russians a great deal, and whatever happens we owe the Persians nothing. If therefore the Russians are determined to protect their southern frontiers by acquiring further territory in north Persia, and if we have no means of preventing it, it would surely be advisable to put the best face we can on the matter.[59]

It would be incorrect to draw the conclusion that Britain was following a policy of appeasement towards the USSR. This argument was levelled in particular against Bullard by US policy makers.[60] British policy in this period was based on an appreciation of the ways in which Britain's own interests could best be served considering the constraints imposed by the war. Developments in Iran were watched with great concern, but the potential threat to Britain from the USSR was probably not appreciated before 1945. Even after this date the British still refused to go beyond what they believed was realistically possible, and never contested the legitimacy of certain Soviet demands in Iran.

Britain's attitude towards the Soviet threat, and the policies it pursued during the occupation of Iran, inevitably contributed towards a further decline of British prestige in Iran. Gradually politicians of the right, who had previously associated themselves with Britain, started to look to the United States for support; those on the left were pushed closer towards the USSR. The British, however, were unrepentant:

The measures that we had to urge on the Persian government were not, for the most part, popular ones. The ruling classes of landowners and merchants found us opposed to their hoarding and speculation and objected to the necessary measures of rationalisation and control . . . The mass of the people who should have benefited by these measures were either too apathetic to care, or only blamed us for the gross corruption and inefficiency which characterised their application.[61]

The tendency to blame Iran for the hardships suffered during the occupation was a constant feature of British policy. This pattern hardly altered even in 1944 when Iran came under extreme Soviet pressure over the oil negotiations. Iranians were still believed to be responsible for their present unhappy condition. There was no element of self-criticism as far as British policy was concerned. Foreign Office dogma had it that Britain simply knew what was best for Iran, and those who believed otherwise were either stupid or evil. The complacency felt by Britain about her great power status was not easily lost. Bevin captured this mood at the Potsdam Conference, while discussing the limits of British influence in the postwar world:

The USA would now replace them as the leading non-Asian power in the Far East and the Pacific. But the Mediterranean and the Middle East were a different matter. Britain's role in that part of the world was of such a long standing that it was taken for granted by most Englishmen as part of the natural order, a belief confirmed by the effort the British had put into its defence during the war as the main theatre of British operations up to the invasion of Europe.[62]

It was not easy for Britain to accept advice about policy making in the Middle East. While American advisers were much sought after, the British remained sceptical as to the Americans' ability to handle Iran's affairs. Paradoxically, they were also somewhat jealous of the consequences. Britain considered itself, and indeed was considered by others as a great power, and although its predominance was fast fading, it was still believed that Britain would be indispensable in the postwar world, and the United States would not be able to manage alone.[63]

On the eve of the 14th majlis elections, the steady growth of American and Soviet interests in Iran had still not seriously shaken Britain's position. Of the four ministries which had held power, all, with the partial exception of that of Qavam, had been favourable to British interests.[64] Perhaps not surprisingly, the British regarded the forthcoming elections with some impatience. The scathing attitude towards the majlis had not been softened, as reflected in remarks made by the Tabriz consul, R.W. Urquhart, who likened it to 'a monkey house where politicians chatter, quarrel and leap about, intent on their immediate consequential whims, without any effective sense of responsibility for the country at large'.[65] Foreign Office comment in London echoed these sentiments, showing little interest in the electoral preparations. It was taken for granted that the authorities in the Soviet zone would use their influence to secure the election of their own candidates, and a similar result was expected from the British zone.[66]

In the event, the elections proved to be something of an anti-climax; foreign influence was not such a decisive factor as many had anticipated. Only a moderate success for pro-Soviet elements was registered, and the return to power of a primarily conservative and traditional majlis meant that Britain's position would not immediately be undermined.

Although the feared increase in pro-Soviet candidates did not materialise, the presence of eight Tudeh members, in a parliament where majorities were rare and political groupings continually fluctuated, was a cause for concern. Britain's links with Sayyid Ziya were discreetly encouraged. One newspaper which published a series of articles against him, linking his activities to the British, was quickly suppressed.[67] There was also evidence of British efforts to effect a reconciliation between the Shah and Sayyid Ziya with the aim of checking the Tudeh. Despite their differences, the Shah agreed to 'work with Sayyid Ziya and try to stop the rot in the administrative machine'.[68]

It was clear that the British had little interest in the elections as a means of providing Iran with a more stable and democratic base. Although these were perhaps the first elections in Iran's history which had been conducted with some degree of freedom, the British did not regard this as a positive development, worthy of sympathetic interest or assistance. In a long dispatch to Eden, then foreign secretary, Bullard wrote that 'western style liberalism meant little to Persians', and that, in any case, the liberal deputies had got the country 'in a mess'. To prevent the Soviet domination of Iran, Bullard recommended a return to the 'Reza Shah type of government', and the moulding of a new generation of Persians with the help of US advisers.[69]

British concern about Soviet influence in Iran had not, thus far, led to any substantial policy changes. Prior to the majlis elections, the Office of Strategic Studies warned that the Irano-Soviet border had been 'virtually removed', and the USSR exercised 'strong control' over northern Iran. American officials in London also called for 'greater British involvement' to stop the Soviet Union from 'carving out her own descent on the Persian Gulf'.[70] Yet until Britain's own position was threatened, the old spheres of influence mentality prevailed. Charles Warner of the Northern Department summed up Britain's position as follows: 'I don't know how we can offset Soviet propaganda. So far as I know north Persia has for years and will always be Russia's for the taking. Nor do I think we should attempt to counter it.'[71]

The establishment of zones of influence and the signing of the Tripartite Treaty had perhaps lulled Britain into a false sense of security regarding its understanding with the USSR in Iran. The Declaration Concerning Iran, issued at the end of the Tehran Conference, was also deceptively reassuring. Britain believed that the conference would produce lasting benefits, and Churchill was credited for bringing greater security to Iran. It was felt that 'no such initiative could have come from Russia, and America was too remote from Iran's problems'.[72] The euphoria produced by the conference was short lived, however, and the 'profound impression created by the great and historical pronouncement', failed to endure until the end of the year. By then all the allies were involved in a scramble for Persian oil which made a mockery of earlier guarantees.

In 1944, British influence still dominated in Iran, as demonstrated during the Tehran Conference, but the process leading to a gradual weakening of Britain's power had already begun. The war itself was perhaps the most important immediate factor, although its impact on Britain's overseas interests was not immediately apparent. While US interests in Iran continued to grow apace, the scope of America's new role was also not fully appreciated. It was clear, however, that the United States would not, in the future, be willing to follow in British footsteps in Iran. Their policies diverged as often as they converged.

The American challenge to Britain could not be compared to that posed by the USSR. It had by now become clear that the Soviet government could no longer be brushed off with vague promises of a sphere of influence in the north. The USSR wanted a more substantial foothold in Iran than Britain was willing to concede. British policy had helped set in motion a process whereby Iran would become the stage for a conflict of interests between the USA and the USSR, and whereby its own interests would be progressively undermined.

Iran's internal condition became more uncertain with every month that passed and Britain's own debilitated condition made it increasingly difficult to meet the different challenges. *Laissez faire* had not worked: British selfishness and indifference had produced an explosive situation in Iran, the consequences of which were made apparent during the oil discussions of 1944. The oil question finally forced a reexamination of policy goals. Here was an issue where British interests were most directly concerned.

The raising of the oil question during the war reflected poorly on allied motives in Iran. Part of the blame certainly lay with the Persian government who had initiated the first discussions with American companies. The Americans, for their part, might have resisted the temptation to mark out their stake in Iran's future, at least until the war was over. Britain was equally culpable, though in a different way. Britain could have acted to postpone such discussions while Iran's freedom of action was clearly so circumscribed. Instead, the government acquiesced to a new bid for Iranian oil being made by a British company.[73] Britain's greed presented the USSR with a golden opportunity to press its own claims. As Britain regarded Soviet influence as inevitable, it probably saw the oil concession as the lesser evil to other forms of penetration. The USSR thus seemed set to gain its foothold in Iran as the result of an undignified allied scramble to press different claims on a weakened Persian government.

Britain's desire to obtain a new oil concession in Iran, in addition to the extensive AIOC concession, helped to explain both the far-reaching Soviet demands, and the USSR's indignation when its petition was turned down. The oil question was to have an important bearing on the Azerbaijan crisis, since the Soviet Union's failure to obtain an oil concession led it to use its position in Azerbaijan as a means of placing further pressure on the government in Tehran. British policy was significant in this respect since a determined initiative to deter all powers from participating in oil discussions could perhaps have forestalled the Kavtaradze mission, or at least deprived it of much of its force, and thereby avoided the chain of unhappy consequences which followed.

Naturally, Britain demurred from joining the Soviet Union in its protest against the majlis decision to postpone the oil discussions, but was guarded in its position on the oil issue as it was also in condemning Soviet policy. Bullard felt that Soviet methods had been 'a mistake', but Britain's overall position on the question as to whether or not Russia should be awarded an oil concession was clear:

As to Russia's need for oil, it is certainly no part of our policy to prevent Russia from obtaining oil in north Persia. Indeed the Soviet Union is the natural market for north Persian oil. We do not wish to put any obstacle in the way of the Russians obtaining a concession in Persia by normal methods if and when the Persians are prepared to negotiate.[74]

Although referring here to 'normal methods' and later to the 'free choice of Iran' on the oil question, Britain's position, effectively, was that whatever the circumstances, it would be a mistake to deny the USSR outright a share in Iranian oil. This attitude was consistent with Britain's own possessions in Iran, and her desire that these should be extended in the future. The British government was more exercised about the possible negative consequences to its own assets as a result of the majlis decision than it was about excluding the USSR from the oil race in Iran. The Ministry of Fuel and Power thought that the Russian proposal should be studied 'very carefully':

We are naturally very concerned that any designs which Russia may have on Persia should not adversely affect our established position there, or the possibility of our getting the additional concession now being negotiated by Shell . . . One wonders if the Persian Government is going to deny the aspirations of the Russians in the north, it might not have the effect of increasing Russian interest in Persia in areas beyond that with which they are apparently not concerned. If means could be found for an amicable negotiation, resulting in the grant of a concession to Russia at the same time as the Persians grant a concession to Shell, one would have thought from the point of view of British interests on oil, that such a solution would have much to recommend it.[75]

The real problem for Britain, as elucidated by W.H. Young at the Foreign Office, was the conflict between Britain's petroleum and political interests.[76] The British government was well aware of the possible political consequences arising from the award of a northern concession to the USSR. As the Ministry of Fuel and Power insisted, if only 'political considerations' could be excluded, the best course would be for Russia to get its concession. Yet petroleum interests prevailed. Although Bullard felt that the risks inherent in the USSR obtaining a northern concession were 'far graver' than the risk of its attempting to cancel the AIOC concession, the Petroleum Division won the day, arguing the financial case for a new British concession.[77] No public statement was made against the Soviet demand, nor did the British government attempt to close the door on future negotiations.

The consequences of British policy on the oil question were various.

Although Sa'id's decision temporarily laid the issue to rest,[78] British policy had helped to contribute to a more aggressive Soviet attitude towards Iran. By refusing also to condemn Soviet methods, and by keeping the oil question open, Britain invited the USSR to later renew its demands. As in the past Britain was not prepared to challenge the Soviet Union. While the internal and international climate remained unfavourable to the Soviet concession, indeed its prospects looked bleak in view of Mussadiq's law banning further concessions, Britain expected and perhaps even hoped that the USSR would revive the question in the near future.[79]

Britain's attitude did not earn her Soviet friendship. On the contrary, in the wake of the majlis decision Britain was subject to hostile attacks in the Soviet press. The belief that Britain was the main obstacle to Soviet designs in Iran had become something of an obsession with the USSR. Clearly, however, the Persian government's decision had little to do with Britain. Although Britain endorsed the actions of the majlis after the event, and subsequently, together with the United States, made representations in Moscow, which according to Bullard dealt the final 'death blow' to the Soviet scheme,[80] it did so not from any commitment to Iranian independence, but because there was no other course open to it at the time. In this respect British policy diverged once again from that of the United States. The latter had consistently opposed Soviet methods and gave the Persian government its unconditional support. Nevertheless, the position of the United States, like Britain, was influenced by the hope that its own companies would return to the bidding table in the future.

In retrospect, the oil debates of 1944 represented a watershed for British interests in Iran, hastening the decline of British influence already set in motion by the events of the war. British policy in the oil crisis helped to accelerate this trend. A more sensitive handling of the crisis might have prevented a confrontation with the USSR, and thereby avoided drawing attention to the oil question, a development which was to prove disastrous to Britain. The majlis ruling and Mussadiq's law which followed it set a powerful precedent for Iran's later struggle to gain control of her own oil resources. Even in 1944, one majlis deputy tried to find supporters for a bill to revoke the AIOC concession.[81] Britain, however, failed to anticipate events, or at least to learn from the experience of 1944. Nothing was done to make its Iranian oil operations more attractive to Iranians. In the summer of 1945, the Foreign Office vetoed a request that a Soviet delegation visit the southern oil fields, one of its reasons being that 'the welfare facilities for Persian labour in the AIOC are not so good that they would be convincing'.[82] Bullard promised to look into the question of the welfare of the Persian workers, but somehow this was neglected. Britain's failure to meet the challenge of 1944, coupled with the AIOC's unsympathetic response to the strikers' demands in 1946, did irreparable damage to British oil interests in Iran, as became apparent when talks on the AIOC concession were resumed later in the decade.

In another way too, the 1944 crisis may be seen as marking the downturn in Britain's position. The old assumption that Britain would dominate decision making in Iran no longer held. This responsibility would now be shared, if not handed over completely to the United States. An opportunity to contain Soviet power had been lost, and the USSR was now committed to a more aggressive policy for which the British were in large part responsible, yet at the same time unable to resist. Unable to meet the Soviet challenge, Britain looked more and more to the United States.

Azerbaijan and the road to British decline

British mismanagement and the parallel growth of Soviet power helped draw the United States into Iran. Recognising the new weakness of their position, there was a change in the manner in which the British regarded their American allies. The condescending attitude which had characterised early British policy gave way to concern at the United States' apparent reluctance to assume greater responsibilities in the region. After the Yalta Conference, in January 1945, failed to produce any Soviet guarantees about its future intentions in Iran, Churchill wrote to Roosevelt warning of the USSR's departure from the Tehran Declaration and of the danger that 'Russia would get what it wanted by use of the big stick'.[83] When Clement Attlee replaced Churchill as prime minister, during the Potsdam Conference in July, he urged that the Iranian question be made the subject of urgent discussions at upcoming allied meetings. Yet while the US position on Iran had changed, the administration was still primarily occupied with European problems and the Far Eastern war. As late as the Moscow Conference at the end of 1945, Bevin was still despairing of the United States' unresponsive attitude to the Soviet threat to countries of its southern flank. The foreign secretary returned from Moscow believing that the US secretary of state still thought of 'bringing off a settlement with the Soviet Union which would allow the Americans to withdraw from Europe and in effect leave the British to get on with the Russians as best they could'.[84]

British foreign policy makers believed that Iran, left to its own devices, was incapable of managing its own affairs or of resisting Soviet influence. American assistance was therefore essential. The surrender, in the autumn and winter of 1945, of government forces in Azerbaijan confirmed this belief. Bullard thought that the bulk of the population were apathetic and unable to act sensibly unless guided by a foreign hand. He compared the Iran of 1945 to the England of 1800: the Iranian electorate would 'use power wildly' if they got it. He was convinced that Iran's only hope lay with the United States.[85]

One possible way of meeting the Soviet threat was to accelerate allied troop withdrawals from Iran and thereby reduce the danger of a prolonged occupation. The Iranians took the first initiative, pleading the case for early troop withdrawals throughout 1945, fearful of renewed Soviet hostility following the majlis oil ruling. Britain later took up the idea since it seemed to offer a way out of the new security dilemma posed by the USSR, but also because it was hoped that a gesture towards early troop withdrawals would create a favourable impression on public opinion, particularly in Iran and America, and thereby help to restore Britian's battered image in Iran.

Bullard seized on the idea, which he thought could preempt a permanent stranglehold on north Persia and prevent the further spread of Soviet influence. Clearly a complete withdrawal was out of the question, at least until the European war was over, and possibly the war with Japan as well, but it was felt that even a partial withdrawal would have great propaganda effect while putting pressure on the USSR. The withdrawal of troops from Tehran, for example, could have served as the first step in a series of *pari passu* withdrawals which could help to reduce the Soviet threat. Bullard warned that if the USSR and Britain could not agree to withdraw from Iran, the result would be continuing spheres of influence involving indefinite military commitment and constant friction. Such an arrangement would, of course, place Britain at a disadvantage, in view of the USSR's physical proximity and vastly superior manpower resources.[86]

Britain doggedly pursued the subject of troop withdrawals from Iran at the various allied conferences. Its efforts, which received only halfhearted American support, and virtually none at all from the USSR, were largely unsuccessful. This outcome was not, however, as disappointing as most accounts might lead one to believe. Although Churchill and Eden and later Attlee and Bevin were united in their commitment to an early evacuation of allied forces there were strong elements in the Foreign and War Offices who were against any precipitate withdrawal. At War Cabinet meetings, in early 1945, it was insisted that British troops would be needed in Iran, both to protect the supply line and Britain's oil interests, at least until the end of the Japanese war.[87] The Indian viceroy warned against premature withdrawals, arguing that as 'neither Russia nor Persia are likely to see our motives as altruistic, we should therefore gain little and lose influence in Persian affairs'.[88]

The maintenance of forces in Iran for Britian, as well as for the USSR, had come to be justified in terms not merely of the war effort, but also of the need to retain influence and secure local interests. Although Bullard had managed to convince many senior officials of the benefits of his proposals, there remained strong pressure groups in the military and Foreign Office who opposed him. Of course, the Soviet attitude was a major stumbling block. As Eden remarked, there was no question of Britain withdrawing without the USSR, and with Molotov still intransigent, there was little Britain could do.[89] Nevertheless, it is noteworthy that despite Britain's talk about the desirability of an early departure from Iran, no concrete proposals to this effect were ever produced, nor was unanimity on the subject achieved even within British government departments.

In the middle of these discussions, Britain was reported to be bringing a new brigade into Iran. The brigade was to form part of the strategic reserves for the Far Eastern theatre, but was to be quartered in southern Iran because of an accommodation shortage. This development made it difficult to see how the USSR could take any British initiative on withdrawal seriously. Bullard described the situation as 'most embarrassing': Britain's negotiating position would be seriously compromised if fresh troops were arriving in Iran, whatever their purpose might be.[90] Meanwhile the whole initiative foundered as even the proposed withdrawal from Tehran was postponed pending discussions over the disposal of British assets.

It appeared increasingly as if Britain's efforts to accelerate troop withdrawals had been little more than a propaganda gesture. In June of 1945 the chiefs of staff still insisted on troops remaining in Iran for security reasons. Bullard confessed that on the basis of British military requirements 'we shall not in fact get beyond the evacuation of Tehran . . . but with careful handling that move should last us over the summer, but the Russians cannot be certain that we don't mean to do more'.[91] With the growing threat of Tudeh influence in the south, any hopes of further progress on the issue were dashed completely. In August, Bullard lamented that Britain was pushing the treaty 'to the limit . . . and will remain in Persia long after any excuse remains for doing so that the public could understand. This would have a profoundly discouraging effect on the population and encourage Tudeh mischief makers.'[92]

The failure to agree on troop withdrawals was significant in terms of later developments. Some arrangement over Iran, which could have coincided with the end of the Japanese war, would have prevented the Azerbaijan Democrats from taking power, and perhaps thereby have avoided the year of crisis which followed. Furthermore, an initiative on allied evacuation from Iran would have done much to reverse the process towards national disintegration which had been precipitated by the allied occupation. Britain, not for the first time, had failed to take the initiative on an issue that was vital to Iran's future independence. By September 1945 there was no conceivable reason for retaining troops in Iran that was related to the war effort. But the retention of troops then had a rationale of its own which quite overrode war considerations. The whole edifice of British power in Iran was confronted by the growing strength of the Tudeh party and the possible generalisation of the effects of the Azerbaijan crisis.

The Soviet-supported rebellions in Azerbaijan were not altogether unexpected. The Foreign Office had been predicting some sort of Soviet attempt to consolidate its hold in north Iran, although it was perhaps surprised by the dramatic turn of events in the autumn of 1945. Unlike the Americans, the British did not give much credibility to the annexationist theory of Soviet policy. Nevertheless the developments in Azerbaijan finally led to the abandonment of the belief that Soviet policy was largely defensive:

Russian activities in Persia do not square with the theory of a defensive policy. They square well with the theory of a tentative, but essentially offensive policy. If the Russians, seizing a moment of Anglo-American discord, chanced their luck and got away with the absorption of Persia without having to fight for it, their position would be immeasurably strengthened, both for defence and for eventual future aggression. They would acquire the warmwater ports which have been almost a pathological craving since Peter the Great. They would interpose between Baku and India a vast defence area . . . They would acquire oil resources of great value, shake Britain's whole position in the Middle East to the point of collapse . . .[93]

The advent of the ADP to power was thus accompanied by a qualitative change in British thinking about Soviet policy in Iran. It also required a policy reorientation. With America still slow to take a decisive stand on the Iranian issue, and with the end of any hope of early troop withdrawals, Britain launched a new policy initiative in the shape of the proposed Tripartite Commission. This, it was hoped, would preempt the further spread of Soviet influence, and allow the allies to reach an amicable agreement over Iran.

Bevin's idea of creating an Anglo-Soviet-American commission to deal with the problems arising from the allied occupation, drew on Bullard's earlier plans to introduce a form of local government in Iran. When events in Azerbaijan started to unfold in the autumn of 1945, Bullard started to press more vigorously for the implementation of provincial councils. The British had few illusions about Pishihvari and saw his Azerbaijan Democratic party as representing a serious threat to Iran and British interests there.[94] Fears about the Democrats' intentions increased when the party newspaper *Azerbaijan* immediately launched an attack against Britain.[95] From Tabriz, Vice-Consul Wall reported that the actions of the Democrats were 'following a pattern which every Russian must know by heart', and that the situation in Azerbaijan was as near to the 'classical pre-revolutionary situation of the Leninist textbooks as nature and art can make it'. He concurred that a new decisive initiative was called for.[96]

By implementing his proposals to establish provincial councils, Bullard
hoped to defuse the Azerbaijan situation, which should not, he claimed, be
treated as a problem of provincial autonomy, but one of provincial
government.[97] He accepted that the USSR had 'all the cards in Azerbaijan'
and that the ADP declaration was ingenious in its talk of liberalism and in its
appeal to Atlantic Charter principles. Bullard argued, however, that Azerbaijan was not the only province which felt neglected: a degree of self-
government would be welcome to most provinces. Since provincial councils
were 'common in most countries' and provided for, in principle at least, by
the Persian Constitution, Bullard hoped to overcome local opposition and
implement them throughout the country.[98]

The most appealing feature of the British ambassador's plan was that it
seemed to offer a possibility of resolving a number of Iran's internal problems
simultaneously. On the one hand, provincial councils would undermine the
Democratic party in Azerbaijan and hopefully forestall the demands from
Tabriz and Kurdistan for still wider concessions. On the other hand, by
resolving provincial grumbles, one of the major sources of anxiety to the
central government would be removed. For Britain, the greatest appeal of the
provincial councils scheme was that the southern provinces, once their pro-
British councils had been elected, would be secure from Soviet or Tudeh
influence.

Bevin's Tripartite Commission proposals, which drew on Bullard's ideas,
were first expounded at the Moscow Conference. They took as their point of
departure the fact that the allied presence in Iran had disturbed Persia's
economy and government. The allies would pledge to respect existing
undertakings regarding Iran and accept responsibility for restoring normal
conditions. The central part of the scheme related to the establishment of
provincial councils. The commission would 'make recommendations',
supervise elections and assist in the creation of such councils 'in accordance
with existing constitutional laws'. The proposals also incorporated a clause to
allow for the use of minority languages for 'educational and other purposes'.
Another clause provided for 'consultation' with the Persian government and
guaranteed that the Commission would not weaken the Persian state.[99]

The British invested great hopes in the Tripartite Commission, but it soon
appeared as though the commission had set itself an impossible task. Apart
from the considerable difficulties which would certainly have arisen in
persuading all the parties involved to work together, the Iranians had
somehow to be convinced of the benefits that provincial councils would bring
them. As discussed in chapter 1, modern Iran was born of the belief that unity
and centralisation were essential for progress; decentralisation in contrast
was equated with weakness and decadence. In the Iran of 1945, a majority of
politicians were opposed to the introduction of provincial councils, to say

nothing of the encouragement of minority languages. A further difficulty lay in the need to persuade the USSR that its interests could be better served by provincial councils than by the already existing autonomous governments. Finally, the United States, the USSR and Iran would all need convincing that the Commission proposals were more than just an attempt by the British government to consolidate its sphere of influence in Iran.

Although none of the above problems seemed readily capable of solution, Bevin's mood in Moscow was optimistic. His proposals met, at first, with cautious interest, but soon encountered the joint obstacles of Soviet resistance and Persian prevarication. The Iranians insisted on having two representatives on the commission, and the USSR refused to accept the principle of consultation with the Iranian government. Deadlock ensued, yet even when the USSR finally bowed out of the plan, it was still hoped to secure Iranian support for an Anglo-US initiative. Hakimi, who was in power at the time, actually gave the order to provincial governors to prepare for local elections, but adverse publicity, and the mounting internal opposition obliged him to abandon the scheme.[100]

Britain had clearly not expected the Tripartite Commission idea to provoke such a negative response, and had underestimated the strength of Iranian feeling against any attempt by foreigners to run the country's affairs. The proposals had generated deep suspicions about Britain's intentions, suspicions which were increased by the news that Britain had also opposed an Iranian appeal to the United Nations Security Council against Soviet interference. Bevin called the Iranian initiative a 'half formed plan', and stressed his anxiety 'not to put too heavy a strain at the outset on the Security Council'. It seems however, that the foreign secretary's main concern was that the UN appeal should not jeopardise the Commission's chances of success.[101] Britain's decision provoked criticism not only from Iran, but also from the United States. Brynes told the British ambassador in Washington that he thought it 'inadvisable for a great power to assume responsibility, as did His Majesty's Government, of dissuading a small country from invoking the machinery of the UNO when it thought fit'.[102] British actions confirmed once again the American belief that the selfish pursuit of its own interests still motivated British policy: 'it would be most unfortunate . . . if the impression which is already prevalent be intensified that the British are lukewarm and desirous merely of protecting their interests in the south'.[103]

The failure of the Commission proposals left Britain and the United States following a 'wait and see' policy in Iran. Future developments now depended on the willingness of the USSR to abide by its treaty obligations and withdraw its forces from Iran by March. There was, of couse, no guarantee that troop withdrawals would, in themselves, resolve the Azerbaijan situation, but they might contribute towards a calmer atmosphere in which reconstruction could begin. These hopes were soon disappointed however. The USSR delayed the evacuation of its forces and Iran plunged still deeper into chaos.

For Britain, continuing anxieties about Soviet policy were combined with fears about the intentions of Ahmad Qavam, who had replaced Hakimi as prime minister in January 1946. Qavam had always been regarded with suspicion by Britain, not only because of his suspected predilection towards the USSR, but because he was a strong individual and something of an opportunist whose name was associated with past attempts to upset the status quo. According to Foreign Office reports, Qavam had been involved in pro-German activities at the beginning of the war. Young thought that Qavam was neither pro-allied nor pro-German but was 'merely concerned to be well in with both sides without committing himself to either – a normal Persian game'.[104] Clearly, whatever pro-German proclivities Qavam may have had were no longer evident by 1946, nevertheless his personality and policies were not likely to endear him to the British.

Qavam's return to power was not then welcome to Britain. Bullard lamented the departure of the old and 'deaf' Hamiki, describing it as an illustration of the 'frivolity and irresponsibility of the Persian character'. The majlis vote which later confirmed Qavam's appointment by the slimmest majority was, he claimed, 'an absurd operation', whereby the Speaker of the Assembly, 'sodden with opium' cast his solitary vote to shift the balance in Qavam's favour.[105] As if to confirm British fears, Qavam's appointment coincided with a considerable increase in anti-British propaganda in Iran. This partly reflected Qavam's own reluctance to proscribe the Tudeh as some of his predecessors had done, but also the general increase in Soviet propaganda as the date drew near for final allied evacuation from Iran. Particularly embarrassing to Britain was the Tudeh demand that British activities in Greece and Indonesia be made the subject of a UN appeal along the lines of the proposed Iranian complaint regarding Soviet behaviour.[106]

While justifying the existence of its troops in Greece and Indonesia, and announcing its readiness to discuss the question if called upon to do so,[107] the British government was none the less placed in an awkward position. This may explain, at least in part, why the British kept a low profile on Iran during the spring of 1946 and were content to let the United States assume the leading role. Nevertheless, the failure of Soviet troops to withdraw from Iran by 2 March led to a strong protest note from Bevin as well as Brynes. Both men were infected with the new Cold War fever which was already affecting allied relations. There was, albeit briefly, talk of war with the USSR over Iran.[108]

The US decision to take on the defence of Iran in the spring of 1946 was met with a mixture of relief and anxiety in British circles. Relief, because the government had been genuinely concerned about the lack of initiative shown by the United States with regard to the Soviet threat in Iran. Anxiety, as before, because of the continuing element of competition, and even hostility between the two Western powers, and because of the realisation that the Americans would not always pursue policies that corresponded to British interests. The two pillars of Britain's Iranian policy, the oil concession and the security of its imperial possessions, were unlikely to be supported by the US government in the long term. On the contrary, the Americans made no secret of their desire to expand US oil interests, or of their intention to assist in the dismantling of imperial possessions.[109]

The assumption by Britain of a less prominent role in Iran did not of course mean that it intended to surrender its interests and involvement there. With regard to oil, at least, the British government hoped to strengthen its position once the present uncertainty was over. Britain thus had a particular interest in the linking of troop withdrawals to the Soviet demand for an oil concession. If the latter were successful, this was a signal to British companies to resume negotiations with the Iranian government. As early as March 1946, representatives of Shell had called at the Foreign Office to suggest that the oil negotiations, interrupted in 1944, should be renewed, and in May, the Ministry of Fuel and Power gave its support to the reinitiation of discussions.[110]

Although Britain had opposed Iran's earlier attempt to appeal to the United Nations, on this occasion the British delegation was instructed to offer Brynes its full support during the deliberations of the Security Council.[111] The outcome was not unfavourable to Britain. The threat to Iran from the USSR was reduced by Stalin's agreement to withdraw his troops, while Britain's oil interests looked secure with the effective bypassing of the 1944 majlis ruling to allow the USSR its share in a joint stock company. In accepting the terms of the Qavam–Sadchikov agreement, however, both Britain and the United States had been party to the further diminishing of Iranian sovereignty.

Britain had pledged that it would not accept any Iranian statement made under duress, or while treaty obligations were being violated,[112] yet both these conditions had clearly prevailed during Qavam's negotiations with the USSR. Britain and the USA had effectively given their seal of approval to the bartering of Iranian sovereignty for what was quite blatantly the extension of Soviet economic and political influence in the northern provinces. Whether or not Qavam believed the oil agreement to be a *fait accompli* is unclear, but the USSR and Britain both believed and hoped that it was. The Irano-Soviet agreement was particularly attractive to Britain in that it opened the way for new British oil concessions in the south. Britain's only objection to the agreement was that the proposed Irano-Soviet company appeared to offer more favourable terms to Iran than did the AIOC. The government might thereby be obliged to change its existing arrangement with respect to the AIOC and to any future concession. In a draft report on the question of southeast Persian oil, the Ministry of Fuel and Power outlined its objections to following the Soviet example:

A mixed company of the kind suggested would make it impossible to secure the essential flexibility in the operation of British oil resources. During the recent war, British and American companies have been able . . . to increase or decrease production as required . . . in the interests of allied strategy. This would not have been possible had the exploitation of the oil resources in question been operated by joint companies through which the local government would have been able to insist upon a rate of output to accord with their view of their own interests . . . It would hamper the British companies at every turn in the task of obtaining the best possible results from an oil field, if the local government were associated with them in the ordinary day-to-day operations in the field.[113]

The fear of drawing undue attention to British oil concessions in Iran, which might compel the AIOC to introduce unwelcome changes, led the British government to oppose an initiative that the whole question of oil concessions in Iran be placed under the control of the United Nations.[114] It was felt that the overseeing of Iran's oil exploitation by an international body would diminish the degree of autonomy which Britain could exercise in managing both its present and future operations in Iran.

There were, of course, no illusions on Britain's side as to the real meaning of the Irano-Soviet agreement. Bullard described as 'ominous' the fact that the three key issues, evacuation of troops, oil and Azerbaijan had been linked. He also noted that the paragraph on the oil agreement was 'sailing rather close to the wind of the 1944 law'.[115] Yet Britain like the USA was unwilling to challenge the outcome of the negotiations, even when they proved, at least in the short term, to be disappointing from the point of view of Western interests. The withdrawal of Soviet troops in May 1946, as noted, did not reduce the level of Tudeh propaganda, nor did it result in the collapse of the autonomous governments. Qavam's interregnum showed growing anti-British, or at least anti-rightist tendencies: Bullard described the arrest of prominent rightists as the 'fruit of Soviet Persian friendship'.[116] In Azerbaijan the British Public Relations Bureau was attacked, while the Azerbaijan government imposed a tax on all incoming AIOC products, and the local AIOC manager was arrested.[117]

With no immediate benefits accruing to Britain's position in Iran as a result of the Irano-Soviet agreement, the government became increasingly alarmed. At a meeting of representatives of the Foreign and India Offices and the Ministry of Fuel and Power it was warned that Britain had to face the unpleasant possibility that a government entirely subservient to the Soviet government might soon be operating in Tehran and that this government might either cancel the AIOC concession, or by stirring up labour trouble make the operation of the concession virtually impossible . . . We had to decide whether to continue to support Persian independence through the United Nations Organisation, or to regard Persian independence as lost and take such steps as are open to us to preserve our interests in southern Persia.[118]

Policy recommendations arising from the meeting included making further efforts to win American support for Britain's position and 'get them an oil stake' with this end in view. By doing this it was hoped that the USSR would no longer see Iran as the 'weak limb in the Anglo-American capitalistic bloc'. Working with the United States and through the United Nations was seen as the preferable route, and the one less likely to excite criticism, but a second line of defence was also proposed which would include 'organising a party to oppose the Tudeh' and 'playing Russia's game and organising an autonomy movement in southwest Persia'.[119]

Before having time to act on any of these recommendations, Britain was shaken by the first direct assault against its position in Iran with the onset of labour troubles in the oil fields. While magnifying fears about Soviet and Tudeh influence in Iran, these events also removed any illusions about Soviet promises that the USSR would not interfere with British oil interests. The call for resistance grew stronger: 'If the Tudeh don't meet with effective resistance their political momentum will allow them to undermine British interests. We musn't be too rigid about non-intervention or we will just hold the ring for the communists and invite them to extend the scope of their campaign'.[120] Le Rougetel, who had replaced Bullard as ambassador, thought that the southern unrest was symptomatic of a new countrywide trend in which the right were losing out to the left. He had just received a message from the governor general of Khuzistan in which the latter warned that he could no longer guarantee the security of the region.[121] The growing threat from the left provided Britain with the opportunity to rally further the support of the United States on issues that had become the chief focus of concern for US policy makers: the Soviet threat and the credibility of the United Nations:

Neither we nor the United States government can view with indifference the prospect of Persia's reduction to the status of a satellite under the very eyes of the Security Council with the consequent weakening of world confidence in the United Nations Organisation. Further, neither of us wish our great oil interests in the Middle East to be at the mercy of the Soviet Union acting through satellite governments or subversive agents. The Soviet campaign of weakening what they regard as the Anglo-US combine has begun with Tudeh agitation against the AIOC and may well be extended to Iraq, Kuwait, Bahrain and Saudi Arabia.[122]

This early British version of the 'domino theory' had special appeal to US policy makers who by now were beginning to formulate their ideas about 'containment' of the USSR. Britain's anxieties over the extent of the US commitment to the region proved needless: the precedent for intervention had been established during the UN debates on Iran. It was only a question of time before the administration would take further steps to check Soviet influence.

Meanwhile Britain still had to cope with what developed into a complete strike among AIOC workers. Khuzistan's governor general proved unable to keep control and the strike, which lasted three days, led to casualties on both sides and created a state of 'extreme alarm'.[123] The consensus at the Foreign Office was that the strike was bogus: the dispute was described as 'political' rather than resulting from genuine labour unrest. However, Bevin and other Labour MPs declared themselves 'impressed' with the economic causes of the strike and urged the implementation of a reform programme.[124] Whatever the strike's origins, no one doubted that Tudeh and Soviet influence was involved, and this gave the British the opportunity to point an accusing finger at Qavam for his toleration of the left and appeasement of the USSR. Paradoxically, despite the initial impact of the strike and the irritation provoked by Qavam's subsequent decision to appoint a 'pro-Tudeh' commission, headed by Firuz, to investigate its origins and start negotiations, the strike actually improved Britain's position in the short term. When order was finally restored after the granting of special powers to the Khuzistan governor general, Britain was able to secure the negation of most of the strike's early achievements. Meanwhile, on the strength of the labour troubles in the oil fields, Attlee secured the approval of parliament for the dispatching of two warships to the Shatt al-Arab, and subsequently moved an Indian brigade to Basra in the event of further unrest.[125]

Perhaps the most important effect of the strike, from Britain's viewpoint, was that it drew attention to the threat posed by the Tudeh. When this threat appeared to be a nationwide, as opposed to a local phenomenon, it produced a strong anti-Tudeh reaction both inside and outside Iran. While this development was helpful to Britain, a parallel development which also drew attention to British activities in southern Iran produced less desirable effects, in that it paved the way for the gradual undermining of Britain's position. In the context of its future oil operations the period 1944–6 was highly damaging to British interests, precipitating an open conflict between the British and Iranian governments. Such a situation might have been avoided if the AIOC had been willing to reform its operations. It was not enough to dismiss the strike as the work of Tudeh agitators. The oil industry in Iran, as Bevin himself pointed out, was a 'fertile field for reform'. He drew attention to the moderation of some of the Tudeh proposals which 'in any ordinary industry would be adopted'.[126] There was little doubt that the company's earlier labour law was in need of reform, and much could be done, argued Bevin, to make the AIOC concession more acceptable to Iranians. What argument could he give, the foreign secretary asked during a conversation with the AIOC chairman William Fraser, to anyone who claimed the right to nationalise Persian oil, while the Labour government was nationalising companies 'left and right' in Britain? He even suggested that Britain abandon its concessionary rights and 'follow the Soviet Union's example in offering a 50–50 deal'.[127]

Acting on Bevin's suggestions a commission was sent to investigate the conditions of the oil field workers. Instead of producing a critical report, however, the commission found that the AIOC's attitude towards labour was 'better than that obtained in other Persian industries'.[128] Effectively the would-be reformers were placed in an almost impossible position. They faced stiff resistance, not only from the AIOC, but also from the Ministry of Fuel and Power, the Treasury and many members of the Foreign Office itself. Instead of reforms some of the latter advocated tougher measures such as suspending or reducing royalties during strikes 'to give the Persian government a financial inducement to prevent strikes'. Nor did they rule out the use of force in the future, although Bevin resisted the possibility of sending British troops to the oil fields 'unless I was convinced there was no other way of saving British lives'.[129] Nevertheless, the impression left by British policy on the oil question, as summed up by the US ambassador, was that 'the AIOC had a great opportunity to take the lead in Iran's labour relations. It has so far missed this opportunity largely for the sake of profits . . .'[130]

The portents were ominous with regard to Britain's future interests in Iran, yet despite Bevin's concern, and the obvious fragility of Britain's position, complacency still prevailed in most government departments. This feeling was encouraged not only by the satisfactory settlement of the oil strike, but also by the rallying of the pro-British southern tribes.

Until the oil fields strike and subsequent inclusion of the Tudeh members in Qavam's cabinet, the question of using the southern tribes of Iran to defend Britain's position had not gone beyond the level of informal discussions at the Foreign or India Offices. Certain British officials in Iran were strongly suspected of maintaining links with tribal leaders as an insurance policy against the possible breakdown of central government authority. Britain's links with the tribes, as already noted, had a long history, and the allegiance of the tribes had always been seen as an important factor in maintaining the security of the oil fields. Prior to the First World War, the India Office had expressed the belief that 'future action in southwest Persia largely depended upon the extent to which the Bakhtiaris, the Lurs, and the tribes of Arabistan could be "utilised" and "strengthened"'.[131] In the critical summer and autumn of 1946, the temptation to mobilise the tribes in support of British interests may have proved irresistible.

Before the oil strike started there had been talk among British officials in Iran of the need to take some retaliatory action against Tudeh influence in the south. The 'tribal union' formed by the Khuzistan Arabs during the strike itself, and the subsequent union of the Bakhtiari and Qashqa'i tribes were both suspected of having British connections. Two Foreign Office minutes were revealing in this respect. The first, written by Orme Sargent advised that in the event of the Tudeh coming to power 'it would be desirable to investigate the possibility of encouraging any demand from the people of SW Persia for provincial autonomy. The success of the Azerbaijan democrats in obtaining local autonomy might lead the peoples and tribes of SW Persia to demand similar.' The second, by Lancelot Pyman, echoed these sentiments, and suggested as a remedy to the spread of Soviet control, the encouragement of local separatism and the development of an 'Azerbaijan' in southwest Persia under British inspiration.[132]

It should be put on record that Bevin, like Bullard, strongly opposed these suggestions. He thought local councils 'acceptable', but refused to entertain the idea of provincial autonomy because it would be 'doing what the Russians do'. Tampering with a secessionist movement, Bevin argued, would put the country 'back to where it was in 1907'.[133] Yet despite these protestations, British involvement in the southern uprisings was strongly implicated. The Americans certainly believed it to be so. Le Rougetel had once confided to the US ambassador that 'old line British officials in Iran are inclined towards arousing the tribes' even if London was opposed. Allen also noted the difficulty between 'Foreign Office officials and representatives of the government of India under Skrine . . . [It was] too much to expect that in view of the recent situation, local Britishers would turn down an offer by the Arab tribes.'[134]

The main personalities behind Britain's efforts to organise the southern tribes were Colonel Underwood, assistant military attaché and political advisor of the AIOC, and Alan Trott and Charles Gault, the British consuls in Ahwaz and Isfahan. According to the US consul in Basra, Underwood had mobilised Khuzistan's Arabs to fight the Tudeh. The consul cited 'British Embassy sources' as stating that a programme of action had yet to be worked out, but that it would favour 'liberal reforms' and demand autonomy similar to that granted to Azerbaijan.[135] The US ambassador, Allen, later spoke of 'Britain's reliance on the local tribal union' whose unacknowledged 'godfather' was Underwood.[136] As the movement gathered pace, Britain reportedly encouraged the tribes to make an appeal to the Arab League in Cairo, a move in which Underwood was almost certainly involved since he was in Cairo at the time. Although the British embassy denied involvement in the subsequent Bakhtiari–Qashqa'i union, Qavam claimed he held written evidence of secret meetings between members of the Isfahan, Ahwaz, and Tehran consulates and the Bakhtiari chiefs.[137]

The Foreign Office admitted that Trott had held contacts with tribal leaders but insisted that these were part of his 'normal duties' and had not included organisation or instigation of the tribes. Le Rougetel also conceded that the British consuls 'knew of a plot, and were approached for assistance, but so far as I am aware gave no reason to believe it would be forthcoming'.[138] Britain's assurances were generally unconvincing, and the delay in issuing a formal denial of complicity cast further doubts on British actions. Even Bevin, who had vetoed any suggestion to incite the tribes, seemed to doubt that his instructions had been carried out. On a Tehran dispatch on the tribal question the foreign secretary minuted: 'Are we quite sure that our people right down there were told of my decision?' The American ambassador also thought that Bevin's delay in making a statement on the tribal question suggested that he was 'not entirely satisfied with reports about Trott's activities and wants more information'.[139]

Although the British government, under strong pressure from both Qavam and the United States,[140] finally made a public statement denying complicity in the southern rebellion,[141] this was largely designed for public consumption and to prevent the embarrassment of recalling consular officials. The ambiguity of Britain's position, the timing of the uprising, and the delay in issuing a statement were regarded by many as sufficient proof of Britain's involvement. Certainly the results of the tribal uprising had assisted Britain in securing its policy goals as described in Tehran's quarterly report to London:

To endeavour to neutralise communist activities and prevent political sabotage in the oil field areas . . . strong pressure has been maintained on the prime minister to suppress subversive activities . . . Our publicity has aimed at influencing Persian public opinion in such a way that the full support of the prime minister could not be given to the Tudeh party before the elections . . .[142]

It could be argued that Qavam was, in any case, preparing to impose restrictions on the activities of the left, and that the tribal uprising merely assisted him in the implementation of policies which he had planned but not yet carried out. Le Rougetel suggested that the 'Isfahan plot' was used to strengthen the position of Qavam's own party, and was thus somehow concocted by the prime minister himself.[143] There is little doubt however that British policies in southern Iran did upset Qavam's plans. Whatever Britain's exact role in southern developments, the tribal rebellion represented a statement of intent by pro-British elements and a warning to Tehran as to what it could expect if it did not change its present policies.

The American role in the southern crisis had been minimal. The uprisings in both north and south Iran had provided the stage for the USSR and Britain to enact their traditional great power roles in Iran. American participation was neither offered nor sought. Nevertheless, events in the south did encourage the US government to insist on a complete break between Qavam and the Tudeh, and to call for the resumption of central government control throughout the country. Britain took a slightly different stand. Le Rougetel still feared the possible extension of Tudeh and Soviet influence, and spoke of the 'prime necessity for establishing a definite frontier between the USSR and Iran'.[144] Just what he meant by this soon became clear when he suggested that the Persian government 'may be wise to run the risk of losing this rich province rather than allow the Azerbaijan communists to enter the new Majlis and jeopardise their national independence'.[145]

Perhaps not surprisingly, American support for Le Rougetel's initiative was not forthcoming. The US ambassador thought that this inclination 'to look with complacency on the loss of Azerbaijan may not reflect London thinking', however, he also reasoned that British policy 'wants to retain the oil concession'.[146] Certainly the British ambassador's statement was illustrative of British thinking on the Iranian question. Britain still undervalued Persian sovereignty and territorial integrity. It was only because the United States did not share Britain's views about spheres of influence that Iran was able to remain independent.

It was left therefore to the United States to take the initiative in encouraging Qavam to dispatch troops to the north. Britain assumed a position of non-interference; the immediate threat to its interests having subsided, Britain was noticeably reticent in condemning Soviet policy. Despite the recent events which had shaken its position, Britain still regarded some degree of Soviet influence in Iran as inevitable. It was felt that British interests would be best served if the majlis gave its approval to the Irano-Soviet oil company. Bevin had anxiously pressed for an American commitment on Iran, when British interests were threatened, and he feared the creation of a vacuum into which Soviet power would move. By the end of 1946 he was 'satisfied': the United States had moved from a position which he described as 'neutrality', to an 'explicit commitment to uphold Iran's independence and sovereignty'.[147] However, as Britain would soon discover, the logic of the American position in Iran was ultimately contradictory to British interests there.

In March 1947 Bevin met Stalin, and assured the Soviet leader that Britain would advise the Persians to live up to their agreements with the USSR. Explaining his decision Bevin told Stalin that Britain held concessions in southern Persia and had no intention of interfering with Persian independence.[148] This private agreement, in which Stalin also assured Bevin that he would respect Britain's oil interests, led to speculation, not for the first time, that Britain and the USSR were conspiring at Iran's expense. The Foreign Office warned Tehran of 'the dangers of giving the impression of acting in collusion with the Russians . . . we must not appear to pursue a "spheres of influence policy" along 1907 lines'.[149] At the same time there was a need to reassure Washington that Britain and the United States were at one in the desire to maintain Persian independence. Their only difference, explained the Foreign Office was 'over policy . . . the United States was more impressed with the possible dangers which might flow from the Soviet concession, while HMG is more worried about the dangers if Persia refused to meet Russian demands'.[150] In reality the gap was, of course, much wider. Britain and the United States were not united over Iran, and over oil matters in particular. Until the majlis decision became known in the autumn of 1947, the British continued to urge the Iranians to keep the oil door open.[151]

The fate of the Soviet oil agreement has already been told. Secure of US support, the majlis overcame British and Soviet pressures and rejected it outright.[152] Predictably, the decision made Britain's position in the south more vulnerable, although many observers, including the AIOC chairman, appeared not to appreciate this at the time.[153] A precedent had been created by which Iran could deny foreigners the right to exploit its oil. Britain was now confronted by a Persian government, which by its own efforts had created the mechanism which would, in due course, undermine the AIOC concession. Britain's policy with regard to its own oil operations did nothing to appease the Persians. On the contrary, the defiance of the AIOC encouraged the infant nationalisation movement to proceed with impunity.

In conclusion, there can be little doubt that Britain's wartime policies towards Iran had been costly and damaging, not only to Iran, but to Britain itself and to allied relations as well. The principles of British policy were based on considerations which were no longer applicable to the postwar world. This was reflected in the dichotomy of interests between Britain and the United States and by the fact that it was American power rather than British which emerged triumphant in 1945. Whatever critiques may be made of US policy, the Americans were, at least in 1947, more interested in retaining Persian territorial integrity and political independence than either of their allies. The fact that this independence was increasingly linked to a close partnership with the United States was as much the result of Britain's wartime policies as it was the result of the threat from the USSR. Britain made the extension of the Cold War to the Middle East desirable and necessary, when the United States was more concerned about European borders, the United Nations and economic reconstruction. The logic of the new US position as a world 'superpower', its conflict with the USSR and its own growing interests in the Near and Middle East, did, to some extent, make the growth of American influence inevitable. However, the degree of this influence and the manner by which it was achieved, owed much to Britain's earlier handling of Iranian affairs.

If British policy helped to define Iran's international alignments and Iran's continuing state of dependence on foreign powers, it also defined Iran's political future, by encouraging the return to an authoritarian regime. Britain's attitude towards the majlis and the resurgence of democratic activities that accompanied the fall of Reza Shah, was to regard them as inappropriate for Iran's particular stage of underdevelopment and therefore unworthy of British encouragement. British and later US policy were in large part responsible for the closing off of political options for Iran. Like the United States, Britain welcomed the return of the conservative-royalist alliance after Qavam's departure. Hakimi, who returned to power for the third time at the end of 1947, was, for all his weaknesses, a more attractive prospect for Britain than the enigmatic Qavam. 'A man who would have sold the pass if left to his own devices', was Le Rougetel's comment on Qavam's two years in power.[154]

In 1941, following the collapse of Persian resistance to the allied occupation, Churchill had remarked: 'We may be glad that in our victory the independence of Persia has been preserved.'[155] Yet neither in 1941, nor less in 1945, could it be claimed that Britain had defended Iran's sovereignty or territorial integrity. Iran's future independence owed little to British efforts. Britain was interested in an independent Iran only in so far as the latter could protect and preserve British interests. Iran's independence was saved by the Persians themselves with the assistance of the United States. It had never been a British priority. In this respect it could be said that British policy in Iran during the war was guided throughout by the twin concepts of spheres of influence and balances of power. It was perhaps the only policy Britain knew; certainly it had served the country well over the years, but was no longer tenable in a postwar world dominated by two new powers, in which European power would be relegated to a poor second place. British influence in Iran did not, of course, disappear overnight. The British government continued to exercise a strong influence in Iran's affairs, the nationalisation of the country's oil resources notwithstanding. Nevertheless, it was US power and influence which gradually became the dominant force in the region, assuming Britain's traditional strategic role and sharing its vast oil wealth.

If Churchill believed that Britain had been instrumental in saving Persian independence, many British officials believed that their well-intentioned policies towards Iran had been misunderstood. 'Persians who ought to have known better suspected Britain of "selling them down the river"', complained Clarmont Skrine.[156] Yet what other conclusion could Persians draw from British policy? While Iran's importance to the allied war effort, especially the maintenance of the supply line to the USSR, cannot be underestimated, British policies were unneccessarily destabilising and their consequences continued to reverberate around the region for many years to come. Britain's obsession with its great power status in Iran, and its continuing efforts to play out that role, left an indelible impression on Iranian life.

Conclusion

The Azerbaijan or 'Iranian' crisis of 1946 now rightly occupies an important place, not only in modern Iranian history, but also in the history of the Cold War. Iranians, particularly those old enough to remember the period, may never have doubted the significance of the turbulent decade of the 1940s in their own history. It has taken a little longer for the Azerbaijan crisis to receive the international recognition it deserves. Yet there is little doubt that events in Iran had lasting repercussions on the relationship between the three wartime allies, and proved to be a landmark, among the many landmarks, in the development of the Cold War:

> For it was the first time that the new tougher American attitude took force as policy. It also represented a shift in the East–West contention from Eastern Europe to a new periphery of conflict that involved a collision in what had been traditionally British and Russian spheres. Finally, it became the first public breach among the superpowers. The United States also took the lead away from Britain and sought to make the Russians back down by playing to the gallery of world opinion.[1]

A turning point in the relationship between the great powers, the Azerbaijan crisis was no less a turning point in Iran's internal development. The resolution of problems arising from the war and the allied occupation had set in motion the process whereby the monarchy was gradually able to reestablish the position it had previously enjoyed. The failure of Iran's experiment in democracy was not in itself the result of events in Azerbaijan, but the consequence of foreign intervention, which had helped to cause the crisis and had hampered the progress of Iran's political development. Allied policies made possible the thirty-eight-year reign of Muhammad Reza Shah.

From this it should not be concluded that the alliance between the United States and the Shah was inevitable. The US administration was not necessarily committed to the restoration of the Pahlavi monarchy. However, the absence of political options, and the Shah's own complaisant attitude, undoubtedly made him the most appealing prospect from the viewpoint of American policy makers in 1946. Yet America's initially ambivalent attitude towards Muhammad Mussadiq during the latter's premiership from 1951 to

177

1953, showed how the US administration was not then totally convinced that the Shah was the only alternative. However, the fear of communism that coloured US attitudes towards any Iranian leader who was not unequivocally anti-Soviet, prompted the final evaluation that Mussadiq, like Qavam, was not the best vehicle for the advancement of US interests in the country. In scenes reminiscent of 1946, when Britain and the USA had discussed with the Shah the possibility of overthrowing Ahmad Qavam, the two Western powers in 1953 together orchestrated the coup which overthrew the nationalist prime minister.

Iran did not, of course, return immediately to the sort of authoritarian regime which had characterised the late Reza Shah period. The 'crisis of democracy' had still to run its course, and only with the fall of Mussadiq, did the royal ascendency prove 'irresistible'.[2] Nevertheless, it has been argued here that any immediate hope for a democratic future had been crushed by 1946. The importance of Iran remaining in the Western camp soon came to override all other considerations. The high-minded principles that had guided US policy at the beginning of the Second World War were all too soon forgotten. Iran's anti-communist stance soon came to be regarded as no less important than the preservation of its political independence.

Pressure from the United States forced the USSR to abandon its ambitions in Iran. These ambitions, contrary to the insistence of some Western Cold War warriors, were not the annexation of Azerbaijan, the acquisition of a warm-water port on the Persian Gulf, nor the menacing of Britain's imperial possessions. Soviet goals in Iran, while undoubtedly influenced by these considerations, were rather related to continuing anxieties over the security of the country's vast borders. 'Friendly governments' whether in Eastern Europe or the Near East, were one way of securing them. Through its occupation of northern Iran, its support for the Tudeh and the Azerbaijan rebels, and its demand for a share in the exploitation of Iranian oil, the Soviet government had tried to shift the balance of forces in Iran in its favour. Yet while willing to go to considerable lengths to secure its goals in Iran, the USSR would not risk conflict with the United States. US intransigence and a hostile international climate made the Soviet Union beat a retreat in Iran.

It has been argued that the relatively complaisant attitude of the USSR reflected its belief that Qavam had been 'won over', and that the oil agreement was to be secured when the 15th majlis convened.[3] Yet it is unlikely that the USSR thought that the combination of local support and the goodwill of the Iranian prime minister would be sufficient to guarantee the passage of the oil bill. Could the USSR have made such a serious miscalculation in its estimation of the Iranian situation? It is more plausible to suggest that it was an understanding of *realpolitik*, rather than its failure 'to appreciate what was going on in the Third World', which explains Soviet policy towards Iran in this period.[4]

Britain had been willing to concede the Soviet Union its desired sphere of influence in Persia, a policy which not only brought her into conflict with the United States, but also produced a complicated series of problems for Britain's own relationship with both the USSR and Iran. For as Britain was forced eventually to accept, a balance of power could no longer operate as in the past, in Iran or anywhere else. By conceding a sphere of influence to the USSR in the north, there was no guarantee that Britain's interest in southern Iran would be safe from Soviet encroachment. The USSR was interested in Azerbaijan, not as an end in itself, but as a means to securing influence throughout Iran. The Iranian experience demonstrated to Britain the new limits of her influence in the postwar world, a world no longer dominated by the great powers but by two emerging 'superpowers'.

Britain's decline was, in many respects, the consequence of war, but in Iran, British policy, characterised by hypocrisy and arrogance, speeded the process. The results of such a policy, as argued, were highly destabilising to Iran, earned Britain the lasting mistrust of the Iranian people, and also contributed to a difficult relationship with Britain's most important ally, the United States. The latter, at least initially, showed little inclination to check the demise of British interests in Iran, as demonstrated by its early reluctance to help Britain out of the troubles it had created for itself over the nationalisation of Iranian oil.[5]

Oil has featured prominently in this account. However, it would be wrong to suppose that events in Iran in this period can be understood merely in terms of the great powers' scramble for the control of the region's oil resources. The Soviet Union may have wanted, and even needed, the extra oil and revenue that an Iranian concession would bring, but it was not the search for petroleum that led the USSR to support Azerbaijan's autonomy, or to retain its troops in Iran in contravention of wartime treaties. Perhaps more important for the USSR was the need for influence in Iran to protect its own oil concerns in the Baku region, the 'Achilles heel' of the country.[6] Nor, despite revisionist attempts to argue the contrary case, was oil the primary American concern in Iran.[7] Clearly the protection of existing and future commercial interests in the region was an important consideration in US policy making in Iran. The United States was, in many respects, a country 'looking for opportunity'.[8] But oil was not a sufficient single explanation for the American decision to 'take on' Iran. An awareness of Iran's strategic importance coupled with the US desire to maintain a balance of power in the region in the light of Britain's waning influence were equally significant.[9] Only in the case of Britain might it be argued that oil, together with traditional considerations of empire security, might be considered a primary determinant of policy. Britain, after all, enjoyed a monopoly over the exploitation of Iran's southern oil reserves, which she was anxious not only to maintain but also to expand. With the weakening of Britain's power during the war, its policy in the Azerbaijan crisis was increasingly conditioned by its position in southern Iran.

For Iran, the Azerbaijan crisis represented the culmination of four years of false starts, frustrated hopes and growing popular disillusionment. The country was unable to act independently of the influence of foreign powers, and its leaders continued to look to external support in their personal struggles for power. The question was no longer that of looking for 'third powers' to offset the traditional Soviet–British rivalry in Iran, for that rivalry was rapidly becoming a thing of the past. The United States, the 'third power', had become the first power and easily outstripped all its rivals. Iran's international relations had entered a new era: that of close and growing alignment with the United States.

Internally, the promise of a new era of political freedom and parliamentary democracy had been frustrated. The occupation had not provided the environment for these conditions to flourish. Foreign intervention had merely helped to pave the way for a return of the old elites. The marriage between the USSR and the country's left-wing parties, notably the Tudeh, struck a death blow at the degree of popular acceptance they had once enjoyed. Soviet interference distorted these movements and distracted them from their original goals. In the case of the Azerbaijan Democrats, it appeared that their very existence was dependent on the exigencies of Soviet policy.

The political demise of Qavam in 1947, like the demise of the left, both to some extent the product of external intervention, represented a serious loss to the Iranian political system. For all his weaknesses and inconsistencies, Qavam had shown his abilities as an independent politician committed to fundamental reforms. He demonstrated his qualities as a statesman, in his handling of Iran's foreign relations in a critical period, and his reforming zeal at home. The real significance of Qavam's defeat was brought home when his successor became known. The reappearance of Ibrahim Hakimi, who took up the premiership for the third time in five years, heralded the return of the conservatives who, secure of American support, could look forward to the future with greater confidence than had been possible at any time during the previous five years.

The Azerbaijan crisis represented the culmination of both an internal and external struggle for the control of Iran. Iran's political future was set on a right-wing course, her foreign alignment on a pro-Western but specifically pro-American course. Events in Azerbaijan were not, of course, the sole explanation for these developments, but they did serve clearly to reveal the different issues at stake in Iran, and proved to be a turning point in Iranian history. They were also a turning point, albeit a more modest one, in the development of the Cold War. The Azerbaijan crisis led to one of the United States' first direct challenges to the USSR. It is true that the United States commitment to Iran was reaffirmed and strengthened following the crisis over the nationalisation of the country's oil resources and the Anglo-US sponsored coup to oust Prime Minister Mussadiq. Yet the origins of this commitment lay in the war and the immediate postwar period.

The early history of the Cold War did not, therefore, unfold in a solely European context. With the United States action in the United Nations in the spring of 1946, the globalisation of the Cold War had already begun. Iran was an early model of how the United States would meet the Soviet challenge and forge new regional partnerships in the developing world. It also provided a good example of the emergent difficulties in the relationship between the United States and Britain. Certainly one of the major conclusions arising from this book, and one shared with those who have studied US–British wartime relations in other areas of the world, is that the Anglo-American alliance was far from being an harmonious one.[10] British policies helped to secure for Iran an important place in the East–West dispute, while also contributing to the decline of British power in the region.[11]

In 1946 the United States helped Iran to preserve its independence and territorial integrity, and this was no insignificant gesture, for the loss to the country of Azerbaijan, or Fars or Khuzistan for that matter, would have been immeasurable. Yet, as events would show, Iran paid a high price for its integrity, and its 'freedom of action',[12] as in the past, was closely conditioned by foreign intervention.[13] Indeed, there were many Iranians who believed, at least until the Khomeini Revolution of 1979, that Iran's partnership with the United States and entry on to the Cold War stage was accompanied by a serious loss of its political independence. Indeed there are few who would disagree that the Iranian Revolution itself was, at least in part, a response to the degree of US influence in Iran's affairs.

Notes

Introduction

1 Shahram Chubin and Sepehr Zabih, *The Foreign Relations of Iran. A Developing State in a Zone of Great Power Conflict* (Berkeley, 1974), p. 37.

2 See for example Ervand Abrahamian, *Iran: Between Two Revolutions* (Princeton, 1982), pp. 398–413. Two works that deal with the crisis in greater detail are: Sepehr Zabih, *The Communist Movement in Iran* (Berkeley, 1966), pp. 98–122; Richard W. Cottam, *Nationalism in Iran* (Pittsburg, 1964), pp. 118–33.

3 Walter LaFeber, *America, Russia, and the Cold War 1945–1984*, 5th ed. (New York, 1985), pp. 34–35; Louis J. Halle, *The Cold War as History* (London, 1967), pp. 99–100.

4 George Lenczowski, *Russia and the West in Iran 1918–1948* (New York, 1949), pp. 286–315; F.S. Fatemi, *The USSR in Iran* (New Jersey, 1980), chapters 3–6.

5 See for example, Bruce R. Kuniholm, *The Origins of the Cold War in the Near East: Great Power Conflict and Diplomacy in Iran, Turkey and Greece* (Princeton, 1980); Anne Deighton, *The Impossible Peace: Britain, the Division of Germany and the Origins of the Cold War* (Oxford, 1990). For a review of the early post-revisionist literature see J.L. Gaddis, 'The emerging post-revisionist synthesis and the origins of the cold war', *Diplomatic History*, VII, 3 (1983), pp. 171–90.

6 Fakhreddin Azimi, *Iran. The Crisis of Democracy* (London, 1989).

7 Kuniholm, *Origins of the Cold War in the Near East*; Daniel Yergin, *The Shattered Peace: The Origins of the Cold War and the National Security State* (London, 1977); Mark H. Lytle, *The Origins of the Iranian–American Alliance* (London, 1987); James F. Goode, *The United States and Iran, 1946–51* (London, 1989); Martin Sicker, *The Bear and the Lion. Soviet Imperialism and Iran* (New York, 1988).

8 Parviz Homayounpour, *L'Affaire d'Azerbaidjan* (Lausanne, 1967); Robert Rossow, 'The Battle of Azerbaijan, 1946', *Middle East Journal*, X, 1 (Winter, 1956) pp. 17–62; E. Abrahamian, 'Communism and Communalism in Iran: the Tudeh and the Firqah-i Dimukrat', *International Journal of Middle Eastern Studies*, I, 4 (October, 1970), pp. 291–316; G.R. Hess, 'The Iranian Crisis of 1945–6 and the Cold War', *Political Science Quarterly*, LXXXIX, 1 (1974), pp. 177–96; R.K. Ramazani, 'The Republic of Azerbaijan and the Kurdish People's Republic', in *The Anatomy of Communist Takeovers* (ed.), T. Hammond (New

Haven, 1975), pp. 448–74; J. Ememi-Yeganeh, 'Iran vs. Azerbaijan (1945–46): divorce, separation or reconciliation?' *Central Asian Survey*, III, 2 (1984), pp. 1–27.

9 See for example, Herbert Feis, *From Trust to Terror. The Onset of the Cold War, 1945–1950* (London, 1970), pp. 63–70, 81–87; Lloyd C. Gardner, *Architects of Illusion: Men and Ideas in American Foreign Policy 1941–1949* (Chicago, 1970), pp. 210–15.

10 On the general view that Britain should be regarded as a major Cold War actor, see further Avi Shlaim, 'Britain, the Berlin Blockade and the Cold War', *International Affairs*, LX (1984), pp. 1–14, and the collection of essays in Anne Deighton (ed.), *Britain and the First Cold War* (London, 1990).

1. The roots of the Azerbaijan crisis

1 See, for example, Mohammad Reza Pahlavi, *Mission for My Country* (London, 1961), p. 118; Hassan Arfa, *Under Five Shahs* (London, 1954), pp. 331–64; Sicker, *The Bear and the Lion*, pp. 68–71.

2 R.K. Ramazani, *Iran's Foreign Policy 1941–1973. A Study of Foreign Policy in Modernizing Nations* (Charlottesville 1975), pp. 112–13; Nikki Keddie, *Roots of Revolution* (London, 1981), pp. 119–20; P. Avery, *Modern Iran* (London, 1965), pp. 387–8; Lytle, *Origins of the Iranian–American Alliance*, p. 141.

3 Abrahamian, *Iran*, pp. 217–18; H. Katouzian, *The Political Economy of Modern Iran 1926–1979* (London, 1981), pp. 150–1; Azimi, *Iran. Crisis of Democracy*, pp. 135–6; M. Reza Ghods, *Iran in the Twentieth Century. A Political History* (London, 1989), pp. 159–78.

4 M.S. Ivanov, *Ocherki Istorii Irana* (Moscow, 1952); M. Sergeyev, 'The struggle of democracy against reaction in Persia', *Bolshevik*, XI (1946), cited in 'Borderlands of Soviet Central Asia. Persia: Part I', *Central Asian Review*, IV, 3 (1956), 317–25.

5 In support of this view see A.K.S. Lambton, 'The Azerbaijan problem', *The World Today* II, 1 (January 1946), 48–57.

6 G.H. Blake and A. Drysdale, *The Middle East and North Africa: A Political Geography* (Oxford, 1985), pp. 46–50; M. Atkin, *Russia and Iran 1780–1828* (Minneapolis, 1980).

7 A. Bennigsen and M. Broxup, *The Islamic Threat to the Soviet State* (London, 1983), p. 110; Muriel Atkin, 'The Islamic Republic and the Soviet Union', in *The Iranian Revolution and the Islamic Republic* (eds.), Nikki R. Keddie and Eric Hooglund (Syracuse, 1986), p. 199; Michael Rywkin, *Moscow's Muslim Challenge. Soviet Central Asia* (London, 1982), p. 151.

8 US Department of State, Record Group 59, Decimal File 891.50, 'Economic Report on Azerbaijan', Tehran, 9 April 1946, National Archives, Washington.

9 Abrahamian, *Iran*, pp. 147, 389–90.

10 A. Afshar, 'The problem of nationality and the national unity of Iran', *Ayandeh*, II (November 1926), 559–69.

11 E.G. Browne, *A Year Among the Persians* (London, 1893), pp. 109–10.

12 Louis Beck, 'Revolutionary Iran and its tribal peoples', in *Sociology of "Developing Societies"*. *The Middle East* (eds.), T. Asad and R. Owen (New York, 1983), pp. 115–7.

13 See W. Eagleton Jr., *The Kurdish Republic of 1946* (London, 1963); A. Roosevelt Jr., 'The Kurdish Republic of Mahabad', *The Middle East Journal*, I, 3 (1947), 247–69; G. Chaliand, ed., *People Without a Country. The Kurds and Kurdistan* (London, 1980), pp. 107–34.

14 F. Kazemi, 'The military and politics in Iran: the uneasy symbiosis', in *Towards a Modern Iran: Studies in Thought, Politics and Society* (eds.), E. Kedourie and S. Haim (London, 1980), pp. 218–19; M.E. Yapp, '1900–1921: the last years of the Qajar dynasty', in *Twentieth Century Iran* (eds.), H. Amirsadeghi and R.W. Ferrier (London, 1977), pp. 1–22.

15 Nikki R. Keddie, *Religion and Rebellion in Iran. The Tobacco Protest of 1891–92* (London, 1966).

16 E.G. Browne, *The Persian Revolution of 1905–1909* (London, 1910).

17 M. Mortazavi, *Le Role de l'Azerbaidjan au cours des XXV siècles d'histoire de l'empire d'Iran* (Tabriz, 1971), pp. 115–16; Browne, *Persian Revolution*, pp. 233–91; A. Kasravi, *Tarikh-i Mashrutah-i Iran* (Tehran, 1937), pp. 676–906.

18 Abrahamian, *Iran*, pp. 97–8.

19 On the role of Britain and Russia in these developments see chapters 4 and 6. For a study of Iran during the First World War, see M. Sepehr, *Iran dar Jang-i Buzurg-i 1914–1918* (Tehran, 1957).

20 Abrahamian, *Iran*, pp. 109–10; H. Nazem, *Russia and Great Britain in Iran 1900–1914* (Tehran, 1975), pp. 104–8.

21 Katouzian, *Political Economy of Modern Iran*, p. 75.

22 Yapp, 'Last years of the Qajar dynasty', p.19.

23 See further below, pp. 83–4.

24 Cottam, *Nationalism in Iran*, pp. 102–6; F. Halliday, 'Revolution in Iran', *Khamsin*, VII (1980), 53–64; Suroosh Irfani, *Iran's Islamic Revolution* (London, 1983), pp. 50–66; S. Ravasani, *Sowjetrepublik Gilan* (Berlin, 1973).

25 Lenczowski, *Russia and the West in Iran*, pp. 54–8.

26 X.J. Eudin and R.C. North, *Soviet Russia and the East, 1920–1927. A Documentary Survey* (Stanford, 1957), p. 98.

27 Sayyid Ziya was a pro-British politician and editor of the newspaper *Ra'd*. Following the *coup d'état*, he briefly held the post of prime minister, but was soon ousted by Reza Khan as the latter consolidated his power.

28 Irfani, *Iran's Islamic Revolution*, pp. 61–3; Abrahamian, *Iran*, pp. 118–19; Katouzian, *Political Economy of Modern Iran*, pp. 76–7.

29 For a comparison of the Gilan and Azerbaijan uprisings, see A.B. Wasserberg, 'The politics of Soviet interference. Soviet policy towards Iran' (City University, New York, Ph.D. thesis, 1979).

30 See A. Azari, *Qiyam-i Khiabani* (Tehran, 1950); Cottam, *Nationalism in Iran*, pp. 122–4; Abrahamian, *Iran*, pp. 122–5.

31 *The Communist International 1919–1943, Documents*, I, (ed.) J. Degras (London, 1956), pp. 105–6.

32 B. Lazitch and M.M. Drachkovitch, *Lenin and the Comintern*, I (Stanford, 1972), p. 408.

33 Basil Dmytryshyn and Frederick Cox, *The Soviet Union and the Middle East. A Documentary Record of Afghanistan, Iran and Turkey 1917–1985* (Princeton, 1987), pp. 260–71.

34 Eudin and North, *Soviet Russia and the East*, pp. 99–102.

35 Yapp, 'Last years of the Qajar dynasty', p. 3.

36 Kazemi, 'Military and politics in Iran', pp. 218–20; W. Knapp, 'The period of Riza Shah, 1921–1941', in *Twentieth Century Iran* (eds.), Amirsadeghi and Ferrier, p. 28; for an outline of some of Kasravi's ideas see Ervand Abrahamian, 'Kasravi, the integrative nationalist of Iran', in Kedourie and Haim (eds.), *Towards a Modern Iran*, pp. 111–17.

37 The Persian Cossack Brigade was created in 1878 by Russian officers at the request of Nasir al-Din Shah. After the Bolshevik Revolution it was commanded by Persian officers, through whose ranks Reza Khan rose to power. See Kazemi, 'Military and politics in Iran', p. 219; Firuz Kazemzadeh, 'The origins and early development of the Persian Cossack Brigade', *American Slavic and East European Review*, XV (1956), 351–63.

38 G.R. Garthwaite, *Khans and Shahs: A Documentary Analysis of the Bakhtiyari in Iran* (London, 1983), pp. 138–9; Louis Beck, *The Qashqa'i of Iran* (London, 1986), pp. 129–42; Donald Wilbur, *Riza Shah Pahlavi: The Resurrection and Reconstruction of Iran: 1878–1944* (New York, 1975), pp. 261–2.

39 Abrahamian, *Iran*, pp. 118–35; Said Amir Arjomand, *The Turban for the Crown: The Islamic Revolution in Iran* (New York, 1988), p. 59.

40 Joseph M. Upton, *The History of Modern Iran. An Interpretation* (Cambridge Mass., 1960), p. 80.

41 Miron Rezun, *The Soviet Union and Iran* (Geneva, 1981), pp. 270–6; Zabih, *Communist Movement in Iran*, pp. 52–5.

42 See chapter 2, pp. 47–8, 50–1.

43 Knapp, 'The period of Riza Shah', p. 50; Keddie, *Roots of Revolution*, pp. 108–10; Katouzian, *Political Economy of Modern Iran*, pp. 98–133; M.H. Pesaran, 'Economic development and revolutionary upheavals in Iran', in *Iran: A Revolution in Turmoil* (ed.), Haleh Afshar (London, 1985), p. 18.

44 Keddie, *Roots of Revolution*, pp. 107–8; Katouzian, *Political Economy of Modern Iran*, pp. 128, 150; Abrahamian, *Iran*, pp. 163–4.

45 L.P. Elwell-Sutton, 'Political parties in Iran: 1941–1948', *The Middle East Journal* III, 1 (January 1949), 49–50.

46 Abrahamian, 'Communism and communalism in Iran', p. 296.

47 British Foreign Office, Class FO371, File 31386, Tehran to FO, 15 January 1946, Public Record Office, London; Roosevelt, 'Kurdish Republic of Mahabad', p. 248.

48 FO371/20830, 'The economic and financial situation in Azerbaijan', Tabriz, 31 December 1936.

49 SD891.00, 'Memorandum on the social and political economy of Azerbaijan', Tabriz, 2 October 1943.

50 Rose L. Greaves, '1942–1976: the reign of Muhammad Riza Shah', in *Twentieth Century Iran* (eds.), Amirsadeghi and Ferrier, p. 54.

51 Zabih, *Communist Movement in Iran*, pp. 64–80; G. Lenczowski, 'The communist movement in Iran', *The Middle East Journal* I, 1 (January 1947), 29–45; Elwell-Sutton, 'Political parties in Iran', pp. 48–52.

52 Abrahamian, *Iran*, p. 177.

53 For a detailed study of the workings of the majlis in this period see Azimi, *Iran: Crisis of Democracy*; see also Avery, *Modern Iran*, pp. 369–71.

54 F.G. Nollau and H.J. Wiehe, *Russia's South Flank* (New York, 1963), p. 29.

55 FO371/27157, press attaché's report, 4 October 1941.

56 FO371/27154, Tabriz consular reports, 7 and 13 September 1941.

57 FO371/27156, Tabriz consular report, 28 September 1941; FO371/27157, press attaché's report, 4 October 1941.

58 Katouzian, *Political Economy of Modern Iran*, p. 150.

59 According to one source, Assyrians and Armenians constituted 3 per cent of the Azerbaijani population. See Fatemi, *USSR in Iran*, p. 78.

60 Abrahamian, *Iran*, p. 175.

61 See A.K.S. Lambton, 'The Azerbaijan problem', *World Today* II, 1 (January, 1946), p. 54; SD891.00, 'Political situation in the Tabriz consular district', 4 January, 1944.

62 FO371/31426, Tabriz consular report, 28 January 1942; Lenczowski, *Russia and the West in Iran*, pp. 189, 205–6.

63 FO371/27152, Eden to Cripps, 23 September 1941; FO371/27154, Tabriz consular report, 7 September 1941; SD891.00, Tehran, 4 October 1941.

64 FO371/35098, Bullard to Eden, 3 May 1943.

65 FO371/27159, Tabriz consular report, 3 November 1941.

66 FO371/27218, Tehran to FO, 16 September 1941; FO371/31426, Tabriz Diary, 28 January–20 February 1942.

67 FO371/31426, Cook to Bullard, 30 November 1941.

68 *Azerbaijan*, various issues, February–March 1942.

69 *Rahbar*, 23 November 1943.

70 FO371/35092, Tabriz Diary, November 1942; FO371/35094, Tabriz Diary, August–September 1943; FO371/40178, Tabriz consular report, 12 August 1944. See also H. Ladjevardi, *Labour Unions and Autocracy in Iran* (Syracuse, 1985), pp. 99–104.

71 FO371/35073, Tabriz consular report, 9 July 1943; A.K.S. Lambton, *Landlord and Peasant in Persia* (London, 1953), p. 396.

72 FO371/35071, Bullard to Eden, 28 May 1943; FO371/35073, Tabriz consular report, 3 August 1943; FO371/35093, Tabriz Diary, June–July 1943; SD891.00, Tabriz, 15 February and 15 July 1943.

73 FO371/35094, Tabriz to Foreign Office, 5 September 1943.

74 FO371/35094, Tabriz Diaries, August and October 1943.

75 FO371/35094, Tehran to Foreign Office, 20 December 1943.

76 FO371/35104. The Declaration was well received by the Iranian press. The Tudeh paper *Razm* (6 December 1943) called it 'a great historical document'; the

Justice party's *Mihr-i Iran* (28 December 1943) said it had made a 'deep impression' on all sections of Iranian society. See also A.H. Hamzavi, 'Iran at the Tehran Conference', *International Affairs*, XX, 2 (April 1944), 192–203.

77 FO371/35117, Bullard to Eden, 23 November 1943.
78 FO371/40177, Tabriz diary, February–March 1944; SD891.00, Tabriz, 15 March 1944.
79 SD891.00, Tabriz, 16 March 1944. See further, pp. 48–9.
80 FO371/40172, War Office report, 23 July 1944.
81 FO371/45432, 'The Tudeh as a party serving the Russians', Tehran, 24 April 1945; Fatemi, *USSR in Iran*, p. 55; Ervand Abrahamian, 'Factionalism in Iran: political groups in the 14th majlis', *Middle Eastern Studies*, XIV (January 1978), 22–55.
82 FO371/40177, Tabriz diary, March 1944.
83 FO371/40178, Lascelles (acting ambassador to Iran), to Eden, 26 August 1944. See also *Rahbar*, 3–15 August which produced daily reports on the conference proceedings.
84 SD891.00, Tabriz, 19 July 1944; for a discussion of events in Tabriz in this period see FO371/40178, Tabriz consular report, 22 August 1944.
85 Ibid.
86 For a discussion of the changing political configurations of the 14th majlis see Abrahamian, *Iran*, pp. 199–244; Azimi, *Iran: Crisis of Democracy*, pp. 99–179.
87 FO371/40172, 'Report from the British Consulate in Isfahan', 24 June 1944, Abrahamian, *Iran*, pp. 206–9; Azimi, *Iran: Crisis of Democracy*, pp. 51–3.
88 See further below pp. 119–20.
89 FO371/40188, Tehran to all consuls, 13 October 1944; FO3712/40241, Tehran to FO, 24 October 1944. For the Tudeh's previous position on the oil question see 'Jang-i Naft', *Rahbar*, 1 August 1944; speech to the majlis by Reza Radmanish, 10 August 1944, cited in FO371/40187, Lascelles to Eden, 26 August 1944.
90 *Rahbar*, 26 November 1945; SD891.00, Tehran, 27 October 1944; ibid, 28 October 1944; FO371/40188, Tehran to Foreign Office, 1 November 1944.
91 *Ra'di Imruz*, cited in FO371/40713, Tehran to Ministry of Information, 8 December 1945.
92 FO371/40178, Tabriz Diary, October–November 1944; Ladjevardi, *Labour Unions and Autocracy*, p. 107.
93 FO371/40242, Tehran to FO, 3 December 1944; L.P. Elwell-Sutton, *Persian Oil: A Study in Power Politics* (London, 1955), pp. 110–11; Homa Katouzian (ed.), *Mussadiq and the Struggle for Power in Iran* (London, 1990), pp. 56–8.
94 FO371/40178, Tabriz Diary, November 1944.
95 FO371/45478, Tabriz Diary, November–December 1944.
96 Ibid., Tabriz Diary, February 1945.
97 Ibid., Tabriz Diaries, January–April 1945; SD891.00, Tabriz, 7 January 1945; Ladjevardi, *Labour Unions and Autocracy*, pp. 105–9.
98 FO371/52710, military attaché's intelligence summary, 11–17 March 1946.
99 See further, p. 122 below.
100 SD891.00, Tabriz, 7 January 1945; FO371/52663, 'Report on conditions in Azerbaijan', August–December 1945.

101 SD891.00, Tabriz, 3, 4 and 23 April 1945; FO371/45458, Intelligence Summary, 2–8 April 1945.

102 FO371/45458, Intelligence Summary, 7–13 May 1945.

103 Ibid., 11–17 June 1945.

104 Ibid., 30 April–6 May 1945; Roosevelt, 'Kurdish Republic of Mahabad', pp. 250–53; Eagleton, *Kurdish Republic of 1946*, pp. 55–6.

105 FO371/45458, Intelligence Summary, 18–24 June 1945; SD891.00, Tabriz, 29 June 1945; Ladjevardi, *Labour Unions and Autocracy*, pp. 108–9.

106 SD891.00, Tabriz, 18 July 1945; *Kharvar-i Now*, 'Dust-i ma ba URSS', 4 August 1945.

107 SD891.00, Tabriz, 14, 15 and 22 August 1945; FO371/54578, Tabriz Diary, July–August 1945; *Kharvar-i Now*, 13 August 1945.

108 SD891.00, Tehran, 19 and 23 August 1945; FO371/52673, 'Review of events of 1945', Tehran, 18 April 1946, Arfa, *Under Five Shahs*, pp. 342–5.

109 SD891.00, Tehran, 30 August and 5 September 1945; Lenczowski, *Russia and the West in Iran*, p. 286; Fatemi, *USSR in Iran*, p. 80.

110 SD891.00, Tabriz, 7 September 1945.

111 FO371/45478, Tabriz Diary, 7–21 September 1945. For the ADP manifesto see Jami, *Guzashtih Chiragh-i Rah-i Ayandih Ast* (Tehran, 1978), pp. 251–4.

112 FO371/45435, Tehran to FO, 9 October 1945; Roosevelt 'Kurdish Republic of Mahabad', pp. 254–5; Eagleton, *Kurdish Republic of 1946*, pp. 43–61.

113 FO371/45478, Tabriz Diary, 16 August–6 September 1945.

114 SD891.00, Tehran 22 November 1945; FO371/45478, Tabriz Diary, 25 October–21 November 1945. See further below, p. 100.

115 FO371/52740, Tabriz Diary, 21 November–31 December 1945; N.Q. Pisiyan, *Marg bud, Bazgasht ham bud* (Tehran, 1949), pp. 26–7; Arfa, *Under Five Shahs*, pp. 346–8.

116 See the preamble to the ADP manifesto in Jami, *Guzashtih*, p. 251; *Azerbaijan*, 5 September 1945.

117 *Azerbaijan*, 25 November 1945.

118 SD891.00, Tehran, 24 September 1945; ibid., Tabriz 25 September 1945.

119 FO371/45435, Wall to Bullard, 24 September 1945; speech by deputy Panahi to the majlis session of 27 September, cited in SD891.00, Tehran 8 October 1945.

120 SD891.00, Tabriz, 17 September 1945.

121 *Kharvari-Now*, 6 October 1945; *Azerbaijan*, 20 October 1945; FO371/45435, Tehran to FO, 12 October 1945.

122 SD891.00, Tehran, 12 October 1945; Abrahamian, *Iran*, p. 220.

123 FO371/45478, Tabriz Diary, 4–25 October 1945; Abrahamian, 'Communism and Communalism', 308–9.

124 FO371/45478, Tabriz Diary, 25 October–21 November 1945; FO371/52663, 'Report on the conditions in Azerbaijan August–December 1945'.

125 *Azerbaijan*, 25 November 1945; FO371/52740, Tabriz Diary, 21 November–31 December 1945.

126 Hakimi's speech to the majlis on 20 November, cited in SD891.00, Tehran, 26 November 1945; FO371/52663, 'Report on conditions in Azerbaijan'.

127 FO371/45437, Tehran to FO, 1 December 1945; FO371/52740, Tabriz Diary, 21 November–31 December 1945.
128 Ibid.; FO371/52663, 'Report on conditions in Azerbaijan'; 'Elections in Azerbaijan', *Iran-i Ma*, 7 December 1945.
129 SD891.00, Tehran, 12 December 1945; Arfa, *Under Five Shahs*, pp. 147–8.
130 FO371/52667, 'Russia and North Persia'; Roosevelt, 'Kurdish Republic of Mahabad', pp. 256–7.

2 The Azerbaijan Democratic party

1 Lenczowski, *Russia and the West in Iran*, pp. 286–7; Cottam, *Nationalism in Iran*, pp. 125–6; A.Z. Rubinstein, *Soviet Policy Toward Turkey, Iran and Afghanistan* (New York, 1982), p. 63.
2 Abrahamian 'Communism and Communalism', pp. 292–316; J. Ememi-Yeganeh, 'Iran vs. Azerbaijan', pp. 1–27; Keddie, *Roots of Revolution*, p. 119.
3 Fatemi, *USSR in Iran*, pp. 80–92; Zabih, *Communist Movement in Iran*, pp. 98–107; Azimi, *Iran: Crisis of Democracy*, pp. 135–7.
4 FO371/45435, Bullard to Foreign Office, 6 November 1945; Homayounpour, *L'Affaire d'Azarbaidjan*, p. 132.
5 FO371/45478, Tabriz Diary, 7–21 September 1945.
6 See Abrahamian, 'Communism and Communalism'.
7 Ibid., pp. 297–8.
8 'Hizb-i Tudeh dar Azerbaijan', *Rahbar*, 23 November 1945.
9 The proceedings of the congress were reported in *Rahbar*, 2 August–7 September 1944. See also FO371/40187, Lascelles to Eden, 26 August 1944.
10 Abrahamian, 'Communism and Communalism', pp. 41–4.
11 See for example, M.A.H. Katouzian, *Khatirat-i Siyasi-yi Khalil-i Maliki* (Tehran, 1981), pp. 371–80.
12 On the split and subsequent developments, see Abrahamian, *Iran*, pp. 305–8; Zabih, *Communist Movement in Iran*, pp. 123–65. Two former Tudeh members later gave their version of events: F. Kishavarz, *Man Muttaham Mikunam* (Tehran, 1978); K. Maliki, *Du Ravish bara-yi Yik Hadaf* (Tehran, 1948).
13 FO371/45478, Tabriz Diary, 30 June–13 July 1945, Katouzian, *Khatirat-i Siyasi*, pp. 363–74.
14 Pisiyan, *Marg bud*, p. 23.
15 Ibid., p. 21.
16 See report on the proceedings of the trial of Khalil Maliki, published in *Kayhan*, 5 March 1966; Abrahamian, 'Communism and Communalism', p. 311.
17 *Sida-yi Iran*, 26 September 1945.
18 *Dad*, 17 October 1945; *Iran-i Ma*, 9 December 1945.
19 *Rahbar*, 28 February 1944; Jami, *Guzashtih*, pp. 251–2.
20 The moderation of the Tudeh programme was remarked upon by the British foreign secretary, Ernest Bevin, who suggested that it should be circulated to the British cabinet 'to show how near their ideas are to labour policy here'. FO371/52705, note by Bevin on a Bullard to Eden dispatch, 21 June 1946.

21 FO371/45434, minute on the Tudeh and ADP programmes, 7 October 1945.
22 *Azarbaijan*, 17 September 1945.
23 *Ittila'at*, 27 November 1945; *Iran-i Ma*, 1 December 1945.
24 *Iran-i Ma*, 10 and 11 December 1945.
25 *Rahbar*, 14 March and 22 April 1946.
26 *Iran-i Ma*, 6 June 1946; *Rahbar*, 15 June 1946; see also A. Amidi-Nuri (ed.), *Azarbaijan-i Dimukrat*, Tehran, 1946.
27 Abrahamian, 'Communism and Communalism', p. 315. Radio broadcasts by the Firqih from the USSR were monitored by the BBC. See *Summary of World Broadcasts*, July–August 1953.
28 Abrahamian, 'Communism and communalism', p. 316. On the changes in Soviet policy towards the nationalist question see, R.E. Kanet (ed.), *The Soviet Union and the Developing Nations* (London, 1974), pp. 21, 28; E.P. Thornton (ed.), *The Third World in Soviet Perspective* (Princeton, 1964), pp. 17–27.
29 SD891.00, 'Memorandum concerning the social and political economy of Azerbaijan', 2 October 1943.
30 Lambton, 'The Azerbaijan problem', pp. 55–6; Homayounpour, *L'Affaire d'Azarbaidjan*, pp. 45.
31 SD891.00, Tehran, 10 December 1945.
32 SD891.00, 'The end of Democrat party control in Azerbaijan', Tehran, 30 December 1946.
33 The committee included: Pishihvari, Javid, Shabistari, Biriya, Padigan, Qiyami, Rafi'i, Ilhami and Shams. Abrahamian, 'Communism and Communalism', pp. 309–10. The list given in *Iran-i Ma* on 7 December omitted Shams and included Mashinchi.
34 Prime minister and acting minister of labour, Pishihvari; minister of the interior, Javid; minister of defence, Kaviyan; minister of education, Biriya; minister of justice, Azima; minister of agriculture, Mahtash; minister of health, Urangi; minister of post and telecommunications, Kabiri; minister of commerce and economy, Rasuli; Supreme Court judge, Qiyami; prosecutor general, Ibrahimi. Sources: *Azarbaijan*, 12 December 1945, cited in Jami, *Guzashtih*; Homayounpour, *L'Affaire d'Azarbaidjan*, p. 77; SD891.00, Tabriz 21 December 1945.
35 Abrahamian, *Iran*, pp. 388–415.
36 Abrahamian, 'Communism and Communalism', pp. 298, 305; Avery, *Modern Iran*, pp. 386–7.
37 Biographical details taken from US Library of Congress, Declassified Documents, Persia, 12C, 'Report to the National Security Council on the position of the United States with respect to Iran', Appendix D ('Significant biographical data'), 21 July 1947; FO371/35070, Tabriz, 9 July 1943; Ladjevardi, *Labour Unions and Autocracy*, p. 255. A. Amir Khizi, *Qiyam-i Azarbaijan va Sattar Khan* (Tabriz, 1960).
38 *Rahbar*, 31 November 1944.
39 Abrahamian, *Iran*, p. 404.
40 FO371/45432, 'The Tudeh as a party serving the Russians', Tehran to FO, 7 May 1945; FO371/40817, 'Report on the first general conference of the Tudeh party' Tehran to FO, 26 August 1944; US Library of Congress, Declassified Docs.,

Persia, 12C, 'Report to the National Security Council'; Ladjevardi, *Labour Unions and Autocracy*, pp. 260–1.

41 FO371/52663, 'Report on conditions in Azerbaijan, August–December 1945', Tehran, 12 January 1946; SD891.00, Tabriz, 16 March 1944 and 28 February 1945, Ladjevardi, *Labour Unions and Autocracy*, p. 256.

42 The US vice-consul, Rossow, claimed incorrectly that Biriya had been killed by an angry crowd in Tabriz. Rossow, 'The battle of Azerbaijan', pp. 30–1.

43 SD891.00, Tabriz, 29 June and 18 July 1945; Abrahamian, *Iran*, pp. 389–93; Homayounpour, *L'Affaire d'Azarbaidjan*, p. 75.

44 SD891.00, Tabriz, 21 December 1945; *Azerbaijan*, 30 November 1945; Abrahamian, 'Communism and Communalism', pp. 309–10.

45 SD891.00, Biographical data on Salamallah Javid, Tehran, 15 July 1946; Abrahamian, *Iran*, p. 398.

46 SD891.00, Tabriz, 12 December 1945; Abrahamian, 'Communism and Communalism', pp. 308, 310.

47 According to some sources, the former Tudeh member, Ghulam Dahishiyan, was involved in the organisation of the Democrats' armed forces. See Ememi-Yeganeh, 'Iran vs. Azerbaijan', p. 15; Homayounpour, *L'Affaire d'Azarbaidjan*, p. 137.

48 On Pishihvari's early life see: J. Pishihvari, 'Sarguzasht-i Man', *Azhir*, 6 December 1943; US Library of Congress, Declassified Docs., Persia, 12C, 'Report to the Security Council'; SD891.00, 'Data on Pishevari' (Taken from various issues of *Azerbaijan*), Tabriz, 21 June 1946; Abrahamian, 'Communism and Communalism', pp. 306–8; Ladjevardi, *Labour Unions and Autocracy*, p. 261.

49 SD891.00, 'Data on Pishevari', Tabriz, 21 June 1946; Nollau and Wiehe, *Russia's South Flank*, pp. 26–8; W. Laqueur, *The Soviet Union and the Middle East* (London, 1959), p. 30.

50 Katouzian, *Khatirat-i Siyasi*, pp. 303–7.

51 *Azhir*, 4 January and 13 June 1944; Abrahamian, 'Communism and Communalism', p. 306.

52 FO371/40187, 'Report on the first General Conference of the Tudeh Party', 26 August 1944.

53 See for example, Fatemi, *USSR in Iran*, p. 59; Zabih, *Communist Movement in Iran*, pp. 87, 98.

54 *Azhir*, 7 September 1944.

55 See for example, F. Alavi, *Pishihvari Chist?* (Tehran, 1946), p. 31.

56 Cottam, *Nationalism in Iran*, pp. 129–30.

57 See Fred Halliday, 'Steppes towards secession?', *The Times Literary Supplement*, 22–8 June 1990, pp. 661–2.

3 The year of crisis: 1946

1 Abrahamian, *Iran*, chapter 5; Azimi, *Iran: Crisis of Democracy*; M. Davudi, *Qavam al-Saltaneh* (Tehran, 1948).

2 *FRUS* (1946), vol. VII, p. 495.

3 Ibid., p. 375.
4 *Azerbaijan*, 26 September 1945.
5 SD891.00, Tehran, 12 December 1945; FO371/44539, FO to Tehran, 14 December 1945.
6 FO371/52740, Tabriz Diary, January 1946; *FRUS* (1946), vol. VII, pp. 564–5.
7 *Azerbaijan*, 25 November 1945; *Rahbar*, 15 June 1946.
8 SD891.00, Tabriz, 24 January 1946.
9 *Azerbaijan*, 27 December 1945.
10 Speeches by Hakimi to the majlis sessions of 12 and 18 December 1945, cited in SD891.00, Tehran, 13 and 19 December 1945; FO371/45440, 'Observation of the Persian government on the text of a Soviet reply to an American note on the situation in Azerbaijan', 12 December 1945.
11 SD891.00, 'Appeal to the US President on behalf of the clerics of Tehran for action in settling the present crisis' (dated 17 December 1945), Tehran, 11 January 1946; Lambton, 'The Azerbaijan problem', p. 55.
12 FO371/45440, Tabriz to Tehran, 20 December 1945; FO371/52661,Tehran to FO, 8 January 1946; *FRUS* (1945), vol. VII, p. 462.
13 FO371/45439, Tehran to FO, 18 December 1945; ibid., FO to Moscow, 22 December 1945; *FRUS* (1945), vol. VII, p. 433.
14 *The Daily Telegraph*, 17 December 1945.
15 FO371/45439, Tehran to all Consuls, 12 December 1945; ibid., Tehran to FO, 18 December 1945.
16 *Kayhan*, 5 December 1945.
17 FO371/45452, Tehran to FO, 22 December 1945.
18 See below p. 101.
19 See further chapter 6.
20 FO371/52667, 'Russia and North Persia'.
21 Mussadiq's speech to the majlis session of 10 January, SD891.00, Tehran, 11 January 1946; Fatemi, *USSR in Iran*, pp. 92, 95–6; F. Diba, *Mohammad Mossadegh. A Political Biography* (London, 1986), p. 81.
22 *Azerbaijan*, 10 January 1946; FO371/52663, Moscow to FO, 22 January 1946.
23 *Dad*, 18 January, 1946; *Azerbaijan*, 8 January 1946.
24 FO371/45440, Tabriz to Tehran, 20 December 1945; FO371/52661, Tehran to FO, 8 January 1946; Homayounpour, *L'Affaire d'Azarbaidjan*, pp. 137–40; Pisiyan, *Marg bud*, pp. 126–9.
25 FO371/52740, Tabriz Diary, January–February 1946; *Azerbaijan*, 8 January 1946.
26 *Dad*, 18 December 1945.
27 FO371/52740, Tabriz Diary, January–February 1946; Fatemi, *USSR in Iran*, p. 89.
28 FO371/52740, Tabriz Diary, November–December 1945.
29 SD891.00, Tabriz, 26 January 1946; Eagleton, *Kurdish Republic of 1946*, pp. 43–6.
30 *Azerbaijan*, 10 January 1946; SD891.00, Tabriz, 15 January 1946.
31 See further Richard W. Van Wagenen, *The United Nations Action. The Iranian Case 1946* (New York, 1952), pp. 30–41.

32 FO371/52710, Intelligence Summaries, December 1945–January 1946; FO371/52662, Tehran to FO, 20 January 1946; *Journal de Tehran*, 31 December 1946.

33 FO371/52664, Tehran to FO, 15 February 1946; Abrahamian, *Iran*, pp. 227–8.

34 Qavam's mission to Moscow is discussed in chapter 5.

35 FO371/52710, Intelligence Summary, 11–17 March 1946, Lenczowski, *Russia and the West in Iran*.

36 *The New York Times*, 27 January 1946.

37 FO371/52710, Intelligence Summary, 11–17 March 1946.

38 Van Wagenen, *The Iranian Case*, pp. 30–65; Kuniholm, *Origins of the Cold War in the Near East*, pp. 326–42; see also chapter 5.

39 R.M. Slusser and J.F. Triska, *A Calendar of Soviet Treaties 1917–1957* (Stanford, 1959), pp. 208–9; see also FO371/52672, Tehran to FO, 5 April 1946, which contains the text with comments by the British ambassador.

40 See chapter 1, p. 30.

41 *FRUS* (1946), vol. VII, p. 371.

42 FO371/52672, Tehran to FO, 15 April 1946.

43 *Jibhih*, 19 April 1946; *Azerbaijan*, 22 May 1946. See further pp. 127–8.

44 SD891.00, Washington, 16 May 1946; FO371/52676, Tehran to FO, 22 May 1946; Ramazani, *Iran's Foreign Policy*, p. 143.

45 FO371/52672, Tehran to FO, 10 April 1946; FO371/52676, 22 May 1946; SD891.00, Tehran, 11 April and 31 May 1946.

46 FO371/45432, 'Statement on British policy in Persia, prepared by Prince Muzaffar Firuz', n.d.

47 Abrahamian, *Iran*, p. 227; Azimi, *Iran: Crisis of Democracy*, pp. 148–9.

48 *Ittila'at*, 23 April 1946; FO371/52710, Intelligence Summary, 22–8 April 1946; Fatemi, *USSR in Iran*, pp. 135–8.

49 *Azerbaijan*, 1 April 1946; *Azad Millat*, 26 April 1946.

50 SD891.00, Tabriz, 24 April 1946; *Azerbaijan*, 15 May 1946.

51 FO371/52740, Tabriz Diary, May 1946.

52 SD891.00, Tabriz, 7 May 1946; Roosevelt, 'Kurdish Republic of Mahabad', pp. 258–9.

53 FO371/52679, Tabriz consular report, 30 July 1946; SD891.00, 25 April 1946.

54 SD891.00, Tehran, 4 and 8 May 1946; Pisiyan, *Marg bud*, p. 219.

55 See further pp. 104–5.

56 *Rahbar*, 15 June 1946; *Azerbaijan*, 15 May 1946.

57 FO371/52710, Intelligence Summaries, May–June 1946.

58 FO371/52714, Tehran to FO, 28 May 1946.

59 FO371/52710, Intelligence Summary, 25 March–7 April 1946; FO371/52676, Tehran to FO, 29 May 1946.

60 FO371/52710, Intelligence Summary, 11–17 March 1946.

61 *Azerbaijan*, 25 June 1946; *Sitarih*, 26 June 1946.

62 SD891.00, Tabriz, 21 June 1946.

63 *Kayhan*, 14 June 1946.

64 FO371/52740, Tabriz Diary, June 1946.

65 *Azerbaijan*, 22 November 1946.

66 N.S. Fatemi, *Oil Diplomacy* (New York, 1954), p. 319.
67 SD891.00, Tehran, 17 June 1946.
68 *Azerbaijan*, 10 January 1946; SD891.00, Tabriz, 4 January 1946.
69 FO371/52740, Tabriz Diary, December 1945.
70 *Azerbaijan*, 18 February 1946.
71 FO371/52740, Tabriz Diary, March 1946; SD891.00, 'General review of conditions in the Iranian province of Azerbaijan', Tabriz, 21 August 1947.
72 Ibid.; FO371/52740, Tabriz Diaries, December 1945–February 1946.
73 *Azerbaijan*, 5 February 1946.
74 FO371/52740, Tabriz Diaries, January–February 1946.
75 Ibid., January and May 1946; FO371/52679, 'Six monthly report', Tabriz, 30 July 1946.
76 *Azerbaijan*, 3 September 1945.
77 Ibid., 18 January 1946; FO371/52740, Tabriz Diary, March 1946.
78 Ibid.; FO371/52679, 'Six monthly report', Tabriz, 30 July 1946. For a study on rural conditions in Iran, see further Lambton, *Landlord and Peasant in Persia*.
79 *Azerbaijan*, 28 May 1946.
80 FO371/52679, 'Six monthly report', Tabriz, 30 July 1946; SD891.00, 'General review of conditions in Azerbaijan', Tabriz, 21 August 1947; Wasserberg, 'Politics of Soviet interference', p. 172.
81 FO371/52740, Tabriz Diary, January 1946; FO371/52679, 'Six monthly report', Tabriz, 30 July 1946; *Azerbaijan*, 16 June 1946.
82 *Dad*, 18 February 1946.
83 FO371/52740, Tabriz Diary, January 1946.
84 Ibid., Tabriz Diary, February 1946; *Azerbaijan*, 7 February 1946.
85 *Azerbaijan*, 21 May 1946.
86 SD891.00, Tabriz, 20 February 1946.
87 Article 13 stated that Kurds living in Azerbaijan would enjoy the advantages of the agreement, and that Kurdish would be the language of instruction for the first years of primary school. *Azerbaijan*, 16 June 1946; Eagleton, *Kurdish Republic of 1946*, pp. 93–94.
88 SD891.00, Tabriz, 24 June and 9 July 1946; FO371/52711, Intelligence Summary, 17–23 June 1946.
89 FO371/52705, 'Summary of the Persian prime minister's new party', 1 July 1946; *Journal de Tehran*, 1 July 1946.
90 *Jibhih*, 30 June 1946.
91 SD891.00, Tehran, 6 August 1946.
92 Pahlavi, *Mission For My Country*, p. 116.
93 FO371/52706, Tehran to FO, 4 August 1946; Fatemi, *USSR in Iran*, p. 140.
94 FO371/52677, Tehran to FO, 9 June 1946; SD891.00, Tehran, 6 August 1946.
95 FO371/526706, Tehran to FO, 20 October 1946; SD891.00, 'Abadan strike news', 15 July 1946.
96 *Rahbar*, 4 August 1946; FO371/52706, Tehran to FO, 20 October 1946.
97 FO371/52706, Tehran to FO, 4 August 1946; Fatemi, *USSR in Iran*, p. 142.
98 FO371/52706, Tehran to FO, 2 August 1946.

99 Ibid., Tehran to FO, 8 August 1946; Azimi, *Iran: Crisis of Democracy*, pp. 155–6.

100 FO371/52706, Tehran to FO, 20 October 1946; SD891.00, 10 and 26 August 1946.

101 FO371/52706, Tehran to FO, 20 October 1946; SD891.00, 13 July 1946.

102 FO371/52710, Intelligence Summaries 22–8 April and 2–12 May 1946.

103 SD891.00, Tehran 12 August 1946.

104 FO371/52710, Intelligence Summaries, August – September 1946; SD891.00, Tehran, 10 September 1946; Pierre Oberling, *The Qashqa'i Nomads of Fars* (The Hague, 1974), pp. 183–90.

105 FO371/52681, Tehran to FO, 13 September 1946; FO371/52706, Tehran to FO, 20 October 1946.

106 FO371/52711, Intelligence Summary, 26 August–1 September 1946.

107 SD891.00, Tehran, 21 September 1946.

108 See further pp. 171–2.

109 FO371/52711, Intelligence Summary, 23–9 September 1946; FO371/52682, Shiraz to Tehran, 19 September 1946; SD891.00, 23 September 1946.

110 Ibid.

111 FO371/52711, Intelligence Summary, 23–9 September 1946.

112 FO371/52711, Intelligence Summary, 30 September–6 October 1946; FO371/52706, 20 October 1946; SD891.00, Tehran 14 October 1946.

113 FO371/52706, Le Rougetel to Bevin, 12 August 1946.

114 *Rahbar*, 7 August 1946.

115 FO371/52706, Le Rougetel to Bevin, 12 August 1946.

116 FO371/52685, Tehran to FO, 12 October 1946; SD891.00, Tehran, 14 October 1946.

117 *Iran-i Ma*, 15 October 1946.

118 SD891.00, Tehran, 18 October 1946; *Rahbar*, 19 October 1946.

119 FO371/52684, Tehran to FO, 16 and 18 October 1946.

120 FO371/52685, Tehran to FO, 28 October 1946.

121 *FRUS* (1946), vol. VII, p. 513.

122 SD891.00, 21 October 1946.

123 SD891.00, Tehran, 21 August 1946.

124 FO371/52740, Tabriz Diaries, August–September 1946.

125 SD891.00, Tehran, 21 August 1946.

126 SD891.00, 'General review of conditions in Azerbaijan', Tabriz, 21 August 1947.

127 SD891.00, Tehran, 10 and 27 August 1946.

128 SD891.00, Tehran, 8 September 1946; FO371/52681, Tehran to FO, 20 September 1946.

129 SD891.00, Tabriz, 27 August 1946; FO371/52682, Tehran to FO, 25 September 1946.

130 FO371/52740, Tabriz Diary, August 1946; SD891.00, Tabriz, 7 August 1946.

131 *Azad Millat*, 25 August 1946; FO371/52740, Tabriz Diary, August 1946.

132 SD891.00, Tabriz, 27 August and 9 September 1946; H.E. Chehabi, *Iranian Politics and Religious Modernism. The Liberation Movement of Iran under the Shah and Khomeini* (London, 1990), p. 119.

133 FO371/52711, Intelligence Summary, 16–22 September 1946.

134 SD891.00, Tehran, 30 September 1946.

135 Ibid., 5 and 14 October 1946.

136 Ibid.; FO371/Tehran to FO, 6 October 1946.

137 *Kayhan*, 17 October 1946.

138 SD891.00, Tehran, 14 October 1946.

139 Ibid., 21 and 24 October 1946.

140 Ibid., 28 October 1946; FO371/52706, Tehran to FO, 6 November 1946.

141 FO371/52685, Tehran to Foreign Office, 29 October 1946.

142 *Monitoring Report*, 21 November 1946; FO371/52686, Tehran to FO, 20 November 1946.

143 *Azerbaijan*, 22 November 1946; SD891.00, 'End of Democrat party control in Azerbaijan', Tabriz, 30 December 1946.

144 *Azad Millat*, 6 November 1946; FO371/52706, Le Rougetel to Bevin, 4 November 1946.

145 SD891.00, 'Political review of the period 23 October to 5 November', Tehran, 21 November 1946.

146 FO371/52711, Intelligence Summary, 18–24 November 1946; SD891.00, Tabriz, 23 November 1946; *Jibhih*, 13 November 1946.

147 *Rahbar*, 28 November 1946; *Azerbaijan*, 25 November 1946.

148 SD891.00, Tehran, 29 November 1946; FO371/52686, Tehran to FO, 27 November 1946.

149 *Azerbaijan*, 27 November 1946.

150 SD891.00, 'End of Democrat party control in Azerbaijan', Tabriz, 30 December 1946, *Azerbaijan*, 26 November 1946.

151 FO371/52686, Tehran to FO, 28 November 1946.

152 Ibid., 2 December 1946.

153 SD891.00, Tehran, 5 December 1946.

154 *Azerbaijan*, 11 December 1946; For the text of Biriya's announcement see SD891.00, 'End of Democrat party control in Azerbaijan', Enclosure No. 2, Tabriz, 30 December 1946.

155 FO371/52688, Tehran to FO, 13 December 1946.

156 SD891.00, Tehran, 8 December 1946.

157 SD891.00, Tabriz, 11 December 1946; *Dad*, 19 December 1946. According to some reports the local population had turned against the Democrats even before the arrival of central government troops. See SD891.00, Tehran, 15 January 1946; Nollau and Wiehe, *Russia's South Flank*, p. 35.

158 SD891.00, Tehran, 24 December 1946; ibid., Tabriz, 20 February 1947.

159 Roosevelt, 'Kurdish Republic of Mahabad', pp. 266–8; Eagleton, *Kurdish Republic of 1946*, pp. 111–29; N.Q. Pisiyan, *Az Mahabad-i Khunin ta Karaniha-yi Aras* (Tehran, 1948), pp. 4–7.

160 SD891.00, Tehran, 5 February 1947; ibid., 'The disintegration of the Democrat-e-Iran party', Tehran, 30 December 1947.

161 SD891.00, Tehran, 9 October 1947; Avery, *Modern Iran*, p. 399.

162 SD891.00, Tehran, 20 December 1946 and 10 February 1947.

163 Kazemi, 'Military and politics in Iran', p. 222. According to one historian, the Shah had taken personal command of the operations leading to the reoccupation of Azerbaijan. See Ramazani, *Iran's Foreign Policy*, pp. 151–2.

164 See p. 139.

165 FO371/61971, Tehran to FO, 23 May 1947.

166 SD891.00, Tehran 26 February and 9 May 1947.

167 Ibid., 3 July 1947; ibid., 'Disintegration of the Democrat-e-Iran party', Tehran, 30 December 1947. For details of the fifteen majlis elections see Azimi, *Iran: Crisis of Democracy*, pp. 164–72.

168 SD891.00, 'Address by Prime Minister Qavam to the Iranian majlis, September 14, 1947', Tehran, 9 October 1947.

169 FO371/61974, *FRUS*, (1947), vol. V, pp. 969–70. See further below, pp. 106–7.

170 Qavam's demise and departure are well described in the December dispatches from Tehran in SD891.00, but see in particular, 'Disintegration of the Democrat-e-Iran party', Tehran, 30 December 1947. See also Azimi, *Iran: Crisis of Democracy*, pp. 175–9.

4 The Soviet challenge

1 FO371/52667, 'Russia and North Persia', Tehran, 3 March 1946.

2 See further Firuz Kazemzadeh, *Russia and Britain in Persia, 1864–1914* (New Haven, 1968); Muriel Atkin, *Russia and Iran, 1780–1828* (Minneapolis, 1980).

3 Firuz Kazemzadeh, 'Russia and the Middle East', in *Russian Foreign Policy, Essays in Historical Perspective* (ed.), I.V. Lederer (London, 1962), p. 508.

4 See below, p. 141.

5 Dmytryshyn and Cox, *Soviet Union and the Middle East*, pp. 244–9.

6 Kazemzadeh, 'Russia and the Middle East', p. 251.

7 Eudin and North, *Soviet Russia and the East*, p. 92.

8 See above pp. 10–11. For a comparison of Soviet methods in Gilan and Azerbaijan, see Wasserberg, 'Politics of Soviet interference'.

9 Ivar Spectar, *The Soviet Union and the Muslim World 1917–1958* (Seattle, 1959), pp. 91–6. See also above p. 13.

10 Eudin and North, *Soviet Russia and the East*, p. 91.

11 Dmytryshyn and Cox, *Soviet Union and the Middle East*, pp. 288–92; Slusser and Triska, *Calendar of Soviet Treaties*, pp. 61–2.

12 See further Rezun, *The Soviet Union and Iran*, pp. 318–35.

13 Dmytryshyn and Cox, *Soviet Union and the Middle East*, pp. 338–9.

14 R. Sontag and J. Beddie (eds.), *Nazi–Soviet Relations, 1939–1941: Documents from the Archives of the German Foreign Office* (Washington, 1948), pp. 258–9.

15 *FRUS*, (1940) vol. III, pp. 621–2.

16 Vojtech Mastny, *Russia's Road to the Cold War: Diplomacy, Warfare and the Politics of Communism, 1941–1945* (New York, 1979), p. xvii.

17 William O. McCagg, *Stalin Embattled, 1943–1948* (Detroit, 1978), p. 39.

18 FO371/35902, Tehran to FO, 30 March 1943.

19 Winston S. Churchill, *The Second World War, III, The Grand Alliance* (London, 1950), p. 430.
20 FO371/27154, Tabriz, 7 September 1941.
21 Churchill, *Grand Alliance*, p. 431.
22 Dmytryshyn and Cox, *Soviet Union and the Middle East*, p. 263.
23 M. Vahdat, 'The Soviet Union and the movement to establish autonomy in Iranian Azerbaijan' (Indiana University, Ph.D. thesis, 1958), p. 83.
24 FO371/31420, Tabriz Diary, July–August 1942.
25 FO371/27155, Tabriz, 31 August 1941.
26 SD891.00, Tabriz, 4 January 1944; FO371/27156, Tabriz, 28 September 1941.
27 FO371/35109, Intelligence Summary, 31 March–6 April 1943; see also Katouzian, *Political Economy of Modern Iran*, p. 152.
28 SD891.00, 'Review of the Azerbaijan political situation', Tabriz, 4 January 1944.
29 FO371/27221, Tabriz, 25 September 1941, FO371/27154, FO minute, 6 October 1941.
30 FO371/27156, Tabriz, 28 September 1941.
31 FO371/27157, press attaché's report, 4 October 1941.
32 See above, pp. 22–3.
33 SD891.00, Tabriz, 16 July 1942.
34 FO371/27219, Tehran to FO, 19 September 1941.
35 FO371/31426, Tabriz, 14 December 1941 and 20 February 1942.
36 Avery, *Modern Iran*, p. 353.
37 FO371/31426, Tabriz Diary, September–October 1942; SD891.00, Tabriz, 24 August 1942.
38 FO371/35109, Intelligence Summary, 10–16 February 1943.
39 SD891.00, Tabriz, 31 August 1943.
40 Ibid., Tabriz, 11 August 1943.
41 SD891.00, Tabriz, 24 July 1943; ibid., Tabriz, 6 September 1942.
42 Ibid., Tabriz, 18 September and 2 October 1943.
43 FO371/20830, 'Report on the economic and financial situation of Azerbaijan', Tabriz, 31 December 1936.
44 SD891.00, Tabriz, 24 July 1943; FO371/40178, Tabriz, 22 August 1944.
45 FO371/27157, Tabriz to Tehran, 13 October 1942.
46 SD891.00, Tabriz, 20 March 1943.
47 FO371/27227, Moscow to FO, 30 September 1941.
48 Sir Llewelyn Woodward, *British Foreign Policy in the Second World War* (London, 1962), p. 316.
49 Winston S. Churchill, *The Second World War, IV, The Hinge of Fate* (London, 1951), pp. 459–60.
50 SD891.00, Tabriz, 30 June 1943.
51 FO371/40178, Tabriz, 22 August 1944.
52 SD891.00, Tehran, 8 March 1943.
53 SD891.00, Tabriz, 10 November 1943.
54 Stalin offered the Shah twenty aircraft, and offered to establish a flying school with Soviet instructors. FO371/40171, Tehran, 27 January 1944; FO371/52667, Tehran, 3 March 1944.

55 Kuniholm, *Cold War in the Near East*, pp. 147–8. See also Mastny, *Russia's Road to the Cold War*, pp. 71–2.

56 *Kharvar-i Now*, 9 July 1944; SD891.00, Tabriz, 20 May and 12 July 1944.

57 Rezun, *The Soviet Union and Iran*, pp. 73–4, 234, 374–5; Elwell Sutton, *Persian Oil*, p. 107.

58 FO371/52667, Tehran to FO, 3 March 1946; Greaves, 'The reign of Muhammad Riza Shah', p. 58.

59 *Rahbar*, 25 October 1944.

60 FO371/40178, Tehran to FO, 2 November 1944. See also pp. 28–9.

61 *Rahbar*, 19 and 26 November 1944; *Pravda* articles cited in FO371/40188, Moscow to FO, 24 October 1944.

62 *New York Times*, 30 October 1944; Kuniholm, *Cold War in the Near East*, p. 197.

63 FO371/40241, Tehran to FO, 3 and 10 October 1944.

64 Elwell Sutton, *Persian Oil*, p. 111.

65 Diane Shaver Clemens, *Yalta* (New York, 1970), pp. 255–8; Kuniholm, *Cold War in the Near East*, pp. 215–16, 272–3; Sicker, *The Bear and the Lion*, pp. 66–8.

66 Sir Anthony Eden, *The Eden Memoirs: The Reckoning* (London, 1965), pp. 595–6.

67 FO371/40178, Tabriz Diaries, September–November 1944.

68 SD891.00, Tabriz, 28 October 1944.

69 FO371/40178, Tabriz Diaries, October–November 1944.

70 FO371/40177, Tabriz Diary, March–April 1944; SD891.00, Tabriz, 5 and 25 September 1944.

71 *Soviet Monitor* (a Foreign Office publication), 26 May 1945; SD891.00, Tabriz, 4 May 1945.

72 FO371/40177, Tabriz Diary, June–July 1944.

73 FO371/45463, Tehran, 27 March 1945; SD891.00, Tabriz, 28 June 1944.

74 FO371/40178, Tabriz, 22 August 1944.

75 SD891.00, Tabriz, 1 February 1944; FO371/40177, Tabriz Diary, 1–14 February 1944.

76 FO371/31426, Tabriz, 18 December 1941; Homayounpour, *L'Affaire d'Azarbaidjan*, pp. 130, 146; Kisharvarz, *Man Muttaham Mikunam*, p. 65.

77 See further, Bennigsen and Broxup, *Islamic Threat to the Soviet State*, pp. 108–17; Marc Ferro, 'Des republiques à la derive', *Le Monde Diplomatique* (May 1990), pp. 10–11.

78 Yergin, *Shattered Peace*, pp. 179–81; Avery, *Modern Iran*, pp. 383–4; Sicker, *Bear and the Lion*, p. 71.

79 Malcolm Yapp, 'Soviet relations with countries of the Northern Tier', in *The Soviet Union and the Middle East* (eds.), A. and K. Dawisha (London, 1982), p. 33.

80 SD891.00, Tabriz, 15 May 1945.

81 FO371/40178, Tabriz, 22 August 1944; SD891.00, Tabriz, 14 March 1945.

82 FO371/45432, Tehran to FO, 11 July 1945.

83 *Pravda*, 9 July 1945, cited in FO371/45432, 12 July 1945.

84 FO371/45430, Tehran 3 January 1945.

85 *Monitoring Report*, 9–10 July 1945; *Kharvar-i Now*, 31 May 1945.

86 FO371/45478, Tabriz Diary, September 1945.

87 Ibid., October 1945.
88 Ibid., October–November 1945; FO371/45437, Ministry of Information report, 25 November 1945.
89 SD891.00, Tabriz, 12 December 1945; Homayounpour, *L'Affaire d'Azarbaidjan*, p. 60; Pisiyan, *Marg bud*, p. 27.
90 B. Abdurazakov, *Prouski Angliiskovo i Americanskovo Imperializma v Irane (1941–1947 godi)*, (Tashkent, 1959), pp. 72–9.
91 *Pravda*, 25 November 1945; *Izvestia*, 27 November 1945; FO371/45459, Intelligence Summary, 19–25 November 1945.
92 FO371/45459 Intelligence Summaries, 26 November–3 December and 4–9 December 1945; SD891.00, Tehran, 18 October 1945.
93 SD891.00, Tehran, 22 November 1945.
94 FO371/52661, Tabriz, 17 December 1945; ibid., Moscow, 3 January 1946.
95 FO371/52662, correspondence concerning discussions on Persia at the Moscow Conference of Foreign Ministers, 18 December 1945.
96 FO371/52662, extract of conversation between Bevin and Molotov, Moscow, 19 January 1946; A. Bullock, *Ernest Bevin, Foreign Secretary 1945–1951* (London, 1983), p. 207.
97 FO371/45471, Moscow, 14 December 1945.
98 SD891.00, Tehran, 26 November 1945.
99 FO371/52667, 'Russia and North Persia', Tehran, 3 March 1946.
100 FO371/52662, Dominions Office circular, 31 December 1945. See further below, p. 164.
101 See above p. 58.
102 Hakimi had been a Persian delegate to the Paris Peace Conference in 1919 when Iran had put forward a request that Baku, Turkestan and Armenistan should be returned to Iran.
103 Van Wagenen, *The Iranian Case*, pp. 30–41; Kuniholm, *Cold War in the Near East*, pp. 306–7.
104 FO371/52665, Moscow, 1 March 1946. See also above p. 59.
105 *FRUS* (1946), vol. VII, p. 335; FO371/52666, Moscow, 7 March 1946.
106 *FRUS* (1946), vol. VII, p. 337.
107 Adam B. Ulam, *Expansion and Coexistence: Soviet Foreign Policy, 1917–1973* (London, 1968), p. 427.
108 SD891.00, Tehran, 24 April and 25 May 1946.
109 FO371/52672, Text of Qavam–Sadchikov communiqué, Tehran to FO, 5 April 1946.
110 *Pravda*, 5 April 1946.
111 See above p. 62.
112 FO371/52673, Foreign Office minute, 15 April 1946.
113 See above p. 74.
114 SD891.00, Tehran, 30 September and 28 October 1946.
115 FO371/52771, Intelligence Summary, 25 November–1 December 1946.
116 C. Sykes, 'Russia and Azerbaijan', *Soundings* (February, 1946), pp. 45–52.
117 *Manchester Guardian*, 10 December 1946.

118 *Pravda*, 1 December 1946; FO371/52686, Tehran to FO, 28 November 1946.
119 FO371/52711, Intelligence Summary, 2–8 December 1946.
120 Ibid., 22–8 April 1946; SD891.00, Tabriz, 5 June 1946. See also above p. 62.
121 FO371/52680, Moscow to FO, 23 and 30 August 1946.
122 See above p. 68.
123 SD891.00, Tehran, 1 December 1946; FO371/75458, 'General review of events in Persia', Tehran, 17 January 1949; Fatemi, *USSR in Iran*, p. 146.
124 *Pravda*, 19 December 1946; SD891.00, Tabriz, 14 and 17 December 1946.
125 One account of Pishihvari's death suggests he was killed on Soviet orders following a disagreement with Baqirov, the communist party chairman in Baku. See Kisharvarz, *Man Muttaham Mikunam*, pp. 64–6; SD891.00, Tehran, 7 August 1947.
126 FO371/61971, Tehran, 23 May 1947.
127 Ibid., Moscow, 5 August 1947.
128 See below, pp. 139–40.
129 FO371/61974, Moscow, 26 October and 6 November 1947.
130 Cited in Ulam, *Expansion and Coexistence*, p. 427.
131 FO371/61974, FO minute, 23 October 1947.
132 FO371/61975, Tehran, 24 November 1947; SD891.00, Tehran, 25 August and 30 November 1947.
133 See further A. Yodafat and M. Abir, *In the Direction of the Persian Gulf* (London, 1977); Sicker, *The Bear and the Lion*, chapters 5 and 6; Zalmay Khalilzad, 'Soviet dilemmas in Khomeini's Iran', in *Iran Since the Revolution. Internal Dynamics, Regional Conflict and the Superpowers* (ed.) Barry M. Rosen (Columbia, 1985), pp. 113–2.
134 See Herbert Feis, *Churchill, Roosevelt, Stalin. The War They Waged and the Peace They Sought* (London, 1957), pp. 448–9; Bullock, *Bevin*, p. 220.

5 America: the origins of a policy

1 Recent works on US–Iran relations in the war and postwar period include: Lytle, *Origins of the Iranian–American Alliance*; Goode, *United States and Iran, 1946–51*; James A. Bill, *The Eagle and the Lion: the Tragedy of American–Iranian Relations* (New Haven, 1988).
2 A. Y. Alexander and A. Nanes (eds.), *The United States and Iran: A Documentary History* (Maryland, 1980), pp. 2–5.
3 A. Yeselson, *United States–Persian Diplomatic Relations 1883–1921* (New Brunswick, NJ, 1956), pp. 105–29; Yapp, 'Last years of the Qajar dynasty', pp. 14–15. For Shuster's own account see Morgan Shuster, *The Strangling of Persia* (London, 1912).
4 Alexander and Nanes (eds.), *United States and Iran*, p. 20.
5 William J. Olson, *Anglo-Iranian Relations During World War I* (London, 1984), p. 19.
6 Yeselson, *United States–Persian Relations*, pp. 196–222; Knapp, 'The period of Riza Shah', pp. 25–6.

7 See 'Memorandum of an audience given to the American minister (Philip) by Reza Shah Pahlavi', 14 April 1927, cited in Alexander and Nanes (eds.), *United States and Iran*, pp. 41–4. For Millspaugh's personal account see Arthur Millspaugh, *The American Task in Persia* (New York, 1925).

8 Alexander and Nanes (eds.), *United States and Iran*, pp. 44–50; Kuniholm, *Cold War in the Near East*, p. 189; Lytle, *Origins of the Iranian–American Alliance*, pp. 5–7.

9 Alexander and Nanes (eds.), *United States and Iran*, pp. 51–7, 60–2.

10 Yeselson, *United States–Persian Relations*, p. 128.

11 SD891.00, memorandum by the Department of Near Eastern Affairs to the Department of State, 18 March 1933.

12 John De Novo, *American Interests and Policies in the Middle East, 1900–1939* (Minneapolis, 1963), pp. 167–208; Kuniholm, *Cold War in the Near East*, pp. 178–80.

13 See Ramazani, *Iran's Foreign Policy*, p. 18; Lytle, *Origins of the Iranian–American Alliance*, pp. 16–32.

14 *New York Daily Mirror*, 8 February 1936; *Brooklyn Eagle*, 13 June 1936, cited in *United States and Iran*, p. 70.

15 SD891.00, Tehran, 19 December 1941; letter from the Shah of Iran to President Roosevelt, 25 August 1941, and memorandum by Walter Murray, Chief of the Division of Near Eastern Affairs, Washington, 26 August 1941, in Alexander and Nanes (eds.), *United States and Iran*, pp. 77–8.

16 Ibid., pp. 79–80.

17 Kuniholm, *Cold War in the Near East*, pp. 158–61; *FRUS* (1941), vol. III, p. 446.

18 Alexander and Nanes (eds.), *United States and Iran*, p. 84.

19 SD891.00, Washington, 8 June 1942.

20 Bullock, *Bevin*, p. 133; SD891.00, Washington, 11 and 21 August 1942.

21 Alexander and Nanes (eds.), *United States and Iran*, p. 91; M.K. Sheehan, *Iran: Impact of United States Interests and Policies, 1941–1954* (Brooklyn, 1968), p. 13.

22 Kuniholm, *Cold War in the Near East*, p. 145; T.H. Vail Motter, *The United States Army in World War II. The Middle East Theater: The Persian Corridor and Aid to Russia* (Washington, 1952).

23 Vail Motter, *Persian Corridor*, p. 163.

24 SD891.00, Washington, 14 August 1942; Alexander and Nanes (eds.), *United States and Iran*, p. 109.

25 For details of the various US missions see Lytle, *Origins of the Iranian–American Alliance*, pp. 27–32; Thomas M. Ricks, 'US military missions to Iran, 1943–1978: the political economy of military assistance', *Iranian Studies*, XII, 3–4 (Summer–Autumn 1979), pp. 163–93.

26 Welles to Roosevelt, 20 October 1942, Alexander and Nanes (eds.), *United States and Iran*, p. 110.

27 SD891.00, 'Notes of possible interest on the Persian Gulf area', Moscow, 26 June 1942; FO371/31420, memorandum by the US Embassy in London, 16 December 1942.

28 SD891.00, Tehran, 21 August 1942; ibid., Washington, 16 November 1942.

29 SD891.00, Washington, 14 December 1942.

30 FO371/31422, Tehran to FO, 21 December 1942.
31 FO371/31431, Tehran to FO, 20 October 1942; SD891.00, Tehran, 21 December 1942; Kuniholm, *Cold War in the Near East*, pp. 154–7.
32 FO371/35177, 'Report on political events in Persia for 1942', Tehran, January 1943.
33 Alexander and Nanes (eds.), *United States and Iran*, p. 101.
34 SD891.00, Tehran, 24 February 1943.
35 FO371/31420, Foreign Office minute, 16 December 1942.
36 SD891.00, Washington 16 November 1942; ibid., Tehran 24 February 1943.
37 Elliot Roosevelt, *As He Saw It* (New York, 1946), p. 37; Cordell Hull, *Memoirs*, II (London, 1948), pp. 1477–8; see also K.W. Thompson, *Cold War Theories*, I (London, 1981), p. 34.
38 SD891.00, Tehran, 24 February 1943.
39 Bullock, *Bevin*, pp. 216–17.
40 FO371/35906, Foreign Office minute, 13 February 1943.
41 Ibid., Tehran to FO, 24 March 1943.
42 FO371/35076, Washington to Foreign Office, 4 October 1943.
43 SD891.00, Tabriz, 20 March 1943; Woodward, *British Foreign Policy*, pp. 291, 316.
44 SD891.00, Tabriz, 1 and 25 February 1943.
45 See above p. 89.
46 SD891.00, Tabriz consular reports, 18 July and 6 September 1942 and 10 March 1943.
47 SD891.00, Tabriz consular reports, 30 June and 24 July 1943; ibid., Tehran, 8 March and 14 April 1943.
48 Ibid., Washington, 16 August 1943.
49 Kuniholm, *Cold War in the Near East*, pp. 149–50, 156; Alexander and Nanes (eds.), *United States and Iran*, pp. 105–6.
50 Alexander and Nanes (eds.), *United States and Iran*, p. 115; Kuniholm, *Cold War in the Near East*, pp. 171–3; Lytle, *Origins of the Iranian–American Alliance*, pp. 112–16.
51 SD891.00, Tabriz, 20 March 1943.
52 Dreyfus to Hull, 14 April 1943, Alexander and Nanes (eds.), *United States and Iran*, p. 101.
53 SD891.00, Tehran, 21 April 1943.
54 Hull to Roosevelt, 16 August 1943, Alexander and Nanes (eds.), *United States and Iran*, pp. 103–4.
55 SD891.00, Washington, 12 January 1944; Hull, *Memoirs*, vol. II, p. 1507.
56 Kuniholm, *Cold War in the Near East*, pp. 192–202; Lytle, *Origins of the Iranian–American Alliance*, pp. 73–8.
57 Woodward, *British Foreign Policy*, pp. 396–8; Kuniholm, *Cold War in the Near East*, p. 184.
58 See above pp. 94–5.
59 SD891.00, Tehran, 27 October 1944; *FRUS* (1944), vol. V, pp. 452–4; Lenczowski, *Russia and the West in Iran*, pp. 218–20.
60 Kuniholm, *Cold War in the Near East*, p. 187.

61 FO371/40242, Washington to FO, 7 November 1944; Woodward, *British Foreign Policy*, p. 316.
62 SD891.00, memorandum by Loy Henderson on US policy towards Iran, 23 August 1945.
63 On the shift in US policy see Lytle, *Origins of the Iranian–American Alliance*, in particular chapters 3 and 8.
64 *FRUS* (1944), vol. V, pp. 470–1.
65 Kuniholm, *Cold War in the Near East*, p. 174; Hess, 'The Iranian Crisis of 1945–6 and the Cold War', pp. 117–46.
66 SD891.00, Tehran, 25 September 1945.
67 'The present situation in Iran with regard to the Millspaugh mission (May–October 1944)', *United States and Iran*, pp. 120–21; Lytle, *Origins of the Iranian–American Alliance*, pp. 112–16. See also Arthur Millspaugh, *Americans in Persia* (Washington, 1946), pp. 129–54.
68 SD891.00, memorandum by the Near Eastern Department on the status of the advisory programmes, 25 August 1945; Alexander and Nanes (eds.), *United States and Iran*, pp. 133–9, 140–2.
69 SD891.00, Tehran, 23 October 1945.
70 Harry S. Truman, *Memoirs: Years of Trial and Hope* (New York, 1956), p. 98.
71 Bullock, *Bevin*, p. 236; Feis, *From Trust to Terror*, pp. 81–7. On the change in US policy see also, Richard Pfau, 'Containment in Iran, 1946: the shift to an active policy', *Diplomatic History*, 1 (Fall, 1977), pp. 359–72; Yergin, *Shattered Peace*, p. 179.
72 Milovan Djilas, *Conversations with Stalin* (New York, 1961), p. 114.
73 SD891.00, Tehran, 24 September 1945; Tabriz, 27 November 1945.
74 Ibid., Tehran, 12 December 1945.
75 See for example record of a conversation between majlis deputy, Dr Shafagh and Harold Minor, SD891.00, Washington, 12 December 1945.
76 *New York Times*, 6 October 1945.
77 SD891.00, Tehran, 16 October 1945.
78 George F. Kennan, *Memoirs, 1925–1950* (London, 1968), p. 287.
79 Yergin, *Shattered Peace*, p. 179; Bullock, *Bevin*, p. 206. For Brynes' own account see James F. Brynes, *Speaking Frankly* (London, 1947), pp. 118–21.
80 Harry S. Truman, *Memoirs: Year of Decisions* (New York, 1955), pp. 550–2.
81 *FRUS* (1946), vol. VII, p. 399.
82 Ibid., p. 340.
83 On US policy towards Greece and Turkey see L.S. Wittner, *American Intervention in Greece, 1943–1949* (New York, 1982); D.J. Alvarez, *Bureaucracy and Cold War Diplomacy: The United States and Turkey* (Thessalonika 1980). For a good comparative study of US policy towards Greece, Turkey and Iran see Kuniholm, *Cold War in the Near East*.
84 Truman, *Year of Decisions*, p. 460.
85 Hess, 'Iranian crisis of 1945–6', p. 117.
86 *FRUS* (1946), vol. VII, pp. 818–19.
87 *New York Times*, 14 March 1946; Feis, *From Trust to Terror*, pp. 82–3.

88 SD891.00, Tabriz, 9 January and 21 February 1946; Kuniholm, *Cold War in the Near East*, p. 318.
89 *FRUS* (1946), vol. VII, p. 342; FO371/52666, Washington to FO, 6 March 1946; ibid., FO minute, 9 March 1946.
90 Rossow, 'The battle for Azerbaijan', pp. 17–32.
91 Brynes, *Speaking Frankly*, p. 126.
92 *FRUS* (1946), vol. VII, pp. 365, 368.
93 Ibid., pp. 381–2. See also above p. 102.
94 Truman, *Years of Trial and Hope*, p. 101.
95 See for example K.A. Samii, 'Truman against Stalin in Iran: a tale of three messages', *Middle Eastern Studies*, XXIII, 1 (January 1987), pp. 95–107.
96 *FRUS* (1946), vol *VII*, p. 426.
97 Ibid., pp. 407–9; Alexander and Nanes (eds.), *United States and Iran*, p. 169; see also above p. 60.
98 *FRUS* (1946), vol. VII, pp. 427–31.
99 Trygve Lie, *In the Cause of Peace* (New York, 1954), p. 80.
100 Kuniholm, *Cold War in the Near East*, pp. 335–77.
101 L.V. Thomas and R.N. Frye, *The United States and Turkey and Iran* (Cambridge, Mass., 1951), pp. 239–40; Alvin Z. Rubinstein, (ed.), *The Foreign Policy of the Soviet Union* (New York, 1960), p. 207.
102 See below p. 164.
103 *FRUS* (1946), vol. VII, p. 378; Yergin, *Shattered Peace*, p. 180.
104 SD891.00, Tehran, 26 March 1946.
105 *New York Times*, 27 January 1946; *New York Herald Tribune*, 17 April 1946.
106 Cited in Habib Ladjevardi, 'The origins of US support for an autocratic Iran', *International Journal of Middle Eastern Studies*, XV (1983), p. 229.
107 SD891.00, Tehran, 6 June 1946.
108 See *United States and Iran*, p. 172; *FRUS* (1946), vol. VII, p. 476.
109 SD891.00, Tehran, 2 April 1946; *FRUS* (1946), vol. VII, p. 480.
110 SD891.00, Washington, 8 April 1946; ibid., 20 April 1946.
111 Memorandum by Brynes, 17 October 1945, *United States and Iran*, p. 153.
112 Ricks, 'US military missions to Iran', p. 173.
113 SD891.00, record of conversation between Allen and the Shah, Tehran, 21 May 1946.
114 Ibid., Tabriz, 30 May 1946 and 13 June 1946.
115 Ibid., Tehran, 17 June 1946.
116 *FRUS* (1946), vol. VII, p. 510; Kuniholm, *Cold War in the Near East*, pp. 303–4.
117 SD891.00, Tehran, 6, 13 and 25 August 1946.
118 FO371/52681, Tehran to FO, 13 September 1946. See also below p. 171.
119 SD891.00, Tehran, 13 September 1946.
120 SD891.00, Tehran, 13 September 1946.
121 Ibid., Tehran, 28 July 1946.
122 FO371/52682, Washington to FO, 27 September 1946.
123 SD891.00, Tehran 28 July 1946.
124 *FRUS* (1946), vol. VII, pp. 500–2.

125 Ibid., p. 495.
126 SD891.00, Tehran, 20 September 1946.
127 Ibid., Tehran, 30 September and 5 October 1946; Kuniholm, *Cold War in the Near East*, p. 393.
128 See above p. 103.
129 SD891.00, Tehran, 30 September 1946.
130 Memorandum of a conversation between Harold Minor, Dean Acheson and Husain Ala, Washington, 8 October 1946. See Alexander and Nanes (eds.), *United States and Iran*, p. 180.
131 Ibid., p. 181.
132 SD891.00, Washington, 11 October 1946.
133 SD891.00, Tehran, 6 and 14 October 1946.
134 Ibid., Letter from Allen to Minor, Tehran, 3 December 1946.
135 Ibid., Tehran, 2 November 1946.
136 Ibid., Tehran, 14 October, 6 and 8 November 1946.
137 Ibid., Tehran, 19 November 1946.
138 Letter from Acheson to Allen, 22 November 1946, Alexander and Nanes (eds.), *United States and Iran*, p. 182.
139 SD891.00, Tehran, 27 November 1946.
140 Ibid., Tehran, 2 December 1946.
141 Ibid., Washington, 2 December 1946.
142 *Azerbaijan*, 9 and 11 December 1946.
143 Alexander and Nanes (eds.), *United States and Iran*, p. 188.
144 SD891.00, 'Report on the end of Democratic party control in Azerbaijan', Tabriz, 30 December 1946.
145 Ibid.
146 *FRUS* (1947), vol. V, pp. 914–16.
147 Ibid., pp. 950–2; *New York Times*, 12 September 1947.
148 *FRUS* (1948), vol. V, pp. 93–4.
149 See, for example, R.K. Ramazani, *The United States and Iran: Patterns of Influence* (New York, 1982), pp. 1–18; Goode, *United States and Iran, 1946–51*, p. viii.

6 British power in Iran

1 See Rose Louise Greaves, *Persia and the Defence of India 1884–1892* (London, 1959); Malcolm E. Yapp, *Strategies of British India: Britain, Iran and Afghanistan 1798–1850* (Oxford, 1980); Ronald W. Ferrier, *The History of the British Petroleum Company: The Developing Years, 1901–1932*, I (Cambridge, 1982).
2 See further D. McLean, *Britain and Her Buffer State* (London, 1979), pp. 73–6; Olson, *Anglo-Iranian Relations During World War I*, pp. 11–23; see also above p. 83.
3 Yapp, 'Last years of the Qajar dynasty', p. 20. On the 1919 agreement see further, M.J. Olson, 'The genesis of the Anglo-Persian Agreement of 1919', in *Towards a Modern Iran*, (eds.) Kedourie and Haim, pp. 185–216.

4 SD641.88, 'The peculiar position of the British in Iran', Washington, 22 August 1950; Martin Wight, *Power Politics* (London, 1978), p. 166.
5 M. Leseur, *Les Anglais en Perse* (Paris, 1923), pp. 149, 173–92; Rezun, *Soviet Union and Iran*, pp. 41–3; Knapp, 'The period of Riza Shah', pp. 24–5.
6 Ferrier, *History of the British Petroleum Company*, p. 202.
7 FO371/24580, Halifax to Amery, 1 August 1940.
8 Sir Percy Sykes, *A History of Persia*, II (London, 1951), p. 414; Sir Hugh Knatchbull-Hugessen, *Diplomat in Peace and War* (London, 1949), p. 81. One of those who defended the Convention was Reader Bullard, see his *Britain and the Middle East* (London, 1951), pp. 57–8.
9 FO371/27233, India Office to War Office, 29 August 1941; FO371/24580, Amery to Halifax, 23 July 1940.
10 Ibid., Halifax to Amery, 1 August 1940.
11 FO371/27230, FO to Tehran, FO371/27211, FO minutes, 6 September 1941; ibid., Churchill to FO, 6 September 1941.
12 FO371/27208, Tehran to FO, 29 August 1941.
13 For a discussion of the circumstances leading to the occupation see F. Eshraghi, 'Anglo-Soviet occupation of Iran in August 1941', *Middle Eastern Studies*, XX, 1 (January, 1984), pp. 27–52.
14 FO371/27180, monthly report on economic conditions, March 1940.
15 FO371/27206, FO to Jeddah, 22 August 1941; FO371/35069, Middle East Security summary, 13 January 1943. See also Rezun, *Soviet Union and Iran*, pp. 319–33; Lenczowski, *Russia and the West in Iran*, pp. 160–2. For one view that German influence in Iran has been overstated see J.L. Wallach (ed.), *Germany and the Middle East 1835–1939* (Tel Aviv, 1975), pp. 117, 141.
16 FO371/27184, Tehran to FO, 15 August 1941; John Barnes and David Nicholson (eds.), *The Empire at Bay. The Leo Amery Diaries 1929–1945* (London, 1988), p. 711; Frank Brenchley, *Britain and the Middle East: An Economic History 1945–1987* (London, 1989), p. 54.
17 FO371/27217, India Office to FO, 14 September 1941. On the Shah's efforts to renegotiate the oil concession see Ferrier, *History of the British Petroleum Company*, pp. 588–631; Fatemi, *Oil Diplomacy*, pp. 172–93.
18 Barnes and Nicholson, *Empire at Bay*, pp. 660, 711.
19 *Summary of World Broadcasts*, August–September 1941; Sir Reader Bullard, *The Camels Must Go. An Autobiography* (London, 1961), p. 230; Avery, *Modern Iran*, pp. 357–8.
20 SD891.00, Tehran, 24 February 1943.
21 Ibid., 21 August 1941; FO371/27220, Tehran to FO, 21 September 1941.
22 FO371/27206, Persian Gulf resident to the Indian government, 16 August 1941.
23 FO371/27155, Tabriz to Tehran, 7 September 1941.
24 FO371/31388, FO minute, 18 January 1942.
25 *Treaty of Alliance between the United Kingdom and the Soviet Union and Iran* (HMSO, 1942).
26 FO371/27233, Memorandum to the Soviet ambassador in London, 27 September 1941. See also below pp. 163–4.

27 Churchill, *Grand Alliance*, p. 432.
28 See further Azimi, *Iran: Crisis of Democracy*, pp. 35–144.
29 FO371/27185, Tehran to FO, 26 September 1941.
30 FO371/52670, Bullard to Bevin, 15 March 1946. Before his posting to Iran in 1939, Bullard had a long record of service in the Middle East and the Balkans as well as the USSR. He became ambassador to Iran when the British legation was raised to the status of embassy at the end of 1943. See further his *The Camels Must Go*.
31 FO371/27169, FO to Tehran, 6 December 1941.
32 FO371/27233, Tehran to FO, 1 October 1941.
33 Olson, *Anglo-Iranian Relations*, p. 2.
34 SD891.00, Washington, 16 November 1942.
35 Raymond Smith, 'Ernest Bevin, British officials and British Soviet policy, 1945–47', in *Britain and the First Cold War* (ed.), Anne Deighton (London, 1990), pp. 32–50.
36 SD891.00, Tehran, 24 February 1943; ibid., Department of State, 14 December 1943. See also Victor Rothwell, *Britain and the Cold War 1941–1947* (London, 1982), p. 7.
37 'Memorandum on American policy in Iran', Washington, 23 January 1943, Alexander and Nanes, *United States and Iran*, pp. 94–9; Katouzian, *Political Economy of Modern Iran*, pp. 141–4.
38 FO371/31836, Tehran to FO, 20 November 1942.
39 Katouzian, *Political Economy of Modern Iran*, p. 143.
40 J. Bharier, *Economic Development in Iran, 1990–1970* (London, 1971), pp. 46–9.
41 FO371/31419, Eden to Clark-Kerr, 3 November 1942.
42 FO371/31416, Churchill to Cadogan, 10 June 1942; ibid., FO minute, 12 June 1942.
43 FO371/31422, Tehran to FO, 17 and 21 October 1942; Keith A.H. Murray, 'Feeding the Middle East in wartime', *Royal Central Asian Journal*, XXXIII, 3–4 (July–October 1945), pp. 233–47. See also above p. 113.
44 FO371/35117, 'Report on political events of 1942', 23 March 1943.
45 FO371/31385, FO minute, 10 April 1942.
46 FO371/27155, Tehran to FO, 22 October 1941.
47 FO371/31385, FO minute, 10 April 1942; ibid., Tehran to FO, 10 and 21 April 1942.
48 SD891.00, Washington, 26 November 1943; ibid., Tehran 1 September 1943.
49 FO371/31386, War Office to FO, 4 November 1942; ibid., FO to War Office, 26 November 1942.
50 FO371/31387, Tehran to Baghdad, 1 December 1942; Bullard, *The Camels Must Go*, pp. 232–4.
51 FO371/Tehran to FO, 3 April 1943; SD891.00, Tehran, 8 August and 2 October 1943.
52 FO371/31388, Kiubyschew to Foreign Office, 18 January 1942.
53 McLean, *Britain and her Buffer State*, p. 75.
54 FO371/31388, FO to Tehran, 19 January 1942.

55 FO371/27233, Memorandum to the Soviet ambassador, 27 September 1941; ibid., India Office to FO, 27 September 1941.
56 FO371/61796, Tehran to FO, 15 March 1946.
57 See above, p. 56.
58 FO371/31413, Tehran to FO, 26 February 1942.
59 Ibid., FO minute, 22 April 1942; FO371/31388, FO minute, 17 January 1943.
60 Wm. Roger Louis, *The British Empire in the Middle East 1945–1951* (Oxford, 1984), pp. 58–64; FO371/45464, comments by Bullard on the withdrawal of British troops from Persia, 30 June 1945.
61 FO371/35117, 'Report on political events of 1942', Tehran, 26 March 1943.
62 Bullock, *Bevin*, p. 113.
63 Rothwell, *Britain and the Cold War*, pp. 2–3, 6–9; David Reynolds, 'Roosevelt, Churchill, and the wartime Anglo-American Alliance, 1939–1945: towards a new synthesis', in *The 'Special Relationship'. Anglo-American Relations Since 1945* (eds.), Wm. Roger Louis and Hedley Bull (Oxford, 1986), pp. 29–30.
64 FO371/35069, FO minute, 14 February 1943.
65 FO371/34093, Tabriz Diary, 16–31 March 1943.
66 FO371/35069, Tehran to FO, 16 March 1943.
67 FO371/35076, Washington to FO, 4 October 1943; FO371/35077, 25 October 1943.
68 FO371/40187, Bullard to Eden, 'Six monthly report on events in Persia', Tehran, 6 July 1944; ibid., Tehran to FO, 27 August 1944.
69 FO371/35098, Tehran to FO, 3 May 1943.
70 FO371/35103, Report by the Office of Strategic Studies on the Soviet government of northern Iran', 13 August 1943; FO371/35096, FO minutes, 9 March 1943.
71 FO371/35096, FO minute, 24 March 1943.
72 FO371/40177, Kermanshah Diary, 17–31 December 1943.
73 For details of the British application, see FO371/40241.
74 FO371/40188, Tehran to FO, 10 November 1944; FO371/43430, Eastern Department minutes, 20 January 1946.
75 FO371/40241, Ministry of Fuel and Power to FO, 10 October 1944; ibid., 18 October 1944.
76 FO371/40241, FO minute, 11 October 1944.
77 FO371/40243, Ministry of Fuel and Power to Cadogan, 15 December 1944; ibid., Tehran to FO, 29 December 1944; FO371/40241, FO minute, 11 October 1944.
78 See above, pp. 28–9
79 FO371/45431, Baxter to Bullard, 10 April 1945.
80 FO371/40242, Tehran to FO, 7 November 1944.
81 FO371/40243, Tehran to FO, 4 December 1944; Elwell Sutton, *Persian Oil*, pp. 111–12.
82 FO371/45433, Tehran to FO, 20 July 1945.
83 FO371/45430, FO to Tehran, 15 January 1945. See further Diane Shaver Clemens, *Yalta* (New York, 1970), pp. 255–8.
84 Bullock, *Bevin*, p. 216. See also above p. 124.

85 FO371/45434, Tehran to FO, 21 August 1945.
86 FO371/45462, Churchill to Eden, 1 January 1945.
87 Ibid., War Cabinet minutes, 2 January 1945; ibid., War Cabinet report on the disposition of allied forces in Persia, 10 January 1945.
88 Ibid., Indian viceroy to secretary of state for India, 12 January 1945.
89 Ibid., Tehran to FO, 19 and 31 January 1945. On Molotov's attitude see further p. 95.
90 FO371/45464, Tehran to FO, 2 June 1945.
91 Ibid., FO minute, 5 June 1945; ibid., Tehran to FO, 2 June 1945.
92 FO371/45467, Tehran to FO, 23 August 1945.
93 FO371/45434, FO minute, 10 July 1945.
94 FO371/40177, Tabriz Diaries, March–April and July 1944.
95 *Azerbaijan*, 5 September 1945.
96 FO371/45478, Tabriz, 'Six monthly report', 23 August 1945.
97 FO371/45437, Tehran to FO, 27 November 1945.
98 FO371/45436, Tehran to FO; Louis, *British Empire in the Middle East*, p. 66.
99 FO371/52667, 'Russia and North Persia', 15 March 1946; FO371/52661, Tehran to FO, 5 January 1946.
100 SD891.00, Tehran, 15 January 1946; Azimi, *Iran: Crisis of Democracy*, pp. 140–1; see also above pp. 56–7.
101 FO371/52661, FO to Tehran, 2 January 1946; ibid., FO to Washington, 5 January 1946. See further Bullock, *Bevin*, p. 219; Louis, *British Empire in the Middle East*, p. 67.
102 FO371/52661, Washington to FO, 7 January 1946.
103 SD891.00, Washington, 11 December 1945.
104 FO371/40180, Tehran to FO, 26 January 1944; ibid., FO minute, 28 March 1944. See also FO371/56278, 'The devious way of Mr. Qavam', 24 April 1946 (report by Michael Foot MP following a visit to Iran).
105 FO371/52667, 'Russia and north Persia', 15 March 1946.
106 FO371/52666, Tabriz to Tehran, 1 January 1946; Bullock, *Bevin*, pp. 219–20; Van Wagenen, *The Iranian Case*, p. 33.
107 FO371/52666, FO minute, 23 January 1946.
108 See above, p. 126.
109 See further, Thompson, *Cold War Theories*, I, p. 34; Kuniholm, *Cold War in the Near East*, pp. 178–89; Bullock, *Bevin*, pp. 35–6.
110 FO371/52728, FO to Tehran, 1 March 1946; ibid., Ministry of Fuel and Power to FO, 3 May 1946.
111 FO371/52667, Dominions Office circular, 16 March 1946; FO371/52671, FO to Tehran, 2 April 1946.
112 FO371/52667, Moscow to FO, 13 March 1946.
113 FO371/52728, Draft report on southeast Persian oil (undated, circa April 1946).
114 FO371/52669, Foreign Office to Tehran, 30 March 1946.
115 FO371/52672, Tehran to FO, 5 April 1946.
116 Ibid., 10 April 1946.
117 FO371/52777, Tabriz to Tehran, 14 March 1946; FO371/52678, Tehran to FO, 20 March 1946; FO371/52672, Tabriz to Tehran, 24 March 1946.

118 FO371/52673, FO minutes, 15 April 1946.
119 Ibid., FO minute, 18 April 1946.
120 FO371/52647, Tehran to FO, 4 May 1946.
121 FO371/52677, Tehran to FO, 9 June 1946.
122 Ibid., Dominions Office circular, 15 June 1946.
123 FO371/52076, 'Three monthly report', Tehran, 20 October 1946; see also comments on the strike by the Ahwaz consul general in FO371/52714, Tehran to FO, 8 June 1946.
124 FO371/52714, Tehran to FO, 8 June 1946.
125 FO371/52706, 'Three monthly report', Tehran, 20 October 1946. See pp. 69–70.
126 FO371/52725, Bevin to FO, Paris, 23 June 1946.
127 FO371/52735, FO minute, 52735, 20 July 1946; Louis, *British Empire in the Middle East*, pp. 69–70.
128 FO371/52716, message to Bevin from the Persian commission, Tehran, 12 June 1946.
129 FO371/52715, FO minute, 20 June 1946; ibid., memorandum by Bevin, 11 July 1946.
130 SD891.00, Tehran, 7 June 1946.
131 McLean, *Britain and her Buffer State*, p. 56.
132 FO371/52715, FO minutes, 18 and 20 June 1946.
133 Ibid., Bevin to FO, Paris, 23 June 1946.
134 SD891.00, Tehran 12 August 1946; Oberling, *The Qashqa'i Nomads of Fars*, p. 186.
135 Ibid., Tehran, 2 and 9 July 1946.
136 Ibid., memorandum on events in Khuzistan, Tehran, 19 July 1946.
137 FO371/52683, Moscow to FO, 27 September 1946; SD891.00, Tehran, 14 September 1946.
138 FO371/52681, Tehran to FO, 13 September 1946; FO371/52682, Tehran to FO, 26 September 1946.
139 FO371/52681, Tehran to FO, 13 September 1946; SD891.00, Tehran, 27 September 1946.
140 FO371/52682, message to the secretary of state, 28 September 1946; ibid., Washington to FO, 27 September 1946.
141 FO371/52683, Tehran to FO, 1 October 1946.
142 FO371/52706, 'Three monthly report', Tehran, 20 October 1946.
143 FO371/52681, Tehran to FO, 13 September 1946; Avery, *Modern Iran*, pp. 396–7.
144 SD891.00, Tehran, 28 July 1946.
145 FO371/52685, Tehran to FO, 29 October 1946.
146 SD891.00, Tehran, 28 July 1946.
147 Bullock, *Bevin*, p. 335.
148 Ibid., p. 381.
149 FO371/61972, FO to Tehran, 2 September 1947.
150 Ibid., FO to Washington, 28 August 1947.
151 Ibid., Tehran to FO, 11 September 1947. See also note from Le Rougetel to Qavam, published in *The Times*, 15 September 1947.

152 See FO371/61974, 'Summary of the Soviet–Persian oil agreement', 13 October 1947. See further p. 82.
153 FO371/61974, minutes of a meeting at the Ministry of Fuel and Power on the Persian situation, 28 October 1947. One observer who correctly predicted the consequences of the majlis decision was Elwell Sutton. See his *Persian Oil*, p. 112.
154 FO371/75458, 'General review of events in Persia, 1947 and 1948', Le Rougetel to Bevin, 17 January 1949.
155 Churchill, *Grand Alliance*, p. 428.
156 Sir Clarmont Skrine, *World War in Iran* (London, 1962), p. 226.

Conclusion

1 Yergin, *Shattered Peace*, p. 179.
2 Azimi, *Crisis of Democracy*, p. 341.
3 See above, p. 106.
4 Thornton, *Third World in Soviet Perspective*, p. 17.
5 Bruce R. Kuniholm, 'U.S. policy in the Near East: the triumphs and tribulations of the Truman administration', in *The Truman Presidency* (ed.), Michael J. Lacey (Cambridge, 1989), pp. 333–4.
6 Fontaine, *History of the Cold War*, vol. I, p. 279.
7 Gardner, *Architects of Illusion*, pp. 210–12; Gabriel Kolko, *The Politics of War. Allied Diplomacy and the World Crisis of 1943–1945* (London, 1969), p. 298.
8 Rothwell, *Britain and the Cold War*, pp. 10–11.
9 Kuniholm, 'U.S. policy in the Near East', pp. 299–301.
10 See for example, Reynolds, 'Roosevelt, Churchill, and the wartime Anglo-American alliance, 1939–1945', pp. 17–41; Robert M. Hathaway, *Ambiguous Partnership. Britain and America, 1944–1947* (New York, 1981).
11 Louise L'Estrange Fawcett, 'Invitation to the Cold War: British policy in Iran, 1941–47', in *Britain and the First Cold War* (ed.), Deighton, p. 199.
12 T. Cuyler Young, 'The race between Russia and reform in Iran', *Foreign Affairs*, XXVIII, 2 (January 1950), p. 278.
13 Marvin Zionis, *The Political Elite of Iran* (Princeton, 1971), p. 304.

Bibliography

Archives

British Foreign Office, Class FO371, Public Record Office, London.
US Department of State, Record Group 59, National Archives, Washington.
US Department of State, Declassified Documents: Iran, Library of Congress, Washington.

Published documents

Alexander, Y., and Nanes, A. (eds.). *The United States and Iran: a Documentary History*, Maryland, 1980.
Cordier, A.W., and Foote, W. (eds.). *Public Papers of the Secretaries General of the United Nations*, London, 1969.
Degras, J. (ed.). *The Communist International 1919–1943. Documents*, London, 1956.
Dmytryshyn, Basil, and Cox, Frederick. *The Soviet Union and the Middle East. A Documentary History of Afghanistan, Iran and Turkey 1917–1985*, Princeton, 1987.
Eudin, Xenia J., and North, Robert C. *Soviet Russia and the East, 1920–1927. A Documentary Survey*, Stanford, 1957.
Hurewitz, J.C. (ed.). *Diplomacy in the Near and Middle East. A Documentary Record 1914–1956*, Princeton, 1956.
Slusser, R.M., and Triska, J.F. *A Calendar of Soviet Treaties 1917–1957*, Stanford, 1959.
Sontag, Raymond, and Beddie, James (eds.), *Nazi–Soviet Relations, 1939–1941: Documents from the Archives of the German Foreign Office*, Washington, 1948.
US Department of State, *Foreign Relations of the United States*, Washington, 1939–47.

Books and articles

Abdurazakov, B. *Prouski Angliiskovo i Amerikanskovo Imperializma v Irane (1941–1947 godi)*, Tashkent 1959.
Abrahamian, Ervand. *Iran: Between Two Revolutions*, Princeton, 1982.
 'The crowd in Iranian politics 1905–53', in Haleh Afshar (ed.), *Iran: A Revolution in Turmoil*, London, 1985.

'Kasravi. The integrative nationalist of Iran', in Kedourie, E. and Haim, S. (eds.), *Towards a Modern Iran: Studies in Thought, Politics and Society*, London, 1980, 96–131.

'Communism and communalism in Iran: the Tudeh and the Firqah-i Dimukrat', *International Journal of Middle Eastern Studies*, I, 4 (October 1970), 291–316.

'Factionalism in Iran: political groups in the 14th Majlis (1944–46), *Middle Eastern Studies*, XIV, 1 (January 1978), 22–55.

Acheson, D. *Present at the Creation: My Years in the State Department*, New York, 1969.

Akhavi, S. *Religion and Politics in Contemporary Iran: Clergy–State Relations in the Pahlavi Period*, New York, 1980.

Alavi, B. *Panjah-u-Sih Nafar*, Tehran, 1944.

Alavi, F. *Pishihvari Chist?*, Tehran, 1946.

Alvarez, D.J. *Bureaucracy and Cold War Diplomacy: The United States and Turkey*, Thessalonika, 1980.

Ambrose, S.E. *Rise to Globalism: American Foreign Policy Since 1938*, London, 1984.

Amidi Nouri, A. (ed.). *Azarbaijan-i Dimukrat*, Tehran, 1946.

Amir Khizi, I. *Qiyam-i Azarbaijan va Sattar Khan*, Tabriz, 1960.

Amirsadeghi, Hossein, and R.W. Ferrier (eds.). *Twentieth Century Iran*, London, 1977.

Amuzegar, H. *Naft va Havades-i Azarabijan*, Tehran 1947.

Arfa, Hasan. *Under Five Shahs*, London, 1954.

Arjomand, Said Amir. *The Turban for the Crown: The Islamic Revolution in Iran*, New York, 1988.

Asad, T. and Owen, R. (eds.). *Sociology of Developing Societies: The Middle East*, New York, 1983.

Atkin, M. *Russia and Iran 1780–1828*, Minneapolis, 1980.

'The Islamic Republic and the Soviet Union', in Nikki R. Keddie and Eric Hooglund (eds.), *The Iranian Revolution and the Islamic Republic*, New York, 1986, 191–208.

Azeri, A. *Qiyam-i Khiabani*, Tehran 1950.

Avery, Peter. *Modern Iran*, London, 1965.

Azimi, Fakhreddin. *Iran. The Crisis of Democracy*, London, 1989.

Banani, A. *The Modernization of Iran*, Princeton, 1984.

Barnes, John and David Nicholson (eds.). *The Empire at Bay. The Leo Amery Diaries 1929–1945*, London, 1988.

Bathold, W. *A Historical Geography of Iran*, Princeton, 1984.

Beck, Louis. 'Revolutionary Iran and its tribal peoples', in Asad, T. and R. Owen (eds.), *Sociology of 'Developing Societies'. The Middle East*, New York, 1983, 115–26.

The Qashqa'i of Iran, London, 1986.

Bennigsen, Alexandre and Marie Broxup. *The Islamic Threat to the Soviet State*, London, 1983.

Bharier, J. *Economic Development in Iran, 1900–1970*, London, 1971.

Bill, James A. *The Eagle and the Lion. The Tragedy of American–Iranian Relations*, New Haven, 1988.

Binder, Leonard. *Iran: Political Development in a Changing Society*, Berkeley, 1962.
Blake, G.H., and Drysdale, A. *The Middle East and North Africa: A Political Geography*, Oxford, 1985.
Brenchley, F. *Britain and the Middle East: An Economic History 1945–1987*, London, 1989.
Brown, Edward Granville. *A Year Among the Persians*, London, 1893.
    The Persian Revolution of 1905–1909, London, 1910.
Brynes, J.F. *Speaking Frankly*, London, 1947.
Bullard, Sir Reader. *The Camels Must Go: an Autobiography*, London, 1961.
    Britain and the Middle East, London, 1951.
Bullock, Alan. *Ernest Bevin: Foreign Secretary 1945–1951*, London, 1983.
Calvocoressi, P. (ed.). *Survey of International Affairs*, London, 1954.
Central Asian Review. 'Borderlands of Soviet Central Asia. Persia: Part 1', *Central Asian Review*, IV, 3 (1956), 287–325.
    'Borderlands of Soviet Central Asia. Persia: Part 2', *Central Asian Review*, IV, 4 (1956), 282–431.
Chaliand, Gerard (ed.). *People Without a Country: the Kurds and Kurdistan*, London, 1980.
Chehabi, H.E. *Iranian Politics and Religious Modernism. The Liberation Movement of Iran under the Shah and Khomeini*, London, 1990.
Chubin, Shahram, and Zabih, Sepehr. *The Foreign Relations of Iran*, Berkeley, 1974.
    Soviet Foreign Policy Towards Iran and the Gulf, Adelphi Paper No. 157, London, 1980.
Churchill, Winston S. *The Second World War*, III, *The Grand Alliance*, London, 1950.
    The Second World War, IV, *The Hinge of Fate*, London, 1951.
    The Second World War, V, *Closing the Ring*, London, 1952.
Clemens, Diane Shaver. *Yalta*, New York, 1970.
Cottam, Richard W. *Nationalism in Iran*, Pittsburg, 1964.
    Iran and the United States. A Cold War Case Study, Pittsburg, 1988.
    'Political party development in Iran', *Iranian Studies*, I, 3 (Summer 1968), 82–95.
Curzon, G.N. *Persia and the Persian Question*, London, 1892.
Davudi, M. *Qavam al-Saltaneh*, Tehran, 1948.
Dawisha, A. and K. (eds.). *The Soviet Union and the Middle East. Policies and Perspectives*, London, 1982.
Degras, J. (ed.). *The Communist International 1919–1943, Documents*, I, London, 1956.
Deighton, Anne (ed.). *Britain and the First Cold War*, Oxford, 1990.
    The Impossible Peace: Britain, the Division of Germany and the Origins of the Cold War, Oxford, 1990.
De Novo, J. *American Interests and Policies in the Middle East 1900–1939*, Minneapolis, 1963.
Diba, Farhad. *Mohammad Mossadegh. A Political Biography*, London, 1986.
Djilas, Milovan. *Conversations with Stalin*, New York, 1961.
Doenecke, Justus, D. 'Revisionists, oil and cold war diplomacy', *Iranian Studies*, III, 1 (Winter 1970), 23–33.

Eagleton, William Jr. *The Kurdish Republic of 1946*, London, 1963.

Eden, Anthony. *The Eden Memoirs: the Reckoning*, London, 1965.

Elwell-Sutton, L.P. *Persian Oil: A Study in Power Politics*, London, 1955.

'Political parties in Iran: 1941–1948', *Middle East Journal*, III, 1 (January 1949), 45–62.

'The Iranian Press, 1941–1947', *Iran*, VI (1968), 65–104.

Emeni-Yeganeh, J. 'Iran vs. Azerbaijan (1945–46): divorce, separation or reconciliation?', *Central Asian Survey*, III, 2 (1984), 1–27.

Eshraghi, F. 'Anglo-Soviet occupation of Iran in August 1941', *Middle Eastern Studies*, XX, 9 (January 1984), 27–52.

'The aftermath of the Anglo-Soviet occupation of Iran', *Middle Eastern Studies*, XX, 3 (July 1984), 324–51.

Fatemi, F.S. *The USSR in Iran*, New Jersey, 1980.

Fatemi, Nasrullah S. *Diplomatic History of Persia 1917–1923*, New York, 1952.

Oil Diplomacy: Powderkeg of Iran, New York, 1952.

Fawcett, Louise L'Estrange. 'Invitation to the Cold War: British policy in Iran, 1941–47', in Anne Deighton (ed.), *Britain and the First Cold War*, London, 1990, 184–200.

Feis, Herbert. *Churchill, Roosevelt, Stalin. The War They Waged and the Peace They Sought*, New Jersey, 1957.

Between War and Peace, the Potsdam Conference, Princeton, 1960.

From Trust to Terror. The Onset of the Cold War, 1945–1950, London, 1970.

Ferrier, R.W. *The History of the British Petroleum Company*, I, *The Developing Years, 1901–1932*, Cambridge, 1982.

'The development of the Iranian oil industry, in Amirsadeghi, H. and Ferrier, R. (eds.). *Twentieth Century Iran*, London 1977, 93–128.

Ferro, M. 'Des républiques à la dérive', *Le Monde Diplomatique*, May 1990, 10–11.

Fontaine, A. *A History of the Cold War*, London, 1965.

Gaddis, J.L. *America and the Origins of the Cold War*, New York, 1972.

'The emerging post-revisionist synthesis on the origins of the cold war', *Diplomatic History*, VII, 3 (Summer 1983), 171–90.

Gardner, Lloyd C. *Architects of Illusion: Men and Ideas in American Foreign Policy 1941–1949*, Chicago, 1970.

Garrod, Oliver. 'The Qashqai Tribe of Fars', *Journal of the Royal Central Asian Society*, XXXIII, 3–4 (July–October 1946), 293–306.

Garthwaite, Gene R. *Khans and Shahs: A Documentary Analysis of the Bakhtiyari in Iran*, London, 1983.

Ghods, M. Reza. *Iran in the Twentieth Century. A Political History*, London, 1989.

'Iranian nationalism and Reza Shah', *The Middle East Journal*, XXVII, 1 (January 1991), 35–45.

Goode, James F. *The United States and Iran, 1946–51*, London, 1989.

Greaves, Rose L. *Persia and Defence of India 1884–1892*, London, 1959.

'British policy in Persia 1892–1903', *Bulletin of the SOAS*, XXVIII (1965), 36–40, 284–307.

'1942–1976: The reign of Muhammad Riza Shah', in Amirsadeghi, H. and Ferrier, R. (eds), *Twentieth Century Iran*, London, 1977, 53–92.

Haas, William S. *Iran, New York, 1946.*
Halle, Louis J. *The Cold War as History*, London, 1967.
Halliday, F. *Iran: Dictatorship and Development*, London, 1979.
    'Revolution in Iran', *Khamsin*, VII (1980), 53–64.
    'Steppes towards seccession', *The Times Literary Supplement*, IV, 551 (22–8 June 1990), 661–2.
Hammond, Thomas (ed.). *The Anatomy of Communist Takeovers*, New Haven, 1975.
Hamzavi, A.H. *Persia and the Powers. An Account of Diplomatic Relations 1941–1946*, London, 1946.
    'Iran at the Tehran Conference', *International Affairs*, XX, 2 (April 1944), 192–203.
Hathaway, Robert M. *Ambiguous Partnership. Britain and America, 1944–1947*, New York, 1981.
Hess, Gary R. 'The Iranian crisis of 1945–6 and the Cold War', *Political Science Quarterly*, 89, 1 (1974), 117–46.
HMSO. *Treaty of Alliance Between the United Kingdom and the Soviet Union and Iran, 1942.*
Homayounpour, Parviz. *L'Affaire d'Azerbaidjan*, Lausanne, 1967.
Hosking, G. *A History of the Soviet Union*, London, 1985.
Hull, Cordell, *Memoirs*, II, London, 1948.
Ivanov, M.S. *Ocherki Istorii Irana*, Moscow, 1952.
Jami, *Guzashtih Chiragh-i Rah-i Ayandih Ast*, Tehran, 1978.
Jazani, Bizhan. *Capitalism and Revolution in Iran*, London, 1980.
Jowdat, H. *Tarikh-i Firqih-i Dimucrat*, Tehran, 1969.
Kanet, R.E. (ed.). *The Soviet Union and the Developing Nations*, London, 1974.
Kasravi, Ahmad. *Azari ya Zaban-i Bastan-i Azarbaijan*, Tehran, n.d.
    Tarikh-i Mashrutih-i Iran, Tehran, 1937.
Katouzian, Homa. *The Political Economy of Modern Iran 1926–1979*, London, 1981.
    Khatirat-i Siyasi-yi Khalil-i Maliki, Tehran, 1981.
    Mussadiq and the Struggle for Power in Iran, London, 1990.
    (ed.). *Mussadiq's Memoirs*, London, 1988.
Kazemi, Farhad. 'The military and politics in Iran: the uneasy symbiosis', in Elie Kedourie and Sylvia Haim (eds.), *Towards a Modern Iran: Studies in Thought, Politics and Society*, London, 1980, 217–40.
Kazemzadeh, Firuz. *Russia and Britain in Persia, 1864–1914*, New Haven, 1968.
    'The origins and early development of the Persian Cossack Brigade', *American Slavic and East European Review*, XV (1956), 351–63.
    'Russia and the Middle East', in Lederer, I.V. (ed.), *Russian Foreign Policy. Essays in Historical Perspective*, London, 1962.
Keddie, Nikki R. *Religion and Rebellion in Iran. The Tobacco Protest of 1891–92*, London, 1966.
    Iran, Religion, Politics and Society, London, 1980.
    Roots of Revolution. An Interpretative History of Modern Iran, London, 1981.
Keddie, Nikki R. and Eric Hooglund (eds.). *The Iranian Revolution and the Islamic Republic*, New York, 1986.
Keddie, Nikki R. and Ganoronski, Mark J. *Neither East Nor West. Iran, the Soviet Union and the United States*, New Haven, 1990.

Kedourie, Elie, and Haim, Sylvia (eds.). *Towards a Modern Iran, Studies in Thought, Politics and Society*, London, 1980.

Kennan, George F. *Memoirs, 1925–1950*, London, 1968.

Kirk, G. *The Middle East in the War*, London, 1952.

(ed.). *Survey of International Affairs: The Middle East 1945–1950*, London, 1954.

Kishavarz, Firaydun. *Man Muttaham Mikunam*, Tehran, 1978.

Knapp, Wilfred. '1921–1941: the period of Riza Shah', in H. Amirsadeghi and R. Ferrier (eds.), *Twentieth Century Iran*, London, 1977.

Knatchbull-Hugessen, Sir Hugh. *Diplomat in Peace and War*, London, 1949.

Kolko, Gabriel. *The Politics of War. Allied Diplomacy and the World Crisis of 1943–1945*, London, 1969.

Kuhiholm, Bruce R. *The Origins of the Cold War in the Near East: Great Power Conflict and Diplomacy in Iran, Turkey and Greece*, Princeton, 1980.

Lacey, Michael J. *The Truman Presidency*, Cambridge, 1989.

Ladjevardi, Habib. *Labour Unions and Autocracy in Iran*, New York, 1985.

'The origins of US support for an autocratic Iran', *International Journal of Middle Eastern Studies*, XV (1983), 225–39.

LaFeber, Walter, *America, Russia, and the Cold War 1945–1984* (5th edition), New York, Alfred A. Knopf, 1985.

Lambton, A.K.S. 'The Azerbaijan problem', *The World Today*, II, 1 (January 1946), 48–57.

'Some of the problems facing Persia', *International Affairs*, XXII, 2 (April 1946), 254–72.

Landlord and Peasant in Persia, London, 1953.

Laqueur, Walter. *The Soviet Union and the Middle East*, London, 1959.

Lawson, Fred H. 'The Iranian crisis of 1945–1946 and the spiral model of international conflict', *International Journal of Middle Eastern Studies*, XXI (1989), 307–26.

Lazitch, Branko, and Drachkovitch, Milorad M. *Lenin and the Comintern*, I, Stanford, 1972.

Lederer, I.V. *Russian Foreign Policy. Essay in Historical Perspective*, London, 1962.

Lenczowski, George. *Russia and the West in Iran 1918–1948*, New York, 1949.

'The communist movement in Iran', *The Middle East Journal*, I, 1 (January 1949), 29–45.

Leseur, M. *Les Anglais en Perse*, Paris, 1923.

Lie, Trygve. *In the Cause of Peace*, New York, 1954.

Louis, Wm. Roger. *The British Empire in the Middle East 1945–1951*, Oxford, 1984.

Louis, Wm. Roger, and Bill, James (eds.). *Mussadiq, Iranian Nationalism and Oil*, London, 1988.

Louis, Wm. Roger, and Bull, Hedley. *The 'Special Relationship'. Anglo-American Relations Since 1945*, Oxford, 1986.

Lytle, Mark Hamilton. *The Origins of the Iranian–American Alliance*, London, 1987.

McCagg, W.O. *Stalin Embattled, 1943–1948*, Detroit, 1978.

McDaniel, R. *The Shuster Mission and the Persian Constitutional Revolution*, Minneapolis, 1974.

McFarland, Stephen L. 'A peripheral view of the origins of the Cold War: the crisis in Iran, 1941–47', *Diplomatic History*, IV, 4 (1980), 333–51.

McLean, D. *Britain and her Buffer State. The Collapse of the Persian Empire 1890–1914*, London, 1979.

Maliki, Khalil. *Du Ravish bara-yi Yik Hadaf*, Tehran, 1948.

Mastny, Vojtech. *Russia's Road to the Cold War: Diplomacy, Warfare and the Politics of Communism, 1941–1945*, New York, 1979.

Millspaugh, Arthur C. *The American Task in Persia*, Washington, 1925.

Americans in Persia, Washington, 1946.

Mortazavi, M. *Le Role de L'Azerbaidjan au cours de XXV siècles d'histoire de L'Empire d'Iran*, Tabriz, 1971

Murray, Keith A.H. 'Feeding the Middle East in wartime', *Royal Central Asian Journal*, XXXII, 3–4 (July–October 1945), 233–47.

Nazem, H. *Russia and Great Britain in Iran 1900–1914*, Tehran, 1975.

Nollau, F. Gunther, and Wiehe, Hans J. *Russia's South Flank: Soviet Operations in Iran, Turkey and Afghanistan*, New York, 1963.

Oberling, Pierre. *The Qashqa'i Nomads of Fars*, The Hague, 1974.

O'Connor, W. *On the Frontier and Beyond: A Record of Thirty Years Service*, London, 1931.

Olson, William J. *Anglo-Iranian Relations during World War I*, London, 1984.

'The genesis of the Anglo-Persian Agreement of 1919', in Elie Kedourie and Sylvia Haim (eds.), *Towards a Modern Iran*, London, 1980, 185–216.

Ovendale, Ritchie (ed.). *The Foreign Policy of the British Labour Governments 1945–1951*, Leicester, 1984.

Pahlavi, Mohammad Reza. *Mission for My Country*, London, 1961.

Pesaran, M.H. 'Economic development and revolutionary upheavals in Iran', in Haleh Afshar (ed.), *Iran: A Revolution in Turmoil*, London, 1985, 15–50.

Pfau, Richard. 'Containment in Iran, 1946: the shift to an active policy', *Diplomatic History*, 1 (Fall, 1977), 359–72.

Pisiyan, N.Q. *Az Mahabad-i Khunin ta Karaniha-yi Aras*, Tehran 1948.

Marg bud. Bazgasht ham bud, Tehran, 1949.

Pourhadi, J.V. *Persian and Afghan Newspapers in the Library of Congress*, Washington, 1979.

Ramazani, Rouhollah K. *The Foreign Policy of Iran; a Developing Country in World Affairs, 1500–1941*, Charlottesville, 1966.

Iran's Foreign Policy 1941–1973. A Study of Foreign Policy in Modernizing Nations, Charlottesville, 1975.

The United States and Iran: Patterns of Influence, New York, 1982.

'The Republic of Azerbaijan and the Kurdish People's Republic', in Thomas Hammond (ed.), *The Anatomy of Communist Takeovers*, New Haven, 1975, 448–74.

'Iran and the United States: an experiment in enduring friendship', *Middle East Journal*, XXX (Summer, 1976), 322–34.

Ravasani, S. *Sowjetrepublik Gilan*, Berlin, 1973.

Reynolds, David. 'Roosevelt, Churchill, and the wartime Anglo–American alliance,

1939–1945: towards a new synthesis', in Wm. Roger Louis and Hedley Bull (eds.), *The 'Special Relationship'. Anglo–American Relations Since 1945*, Oxford, 1986, 17–41.

Rezun, Miron. *The Soviet Union and Iran. Soviet Policy in Iran from the Beginnings of the Pahlavi Dynasty until the Soviet Invasion in 1941*, Geneva, 1981.

Ricks, Thomas, M. 'US military missions to Iran, 1943–1978: the political economy of military assistance', *Iranian Studies*, XII, 3–4 (Summer–Autumn 1979), 163–94.

Roosevelt, Archie Jr. 'The Kurdish Republic of Mahabad', *The Middle East Journal*, I, 3 (July 1947), 247–69.

Roosevelt, Elliot. *As He Saw It*, New York, 1946.

Rossow, Robert. 'The Battle of Azerbaijan, 1946', *Middle East Journal*, X, 1 (Winter 1956), 17–32.

Rothwell, Victor. *Britain and the Cold War 1941–1947*, London, 1982.

Rubin, Barry. *Paved with Good Intentions. The American Experience in Iran*, Oxford, 1980.

The Great Powers in the Middle East 1941–1947, London, 1982.

Rubinstein, Alvin Z. *The Foreign Policy of the Soviet Union*, New York, 1960.

Soviet Policy Toward Turkey, Iran and Afghanistan, New York, 1982.

'The Soviet Union and Iran under Khomeini', *International Affairs*, LVII (Autumn 1981), pp. 599–617.

Rywkin, Michael. *Moscow's Muslim Challenge. Soviet Central Asia*, London, 1982.

Sabih, Houshang, *British Policy in Persia 1918–1925*, London, 1990.

Samii, Kuross, A. *Involvement by Invitation. American Strategies of Containment in Iran*, Pennsylvania, 1987.

'Truman against Stalin in Iran: a tale of three messages', *Middle Eastern Studies*, XXIII, 1 (January 1987), 95–107.

Saunders, David. *Losing an Empire, Finding a Role. British Foreign Policy since 1945*, London, 1990.

Sepehr, M. *Iran dar Jang-i Buzurg-i 1914–1918*, Tehran, 1957.

Sheehan, Michael K. *Iran: Impact of United States Interests and Policies, 1941–1954*, New York, 1968.

Shlaim, Avi. 'Britain, the Berlin Blockade and the Cold War', *International Affairs*, LX (1984), 1–14.

Shuster, Morgan. *The Strangling of Persia*, London, 1912.

Sicker, Martin. *The Bear and the Lion. Soviet Imperialism and Iran*, New York, 1988.

Skrine, Sir Clarmont. *World War in Iran*, London, 1962.

Spector, Ivar. *The Soviet Union and the Muslim World 1917–1958*, Seattle, 1959.

Stettinius, Edward R. *Roosevelt and the Russians: The Yalta Conference*, New York, 1949.

Suny, R.G. *The Baku Commune, 1917–1918*, Princeton, 1972.

Sykes, Christopher. 'Russia and Azerbaijan', *Soundings*, February 1946.

Sykes, Sir Percy. *A History of Persia*, London, 1951.

Thomas, Lewis V., and Frye, Richard N. *The United States and Turkey and Iran*, Cambridge, MA, 1951.

Thompson, K.W. *Cold War Theories*, London, 1981.

Thornton, E.P. *The Third World in Soviet Perspective*, Princeton, 1964.
Ulam, Adam B. *Expansion and Coexistence: Soviet Foreign Policy, 1917–1967*, London, 1968.
Upton, Joseph M. *The History of Modern Iran. An Interpretation*, Cambridge MA, 1960.
Vail Motter, T.H. *The United States Army in World War II: The Middle East Theater, the Persian Corridor and Aid to Russia*, Washington, 1952.
Van Wagenen, Richard W. *The United Nations Action: The Iranian Case 1946*, New York, 1952.
Wallach, J.L. (ed.). *Germany and the Middle East 1835–1939*, Tel Aviv, 1975.
Wheeler-Bennett, John W. and Nicholls, Anthony. *The Semblance of Peace: The Political Settlement After the Second World War*, London, 1972.
Wight, Martin. *Power Politics*, London, 1978.
Wilbur, Donald N. *Riza Shah Pahlavi: The Resurrection and Reconstruction of Iran: 1878–1944*, New York, 1975.
Wittner, L.S. *American Intervention in Greece, 1943–1949*, New York, 1982.
Woodward, Sir Llewelyn. *British Foreign Policy in the Second World War*, London, 1962.
Wright, Sir Denis A.H. *The British Amongst the Persians During the Qajar Period 1787–1921*, London, 1977.
Yapp, Malcolm E. *Strategies of British India: Britain, Iran and Afghanistan 1798–1850*, Oxford, 1980.
'1900–1921: the last years of the Qajar dynasty', in Amirsadeghi, H., and Ferrier, R.W. (eds.). *Twentieth Century Iran*, London, 1977, 1–22.
'Soviet relations with countries of the Northern Tier', in Dawisha, A. and K. (eds.), *The Soviet Union and the Middle East*, London, 1982, 24–44.
Yergin, Daniel. *The Shattered Peace: The Origins of the Cold War and the National Security State*, London, 1977.
Yeselson, Abraham. *United States–Persian Diplomatic Relations 1883–1921*, New Brunswick, NJ, 1956.
Yodafat, Aryeh. *The Soviet Union and Revolutionary Iran*, London, 1984.
Yodafat, Aryeh and Abir, M. *In the Direction of the Persian Gulf*, London, 1977.
Young, T. Cuyler. 'The race between Russia and reform in Iran', *Foreign Affairs*, XXVIII, 2 (January 1950), 278–89.
Zabih, Sepehr. *The Communist Movement in Iran*, Berkeley, 1966.
Zionis, Marvin. *The Political Elite of Iran*, Princeton, 1971.

Dissertations

Atabaki, Turaj, 'Ethnicity and autonomy in Iranian Azarbayjan', University of Utrecht, Ph.D. thesis, 1991.
Azimi, Fakhreddin. 'The politics of dynamic stalemate: Iran 1944–1953', Oxford University D.Phil thesis, 1984.
Benab, Y. 'The Soviet Union and Britain in Iran 1917–27. A case study of the impact of East–West rivalry', Catholic University of America, Ph.D. thesis, 1974.

Fawcett, Louise L'Estrange. 'The struggle for Persia. The Azerbaijan Crisis of 1946', Oxford University, D.Phil. thesis, 1988.

Ghodad, I. 'The Azerbaijan Crisis 1945–6. An option analysis of US policy', University of Maryland, Ph.D. thesis, 1973.

Hekmat, H. 'Iran's response to Soviet–American rivalry, 1951–1961: a comparative study', University of Columbia, Ph.D. thesis, 1974.

Kittner, N.F. 'Issues in Anglo-Persian diplomatic relations 1921–1933', SOAS, Ph.D. thesis, 1980.

Kovac, J.E. 'Iran and the beginning of the Cold War: a case study in the dynamics of international politics', Utah University, Ph.D. thesis, 1970.

Ladjevardi, H. 'Politics and labour in Iran 1941–1949', Oxford University D.Phil. thesis, 1981.

Mojtehedi, M. 'La Question d'Azarbaidjan: la mouvement des Democrats et les efforts de l'ONA', University of Paris, doctoral thesis, 1952.

Nezam-Mafi, M.E. 'Origin and development of political parties in Persia 1906–1911', Edinburgh University, D.Phil. thesis, 1979.

Pfau, Richard, 'The United States and Iran, 1941–1947: origins of a partnership', University of Virginia, Ph.D. thesis, 1975.

Tabari, K. 'Iran's policies towards the United States during the Anglo-Russian occupation 1941–46', Columbia University, Ph.D. thesis, 1967.

Thorpe, J. 'The mission of Arthur C. Millspaugh to Iran 1943–1945', University of Wisconsin, Ph.D. thesis, 1973.

Vahdat, M. 'The Soviet Union and the movement to establish autonomy in Iranian Azerbaijan', Indiana University, Ph.D. thesis, 1958.

Wasserberg, A.B. 'The politics of Soviet interference. Soviet policy towards Iran', City University, New York, Ph.D. thesis, 1979.

Weaver, P.W. 'Soviet strategy in Iran, 1941–1947', The American University, Washington, Ph.D. thesis, 1958.

Newspapers

Akhtar-i Shumal
Azad Millat
Azerbaijan
Azhir
Dad
Darya
Iran-i Ma
Ittila'at
Izvestia
Jibhih
Journal de Tehran
Kayhan
Kharvar-i Now
The Manchester Guardian

Mihr-i Iran
Monitoring Report (BBC Publication)
Pravda
Ra'd-i Imruz
Rahbar
Razm
Sida-yi Iran
Sitarih
Summary of World Broadcasts (BBC Publication)
The Daily Telegraph
The New York Times
The Times
Zafar

Index

Index